SLINGSHOT TO THE JUGGERNAUT

TOTAL RESISTANCE TO THE DEATH MACHINE MEANS COMPLETE LOVE OF THE TRUTH

SANDER HICKS

SOFT SKULL PRESS

AN IMPRINT OF COUNTERPOINT

Library of Congress Cataloging-in-Publication Data is available.

ISBN: 978-1-59376-423-4

Soft Skull Press
An imprint of COUNTERPOINT
1919 Fifth Street
Berkeley, CA 94710
www.softskull.com

Distributed by Publishers Group West
Cover design by: Christopher Baima
Interior design by: Tabitha Lahr

10 9 8 7 6 5 4 3 2 1

To David

CONTENTS

PART THREE

PART FOUR

PART FIVE

OPENING INVOCATION

Let's stop and do a visualization together.

Take a deep breath.

Hunch up and relax your shoulders. Exhale.

Close your eyes for a moment. Put yourself in the presence of the deeper truth. Connect to the higher power you recognize, whether it's God, peace, nature, the earth, or the universe.

Now, visualize a future where the United States is a global leader in exporting peace, a leader in the science of conflict resolution. Visualize a new kind of country, one that is about empowering its citizens and the citizens of the world rather than intimidating them. Imagine the United States as a country best at figuring out how to meet the needs of all parties in a conflict. Instead of being number one at war, we become number one at fostering peace.

In New York Harbor, we have a former military base, Governor's Island, that was converted into a public park for art and music. Simply visualize that happening on a global scale. See the U.S. military bases and the entire crony-capitalist empire converted into a better life-giving infrastructure. Imagine the U.S. Army coming home and retraining as professionals with expertise in nonviolence and communication, empathy and justice, diplomacy and civil engineering.

See it. Taste it.

Right now we have a president who is calm, cool, understated, and completely amoral, capable of fooling much of the country and some of the world into believing we're moving toward peace, all while keeping several illegal wars going strong (and launching a few new ones). The vision I outline is very different from what we *do* today. But it's a vision that's not really all that different from who we really *are*—it's a vision similar to that of Enlightenment thinkers who foresaw America's revolutionary, transformational promise.

This is a visualization I just did coast to coast, at the beginning of each of my gigs, on my 2011 national tour. I talked about this, my new book to come. But doing these visualizations and having conversations helped write this book. This book is a collective effort. The vision is not just my own. It's in this vision of peace that we are building up a new political party, the Truth Party.

This book is a door. We are going to go through it to a new place. These are ideas that resurrect the dead. If you are spiritually dead, it's time to wake up! We are all a little deadened by the crushing death that surrounds us. It's time to go from death into life. We are going to examine a tragedy and a cover-up. But that is not all.

I promise you a pathway to something greater.

Welcome to *Slingshot to the Juggernaut*.

Come in.

PART ONE

PICK UP A SLINGSHOT

1 DAVID AND GOLIATH

Remember the story of David and Goliath?

We can all relate to the underdog, the scrawny shepherd boy who with a strange self-assurance takes on a bloodthirsty giant. The stage is set for tragedy, because Goliath is an undefeated champion warrior. But in a shocking upset, the little guy wins.

How did that happen? How did a kid knock out a towering, fearsome ogre using just a slingshot?

Certain details of the David story are often overlooked. David had faith that he could do the job because he had some experience fighting off lions as a shepherd. He felt a divine power over him in those struggles. He had faith that the divine power was real, that God was inside him. God wasn't some postmodern master narrative; David believed in what he was doing. And people who believe in what they are doing are undefeatable. David will keep reappearing, to prove this point, through the lives of many individuals in this book.

When David volunteered to do the impossible, he was at first gussied up in the armor of the Israelites. But he couldn't move around. He said, "I cannot go in these because I have never tried them before." A modern translation could be "Dude, I can't even breathe in this gear—forget it. Let me try something." So he put away the professional weapons and armor. He went to a dry creek bed and picked out five smooth stones.

Goliath, for his part, was loud and obnoxious. He was a trash talker. He mocked the God of Israel. He blasphemed so obscenely, David was filled with a special kind of rage. David's rage was holy. You see, David loved God. He loved the truth and the poetry of God. We know this because of the songs he wrote, the Psalms. Radical, antimaterialist, antiwar stuff, like:

> *Trampling under foot the pieces of silver*
> *God has scattered the peoples who delight in war.*[1]

So, even if you, my reader, don't believe in God, or don't believe in "the God" of ancient Israel, I think you can still relate to David's situation. Goliath had already killed a lot of David's friends and countrymen, but when he mocked God, David's foundational beliefs, it hit David in the gut. And that was the beginning of Goliath's end.

The juxtaposition must have been startling: Next to his enemy, David appeared practically naked. David was "stone cold" terrified as he looked out at the battlefield that day. The famous statue *David* by Michelangelo reminds us of this. Many people have joked about how small David's penis and testicles look in that work, but that, too, is a telling detail: His fear of death was so intense, David's genitals shrank up as a natural protective measure. David's face was trying to look cool, while his body was contracting, terrified. We guys can relate.

And yet despite the fear, and the odds, and the unequal weaponry, David won. He felt fear but worked through it. He put his faith in the holiness of truth, the divine poetry, the God that was within him, coursing through his veins as the Spirit of Revolution flows in the heart of history. God is the history of all history, and the Spirit of History tends to love subversive underdogs.

History teaches us we can beat a brutal military juggernaut with a slingshot. God is an anarchist. Throughout history, kings have claimed that God has given them their authority, but a close read of the Bible shows that God does not love human power. God loves truth. God sends the electrical, fiery power of language out through prophets. God sends activists, catalysts like David, Daniel, and Jesus, to completely subvert human power and the corruption of our kings. But as the prophet Daniel said to King Belshazzar of Babylon, you have to learn how to read the writing on the wall.

This book is my slingshot. There's a Goliath in our midst. That Goliath is the status quo reality of war and lies. It's an America that doesn't know what it stands for. It's an American politics that is locked in its addiction to self-destructive, wasteful cycles. It's a war machine that has not only killed millions already but has also grown expert in the realm of spectacle creation. The war machine kills people, but it also kills truth. It molds public opinion to support wars that normally we regular, peace-loving people would never support.

Our current politics, foreign policy, and domestic "antiterror" police tactics are brutally executed in the name of 9/11. But 9/11 is a rotten onion. When you hold up this "defining event," you find not a definitive story but a complex, rotting vegetable. Peel back any layer, and every one stinks. It's soft and can't be supported logically, but we're all too scared to talk about the truth. Instead, we as a country keep killing and killing. In the past year alone we have killed bin Laden, and American citizen Anwar Awlaki, for being in the so-called "Al Qaeda" movement.

As a country, we have been put through an emotional multimedia wringer, where an authoritarian government/media machine has pounded certain images—and explanations, and justifications, and scapegoats—into our heads with such repetition and such intensity that the fact that anyone has rebelled is surprising. It's a miracle that the American people have not been fooled, all of us, 100 percent, en masse. The 9/11 Truth Movement, the We Are Change network, and the Occupy Wall Street movement are all testaments to the will of the people to not be fooled by a system based on secrecy.

A uniformed, angry voice has boomed out, telling us to blame Arabs, blame bin Laden, give up our rights, endorse torture. The voice of tyranny wants America to become a permanent national-security state. But a heartening amount of the American people are not buying it. Major polls show a significant and growing level of skepticism about 9/11. (Look at the Scripps/Howard/Ohio University poll or the *New York Times*/CBS poll from 2006.[2] In 2011, 48 percent of New Yorkers supported a new investigation of World Trade Center Building 7.[3])

Globally, recent data shows that once you get outside the influence of the U.S. media antennae, an even bigger swath of Earth's good people reject the flimsy assertion that nineteen young dudes with box cutters could defeat the world's strongest nation. According to the University of Maryland's World Public Opinion Poll, majorities in only nine of the seventeen countries believe Al Qaeda carried out the attacks.[4]

The 9/11 official story is an old model of power: Create an event, blame an enemy, go to war, and make money. But that old model doesn't work in a world in which more people have access to information. Social-networking technology and good old mass organizing helped to bring down dictators in Tunisia and Egypt. The U.S. State Department had some influence in those struggles there, yes, but these same revolutionary forces have now come back to live in the streets and parks of every major U.S. city, a permanent encampment for democracy, radical sharing, freethinking, and human spontaneity. It's the Occupy movement, and it's a beautiful thing.

Why is this happening? Many of us at first thought that Barack Obama was a David. We are just beginning to admit that the president is in fact a Goliath. The truth is, Barack Obama is an exemplar of the status quo juggernaut of U.S. power. The Occupy movement is what happens when major hopes are raised and then dashed. We have decided to become the change we thought we could get from someone else.

It's important, though, to not forget that the promise of true change was tragically betrayed by one who spoke so well and acted so little. As I will discuss in this book, Barack Obama has these deep family ties to the CIA, USAID, the U.S. military, and other agents of power. Exposing his bait and switch helps to expose a key systemic flaw in America. Obama has bent over backward to preserve illegal wiretapping, the official cover-up of 9/11 and anthrax; he has perpetuated the use of renditions and torture; and he has expanded America's illegal wars. If he were what he sold himself to be, the Occupiers wouldn't be so committed and mobilized. Both the 9/11 Truth movement and the Occupy movement show that the people, the 99 percent, across the spectrum, have more in common than the old notions of left and right wings. The game has changed.

America is aching for meaning. It's aching for some new revolutionary ideas. We Americans are a practical people; we make our pragmatism our philosophy. We take our theories from action, not academies. So I will express my philosophy by holding up the great examples I have found in the action of others, in history and in my own time. It's these people I strive to be more like.

Slingshot to the Juggernaut is dedicated to David, and I mean that in a number of ways. I dedicate this book to the David who slew Goliath, the David who wrote great songs of peace and justice. I write this to call forth your own inner David.[5]

I also dedicate this book to a new David, Dr. David M. Graham. Although this David is a hero I never met, I have studied his inspiring life and death for the past five years. In his native Shreveport, Louisiana, David Graham met two of the 9/11 hijackers ten months before 9/11. David had sharp suspicions about them, but when he tried to report his meetings, the FBI threatened and bullied him.

After 9/11, David was shocked to see the two young Arabs he had met pop up suddenly in the mug shots of the nineteen hijackers. He wrote a book about whom he had met, what he had seen, and when. He reported the truth: that the system, for some reason, deliberately *would not listen*. He was constantly in touch with the Shreveport FBI, before and after 9/11, and they were adamant that he not publish his book. David feared for his life, but he acted despite his fear. In 2005, he was only beginning to really put the puzzle of 9/11 together. But on the verge of publishing his book, Graham was mysteriously poisoned.

Yet his story lives on. His resurrection is in the hearts of all who remain curious about 9/11. He urges us on. His death tells us we are on the right track. Graham was crucified for our lack of courage. Graham shows us that Jesus was not supposed to become a spiritual mascot for the "genocide-for-oil" program of U.S. military adventures. Jesus, as Graham showed, is fearlessness in a pure form—a fearlessness that is here today for all of us to use.

Graham would want us to be free, to use the crisis of our current time to renew our dedication to the truth. So, even in the crush of his death, there's an opportunity for new life. The story of a martyr is a powerful motivator. When someone shows fearlessness against the juggernaut, it's important for that person's story to be shouted from the rooftops. If political resistance can be combined with careful, compassionate, mindful spiritual practice, then the revolution of social justice becomes unstoppable. Both Davids show us this, across time.

A FELLOWSHIP OF DAVIDS

David Graham was not the only David to teach us how to use a slingshot. In this book, we will meet Lt. Col. Anthony Shaffer, who stood up against an entire Pentagon cover-up around 9/11. I will talk about my community media café, Vox Pop, and I'll flesh out some of the stories that were originally started in our newspaper, the *New York Megaphone*. We will meet Barry Kissin, a columnist and lawyer in Maryland who writes with passion against the anthrax cover-up. We will meet Kevin Ryan, a scientist who has called attention to the CIA contractor that makes both anthrax *and* the kind of rare high-grade explosives that were found in trace amounts in the rubble of the Twin Towers.

Is it just a coincidence that all four of the heroes mentioned above are men of science *and* men of faith? I am beginning to see a pattern here. The revolutionaries of the future are not atheists, but people of rigorous honesty. People who respect the higher power, the truth, a truth it's okay to call God. A God with many names and many faces. A Spirit of Truth that is a requisite for figuring out how to see a future of hope and fix our broken world.

This is a book for all people. For those who are religious and spiritual, and those who are not. I gladly give a nod to all the atheists and say yes, the Old Testament is full of blood, gore, genocide, homophobia, misogyny, historical contradictions, and a "jealous God" who is willing to exterminate whole races. I know. Twelve years of Catholic school drilled that into my head. How could there be anything of value here?

In the Bible, there are the signs and stories that point toward a revolutionary solution to our problems. Finding our higher power is part of becoming more merciful. God is mercy at its purest. Potential revolutionaries are robbing themselves of some powerful magic by completely throwing out the Bible.

I aspire to be a revolutionary. But, like the original David, I'm not interested in big guns. There are better weapons for the struggle I am going to describe. It's like David said before he used his slingshot: "All this multitude, too, shall learn that it is not by sword or spear that the Lord saves."

It's not from violence, the Pentagon, the White House, or the media that the truth comes out; it's from a truth that is in each of our hearts. Each of the Davids I've mentioned so far has shared a deep devotion to truth seeking and, in sharing a message of truth, has produced a prophetic message that has inspired others.

I strive to make this a book of prophetic political philosophy. I say "prophetic" because this is a work of history but also a work that projects a new future, based on where we've been. In the Old Testament, we see that the prophet's work is to be able to bounce back and forth, to float like a hip-hop MC on the waves of language, to look back into history, see the promises his or her people have made, and then call for a future that returns to those core promises.

This is a book for all people, for those who are spiritual just as much as for those who are not. My life has a foot in each camp. I have been an atheist and a Catholic, and I have learned the language of each. If you know where to look, the Bible holds signs and stories that overlap with scientific and secular solutions to our problems. Wisdom is like that.

I have been dedicated to exposing the Bush-Cheney 9/11 cover-up for ten years now, but what really turns me on is that a whole new political practice has emerged inside the movement for truth. The old borders of Right and Left are less relevant as a potential means of uniting huge amounts of people around universal values of peace and truth. Rather than frame the world in the paradigms of "Democrat versus Republican" or "liberal versus conservative," the new struggle to come will be "the people versus the elite." Or, to put it in rawer terms, a bumper sticker I saw recently proposed that it's all about "People versus Pigs." That's true, and yet I'm also talking about ideas that can turn pigs back into people again. God, Mercy, Jesus, Buddha, compassion, revolution . . . these things are not concepts, they are practices that bring about redemption and serious social change.

I'm not afraid of contradictions. I graduated college with a postmodern, poststructuralist education in downtown New York City, but I went on to form two corporations before I was forty. One was a fair-trade cof-feehouse company that helped transform a crime-ridden neighborhood into a safer, more vibrant community. The other was a book publisher with a quirky name. Soft Skull Press started out under the counter at the local Kinko's near my college, the New School, in the Village.

Both businesses I have run were a mix of ecstatic risk, swagger, service, and love. They both resulted in a mix of success and failure. The experience taught me more than a PhD or an MBA.

Back at Kinko's, I had a great business mentor. He was also a lefty-capitalist hybrid thinker. When I started Soft Skull Press in 1992, it was a lark; I never thought it would grow up, be run by other great people, and, one dark day in the Great Recession, come back home and give me a book deal. But it has, and look, this book is the proof.

In the late '90s at Soft Skull, I published hot little books of poetry by alternative-rock people and new breeds of social activism (titles like *No More Prisons* and *Saving Private Power*). So, when an opportunity arose to acquire and republish a battered, heavily criticized biography of Dubya Bush, I grabbed it. The company was being distributed nationally at this point, and we printed forty-five thousand copies of what we felt was a set of neglected truths about young Bush. The experience was like a roller coaster. Could the First Amendment and the free flow of information be a slingshot against the juggernaut of lies, media manipulation, and cover-ups that has become the trademark of the CIA/Iran-Contra/Bush family? The results were mixed. The low point was when Bush biographer Jim Hatfield died in the summer of 2001, a month and a half before 9/11. At the time, Hatfield's alcoholism and despair inclined me to believe that he committed suicide. But did he really decide to kill himself right before 9/11? Ten years later, the timing sure seems odd.

Jim Hatfield had stuff on the Bush–bin Laden business history in the book we published back in 1999. Thanks to this, I feel like I've been a "Truther" since 1999, two years before 9/11. Again, from his death comes new life—his work and his sacrifice helped shape the last ten years of my own journalism and independent detective work.

If you are married to parts of the official story, it will take some cour-age to confront the facts that I have dug up. But once you have read *Sling-*

shot in its entirety, I hope you will feel more awake, more determined to seek out the facts for yourself, more energized to take action in your circle and in our world. Certain practices are stronger than death. Love is stronger than death. Love of truth is one of the greatest loves we can know.

I don't know what your spiritual life is like. Maybe you're a Mormon, a Muslim, or an atheist. Maybe your "higher power" is simply the kindness of other people. I see the face of God most clearly there myself.

I myself have had a lifelong rocky relationship with Catholicism. However, I still love Jesus, and I combine my Christian prayer life with the practice of Zen Buddhism. Jesus said he would send us the Spirit of Truth. In this book we'll explore what that spirit is, and how to find it even in the silence of Zen meditation.

Evil exists. No one of us can confront it alone. Miracles happen when we become so in love with life, and truth, that we lose our fear of death. We need to support each other. And as individuals, we all need to work on our connection to our higher power. This is how we get away from living in fantasies, being addicted to illusions, suffering for things that are ultimately empty. We are all called to come higher, to be something greater than we are.

Throughout the book I will be fleshing out my controversial assertions about 9/11. I will make the strongest possible case that the attacks came from deep inside the U.S. war machine. But again, as weird as it may seem, this is not a reason to give up or go back to believing a racist lie that blames innocent Muslims. The topic is actually an opportunity for hope.

How? Well, the American people, in their wisdom, don't like war. We don't want it. We as a people are eager to figure out how to ban it once and for all. The study of the truth about 9/11 is essential to understanding modern history. You start to see a pattern: We had to be hoodwinked into Vietnam, World War I, World War II, the Spanish-American War, the Mexican-American War, et cetera. The U.S. government's use of traumatizing spectacle to mold public opinion is well documented. This fact shows that war is obsolete. And the system knows it.

Once you understand just how calculating and cold the U.S. war machine has become, you will be liberated from having the same old fears.

The fears are fake; they are manufactured like junk food, marketed like drugs. In a country addicted to war, we need a new kind of sobriety.

I believe the work of truth and peace runs counter to the interests of the modern national security state. The highest ethical calling, therefore, is to envision a revolutionary new state. The need for the current war state, as we know it, is itself obsolete. The future of the U.S. state is no state. Yes, we need a revolutionary time and a revolutionary process of dismantling the gigantic "homicide bomber" that is the current U.S. state. And yet this is the natural next step for the Enlightenment-based product of the Renaissance, this federation of liberty-loving associations that America was chartered to be. The future belongs to a place where the best minds of the revolutionary Left, the anarchists, the patriots, the spiritual communities, and the libertarian Right all intersect and cross-pollinate. The future is wide open.

The modern national security state, in the form of Obama's White House, has begun to target 9/11 Truth activists specifically. They attempt to manage "reality" and disrupt the "online and real-space political activity" of those who dare to foment "conspiracy theories." (The quotations there are from the Obama White Houses's own Cass Sunstein, whom we will confront below.) Obama's postmodern "progressives" are taking technocratic police-state oppression to a new low, so we need a new high. What would a revolutionary new form of democratic self-organization look like?

America went through a rough time in the twentieth century; it was a period of intense growth at a rapid pace. Suddenly, we find ourselves running a global empire with over six hundred military bases around the world. Is this what we were destined to become at our founding? Or did we go horribly off track somewhere along the way? What will the twenty-first century mean for America as new global superpowers emerge and the U.S. dollar's strength begins to wane? Is it a crisis that must lead to war, or is it an opportunity for a new high in peace?

The 9/11 Commission Report has one true statement: "The USA needs to figure out what it stands for." The Commission was not up for trying to fix the problem, but you and I will do so through the experience of writing and reading this book. The United States needs a special kind of revolution. We need new Davids to come forth, to say, "This armor isn't working." We need to go beyond Left and Right, beyond Democrat and Republican, to expand our hearts, to nurture our spirits and our spirituality, and to create a renewal of the American spirit.

Out of this spiritual renewal will come powerful new ideas that empower people. We will rejuvenate our democracy and our economy. I have found that it's not hard to learn the language of capitalism, to appreciate what's good about capitalism, without giving up on the idea that capitalism must change, in a fundamental way, if the working class, the people as a whole, and our planet are going to survive. Once we learn this language, we can talk about ways to democratize capital itself. Once you forsake violence, new ideas are possible: new forms of freedom and democracy that can also integrate (without being dominated by) the interests of capital. It is in the interests of both capital and labor to create a whole new set of relationships around human needs, collaboration, capital, markets, investors, and entrepreneurs. I will expand upon these ideas in my section on public interest venture capital and the Occupy Business School.

I believe it's okay to love America. We need to work on a sane love, a love that makes sense. What if America were something that radicals, peace lovers, libertarians, and lefties could be proud of again? July Fourth weekend of 2011, the flag fell down in a storm where I was staying with my son. I found myself going back to Boy Scout code, picking up the flag. When I realized it was soiled, I folded up the flag in that special triangle way. I took it inside and laid it on the washer in the laundry room. You can call me an anarchist, but I love America.

Anger is a cup of poison, and hatred only breeds hatred. If our thinking about America focuses only on the dark side, on the sins of war and the injustice of imperialism, we cheat ourselves of the full picture. Too many on the Left do this. I will be asking everyone, especially the people on the Left, to go further in their thinking about history, economics, and power. I am coming from the Left, but I'm not constrained by any one ideology. The more I step outside the bounds of leftist orthodoxy, the better the ideas I come up with, ideas that will contribute to a larger dialogue about how we can save America—and the world.

Contradictions don't last forever. They lead to a beautiful moment of climax called synthesis. This book will end with a new practice, a proposal for a new way to be. I want the Truth Party to be about creating community, about people coming together and talking, with rigorous honesty, about how we can bring more truth, beauty, and liberty into our lives. We need to do it in our circles and simultaneously talk about how we can do it as a nation. A top-down political party would talk about something like this only at a national level, while some people I have met in Zen say you can affect only your immediate circle. I say they are both right. This vision of a new era of American nonviolence is worthwhile. It's worth doing all we can, with all our mind, and all our heart.

Turn the page, and become like David.

Go to the dry creek bed.

Pick out five perfect stones.

Goliath is loud, but he is about to fall.

2 TRUTHER AS COURT REPORTER: HOW AMERICA'S NUMBER ONE TABOO TOPIC IS MISTREATED IN THE "HALLS OF JUSTICE"

Let's look at and compare two numbers.

The first one is fourteen million. That's how many dollars were spent in the 9/11 Commission's "official investigation" of the 9/11 attacks. Fourteen million dollars is less than one third of the amount spent on Ken Starr's investigation of President Clinton.

Our next number is five hundred times larger. It's seven *billion*. That's the sum total spent by the September 11th Victim Compensation Fund. The serious money was put into a hush-fund vehicle that paid the victims' families not to sue.

With 9/11, the powers that be did a quick investigation that blamed no one and said nothing. The government then spent five hundred times more on shutting people up. The real cover-up was not the Washington, D.C., insiders who wrote a ridiculous and spotty 9/11 report; it was preventing justice in the courts by muzzling the victims who in their limitless grief would of course attempt to find relief by suing the U.S. government, the airlines, and the intelligence agencies that either "failed us" through "incompetence" or did something much more nefarious.

If you compare the two numbers as a ratio, you see that the 9/11 Commission was funded with 0.2% of what we spent on the victims' hush fund. Seven billion dollars can pack a wallop. But not everyone has been hushed up, and there's the real story. This chapter will look at three heroic Davids who dared take on Goliath. These activists and attorneys sought to overturn one juggernaut of a well-capitalized cover-up.

In the United States, people are raised to believe that "everyone can get their day in court." But with 9/11, each time evidence was presented that something was terribly wrong, the dispensers of American justice reacted by moving to crush the plaintiffs.

NYC CAN

In 2009, I served as the canvass director of the New York City Coalition for Accountability Now (NYC CAN). NYC CAN was an effort to rejuvenate the stalled NYC 9/11 Ballot Initiative. The founders of New York 9/11 Truth had made some progress collecting signatures to put the 9/11 investigation question on the NYC ballot. But at the outset of 2009, the new NYC CAN director, Ted Walter, and friends decided that "NYC 9/11 Ballot Initiative" needed to be rebranded as something a bit more palatable, a bit more acceptable to the average New York voter. The new name, NYC CAN, was upbeat and positive. It was trendy, and felt in rhythm with Obama's pert slogan "yes we can." In fact, that year, some activists even dared to dream that Obama himself might open a new 9/11 investigation.

Part of the new mission at NYC CAN was to simplify the message. Our new style would be to coolly and calmly present the request for a voter's signature, to allow voters in New York City a chance to vote on a 9/11 independent investigation. No long debates.

Ted and I ran a tight operation. We had T-shirts and a training manual. We gathered the required signatures, over eighty thousand. We were optimistic that we could overcome the systemic biases in the legal system against 9/11 skepticism. We were wrong.

The ballot access laws in New York State required fifty thousand valid signatures for a popular referendum to be placed on New York City's ballot. But the New York Supreme Court judge decided not to allow us to ask the voters the question about a new 9/11 investigation. The legal decision, when you read it, is twisted and tense, both sad and funny.[6] At one point the court says that this would have been too much "direct democracy," and that this just isn't done in New York State.

The judge accused us of "tortured reasoning," but he himself seems to have been suffering from prejudiced assumptions. The court shows its hand in this regard by referring to the "international terrorists" that it assumes were responsible for 9/11. If the court already had a culprit, why would it have let us open a new investigation into just who those "terrorists" were?

There were some legal gray areas from the first draft of the NYC 9/11 Ballot Initiative that did come back to haunt us. For example, we projected quite a large budget, and we claimed we could raise the $14 million all from private donations. The judge didn't think this was realistic. But who knows—this judge was clearly uninformed about the size of the potential base of supporters.

At one point, our attorney asked the judge about Building 7. The judge answered, "Building what?" That comment inspired NYC CAN to start a new TV ad campaign to raise awareness about one of 9/11's smoking guns, WTC Building 7, which imploded at free-fall speed around 5:21 PM on 9/11, without having been hit by a plane. WTC leaseholder Larry Silverstein even admitted on PBS that he had decided to "pull it," but the media and the courts and even the giant insurance agency all decided to let that odd comment slide.

NYC CAN's leadership made a tragic decision not to appeal the New York State Supreme Court's ruling. It's not the decision I would have made, but my job was already over, and Ted had a commitment to attend grad school out of state.

We lost that battle, but we haven't lost the war. The NYC CAN experience made me a student of how the courts can possibly be used to simply investigate the biggest trauma of our lifetimes.

In the next ten years of 9/11 Truth, I predict we will see less activism in the streets and more court cases. That's because more admissible evidence comes out every year. This change is already underway. With lawyers like William Veale and the Center for 9/11 Justice, we *will* have our day.

Before we dive in and learn more about California attorney William Veale, let's head out from New York City, across the Hudson River, into New Jersey, where citizen litigator Don Meserlian is representing himself in a series of tussles with his local municipal court.

DON QUIXOTE IS
A FORENSICS ENGINEER

On February 4, 2010, forensics engineer Don Meserlian was brought to court in Fairfield, New Jersey, on charges of "harassment" of police chief Mark Deuer. Meserlian had tried to compel Deuer to review an accusation of "treason" in regard to the 9/11 attacks. He presented New York–area seismic records from September 11, 2001, and a scientific study published by physicists at Bentham.org. This peer-reviewed study of the dust from the World Trade Center compelled Meserlian to claim that 9/11 was a crime, and to suspect that it was an inside job. The reason he had "harassed" Chief Deuer was that Meserlian understood certain laws compelled everyone to notify local authorities in any situation where "treason" occurs. I put "treason" in quotes because it's an exact term, a precise word, that denotes a crime carefully defined in the U.S. Constitution.

Meserlian has dug up an old federal law still on the books: U.S. Code 18 (Sec. 2382). This law prohibits "misprision of treason" and applies to all U.S. citizens and judges: No one can fail to act when presented with strong evidence of treason. Meserlian tested his interpretation of the law by phoning U.S. attorney David Foster, who agreed that the law gives any citizen the duty to alert any judge regarding treason.

In Fairfield Municipal Court that day, however, prosecution, police, and Judge Pomaco countered that the eighty-two-year-old Meserlian had been so "annoying" to the police that he was guilty of "harassment." Even though Meserlian would lose his case, at the end of the trial, Judge Pomaco called Meserlian a "patriot." He allowed Meserlian ample time to make his case, over the objections of the prosecution.

Maybe the judge realized that the case law was on Meserlian's side. The same misprision statute has been used in two cases from the Civil War era. In those cases, the judges pointed out that "treason" stands alone as the sole felony our founding fathers saw important enough to define in the Constitution, which states that the primary definition of treason is to "levy war" against the United States. "Levy war" is defined in the case law as that which "wages" or "causes or compels" the United States to go to war.

Following that logic, then, since 9/11 compelled two long wars, and since credible parties have asserted that the attacks may have been an inside job, the 9/11 issue is really a legal question of treason. A close reading of our Constitution, therefore, would compel us to investigate that which caused and compelled us to war. Even if the notion that the attacks may have been an inside job is absurd or atrocious to some, the U.S. Constitution advises to carefully examine any accusations of treason.

But in court, Judge Pomaco wasn't buying it. He kept directing the trial back to the accusation of "harrasment" against Mr. Meserlian. Meserlian, for his part, kept trying to talk U.S. Constitution. The court's refusal to consider his evidence of treason seemed to show that the court was prejudiced against his controversial line of thinking. The judge found Meserlian guilty, but levied no fine.

At the end of the trial, Judge Pomaco gave an interesting speech: Don Meserlian was a dedicated family man, an upstanding citizen, and a "patriot." Pomaco went so far as to describe the 9/11 attacks as "serious" and "a terrible tragedy."

However, Meserlian never asserted that 9/11 was merely "tragic." Beyond Pomaco's maudlin speech, the 9/11 event, and the subsequent lack of scientific, unbiased investigation are serious crimes. In both the NYC CAN case and the more local Meserlian trial, the courts seemed to be wearing a form of mental blinder; the Bush-Cheney story about 9/11 was somehow sacrosanct. The same men who, it is widely acknowledged, lied and manipulated us into the Iraq War are somehow presumed innocent of any malfeasance about bin Laden, anthrax, and the collapse of three towers from two planes.

Rational analysis of 9/11 shows a masterful crime that demands masterful investigation. As the Bible says, when injustice is perpetuated for so long, even the stones will begin to cry out for justice. In court that day, it was sad to see Judge Pomoco smiling at Meserlian and trying to show some kind of integrity, some kind of humanity and virtue. The man was simply unable to sidestep his prior assumptions about 9/11. His substitution of sentimentality for a dispassionate review of evidence itself shows prejudice. The stones cry out. The cool blue fluorescent lights of the New Jersey courthouse seemed to mask the sound of the U.S. Constitution being ripped apart in the back room.

As 9/11 justice activism heads increasingly to the courts, future judges will have this problem: The 9/11 Truth movement's evidence is compelling, scientific, and verifiable. Meserlian, national director of a new group called the Citizens' Committee for a 9/11 Grand Jury, is a lifelong forensics engineer. In his thirty-five years of giving testimonies, he has never lost a case.

September 11 is remarkable for its emotive power, but also for the crime's complexity and for its curious lack of judicial review. Rational, clear-headed analysis of 9/11 has led an entire movement of intelligent citizens to conclude that the perpetrators of the 9/11 attacks remain unindicted inside U.S. military and intelligence. They have evaded scrutiny by most media. Yet domestic and international public opinion shows a sharp break with the Bush-Cheney-Obama official story.

The Meserlian trial is historic. It brought about a new era for U.S. citizens who are skeptical about 9/11. Meserlian is one tough cookie, and a bit of an eccentric. He's also a charming guy who plays a mean violin and can jam with you at the drop of a hat. Meserlian has done the world a favor. He has more guts than we did at NYC CAN. He raises the stakes and points us to laws to remedy our need to investigate that which we can no longer ignore: *treason.* Say it out loud, now: "Treason!"

This case must now be picked up and made to judges of similar but even greater sympathy than Judge Pomaco. We want the sympathy without the sentimentality. We want rigor; we want the crucible of cross-examination. In the court of the mass media, our evidence is not considered. Instead, the sneering Washington consensus pats itself on the back for making dismissive generalizations. They call us "cranks" and "kooks." Meanwhile, we prepare for our next day in court.

The authors of the U.S. Constitution wanted accusations of treason to be treated with exquisite care. Even among our broken judiciary, surely there is a judge who understands this. Maybe it's up to you and me, my dear reader, to go out and find that judge. Because if the fate of NYC CAN and Don Meserlian don't inspire you to action, look at what the system did to attorney William Veale: It sought to crucify him for his love of justice.

MEETING BILL VEALE

In the spring of 2010, I met attorney William Veale in Valley Forge, Pennsylvania, at the aptly named Treason in America conference. We had been in touch via email, but at the conference, we gave a speech together about how an ad hoc "citizens grand jury investigation" could be formed and given actual subpoena power and legitimacy by the system.

Veal's logic is based on the Fifth Amendment:

> *No person shall be held to answer for a capital, or otherwise infamous crime, unless on a presentment or indictment of a Grand Jury . . .*

Veale explained what he meant by use of "presentment" in a memo I asked him to write:

> *The first provision of the Amendment has to do with Grand Juries, requiring an Indictment, which is a legal accusation requested by a prosecutor or a Presentment, which is a charge made by a Grand Jury without the request of a prosecutor. Presentments have had a rich history in this country, but fell into disrepute under varying circumstances. There is no mention of presentments in the Federal Criminal Code, and there hasn't been since the late forties. There can, however, be no sounder basis of legal action in this country than the words of the Fifth Amendment. The presence of the word "presentment" in the Amendment means there must of necessity be a mechanism for its use, no matter how desperately the writers of the Criminal Code may have wanted it to vanish.*

Aha! So, that means at the bedrock of the Constitution is the power of the people to indict criminals, without using a prosecutor. We already have a tool to create a grand jury of citizens. That should make every skeptic, every Truther, excited about getting real justice. Veale adds:

> The grand jury is in its essence a democratic institution. It was designed to be a rein on the government, putting between it and an accused citizen another group of citizens who would decide whether or not the government prosecutor was acting with cause. Since the representatives of the citizens are not discharging their obligations as some of us have envisioned, we are not in a position to look to our elected representatives for justice in the instance of 9/11. We may look to history for a procedure to follow. In colonial days and after the revolution, communities were small enough that town hall meetings played an important role in governance. In the case of local corruption, where the prosecutor was engaged in criminal activity, the people themselves would convene a grand jury for the purpose of investigating and prosecuting an offending official."

As a part of our presentation at the Treason in America conference, Veale and I handed out a "Truth over Treason" form, on two-part NCR paper. It was a kind of legal document, which forty-four individuals that day agreed to sign. By signing, they agreed to contact their local judges and attempt to find a judge willing to look at the evidence of treason.

In the meantime, Veale was preparing for the trial of April Gallop, a soldier and 9/11 victim who suffered injuries in the Pentagon that day.

GALLOP V. CHENEY

The Navajo say, "You can't wake a person pretending to be asleep." Some refuse to even look at evidence of wrongdoing on 9/11. Veale calls that thing the "fortress of denial." On the website of the Center for 9/11 Justice, he and his team of attorneys explain:

The attacks of September 11th were part of a complex and elaborate psychological operation that created in each citizen to a greater or lesser degree a fortress of denial, which has prevented many from any forthright attempt to investigate the truth about 9/11. Before justice will be allowed to breathe, that fortress must be destroyed.

Veale's client is former Pentagon soldier April Gallop. Alongside her two-month-old infant son, Elisha, Gallop was injured in the Pentagon that day.

If the official story were correct, Gallop would be dead. On the first floor, in the fifth corridor of the Pentagon's E ring, her desk and her baby boy were in the direct pathway of one of Flight 77's 2.3-ton jet engines. Instead, Gallop was knocked unconscious and came to in a disaster. Office debris was everywhere, but plane parts were not.

"I didn't see any seats, any metal, any baggage; I wasn't covered in jet fuel."

In a 2007 speech in Irvine, California, Gallop told the audience, "Most of the debris we were encompassed with was pertaining to office things: concrete, books, computers, tables, things to that effect. . . . With that in mind, I would have never believed that it was a plane, simply because I didn't see particular things. According to the Pentagon renovation team [who mapped out where everyone was], we were thirty-five to forty-five feet away from the place of impact."

Representatives from the Army, Navy, Air Force, and Marines visited Gallop in the hospital to discuss what her public statements would and would not say. "They wanted to train us, or specifically communicate to us how they wanted us to express the story, what happened, but I couldn't do that. . . . They wanted to ensure that we communicated things as they made the official story. I just couldn't do that based on what I saw on the inside."

In a military hospital, a captain from the U.S. Army suggested things to add to her story. Gallop objected. According to Gallop, the captain's parting words were "I'm going to leave you with this. This is what it was, this is what you saw, and this is what you're going to say you saw. And we'll be back to transport you to Walter Reade."

"Life afterwards has been just as traumatizing as having the experience," reports Gallop. A female Fox News reporter let slip that the Pentagon was telling the media not to speak with Gallop. Fox News, fearing exclusion from future Pentagon news feeds, complied with the request.

The lawsuit that William Veale and company eventually filed on behalf of Gallop is a great opportunity for historians to pause and reflect just how many strange anomalies there are around 9/11 and the Pentagon. The primary smoking gun cited in *Gallop v. Cheney* is that transportation secretary Norman Mineta testified to the 9/11 Commission that Dick Cheney was in an underground bunker at the White House that morning by nine thirty. Cheney was monitoring radar, and beside him was a young male aide. As the wayward "Flight 77" (if that is what it was) wandered out to the West Virginia area and back, the aide built the tension by telling the VP, "The plane is fifty miles out; it's now forty miles out . . . do the orders still stand?" Cheney whipped his head around and said, "Of course the orders still stand—have you heard *anything* to the contrary?"

This testimony was deleted from the 9/11 Commission website, and, when later asked about the oversight by a camera crew from the movie *Loose Change*, former secretary Mineta was surprised to hear it had been left out.

There's also the problem that the National Transportation Safety Board and the 9/11 Commission Report could not agree on the final flight path of Flight 77. In a similar way, 9/11 researchers Citizens' Investigation Team went to Arlington Cemetery, around the Pentagon, and found eyewitnesses who said the plane came from a more westerly direction, over the Navy Annex building and north of the Citgo station. The official flight path has the plane coming up in a more northeast direction, smacking into a light pole that then somehow inserted itself perfectly into the windshield of local cab driver Lloyd English.

Flight 77's flight data recorder showed the massive jetliner descending at a sharp angle; then, before impact, the recorder mysteriously stopped recording data. This information is inconsistent with the "five frames" of blurry video released by the Pentagon, which show a flat blur parallel to the ground slamming into the Pentagon wall.

Or, let's recall that Clinton holdover Richard Clarke testified that Rumsfeld and Myers were in the Pentagon, running the show, recorded via video conference, as the Pentagon plane was approaching.

As Veale puts it, "Whatever efforts they made to prevent the attack on the Pentagon were unsuccessful, even though sufficient time and armaments existed to mount a defense. If they were in the National Military Command Center, in full view by Richard Clarke, and presumably taped on a video-teleconference screen, they cannot avoid the scrutiny that ordinarily follows failure in the line of duty."

"CYNICAL DELUSION AND FANTASY"

On March 14, 2010, Second Circuit judge Denny Chin dismissed Gallop's suit with prejudice and heated denunciation. He ignored the sixty-five pages of evidence that court procedures required him to treat as presumed true. He ignored the anomalies about what Cheney, Rumsfeld, and Myers were doing on 9/11, and what they said and did about it afterward. In fact, Chin avoided mentioning any of those three by name altogether. Veale later said, "It was like discussing the indictment of someone for robbing a liquor store without ever naming the suspect." But Chin was content to ignore much and dismiss the entire suit as "cynical delusion and fantasy."

Perhaps it's fortunate that Chin levied such incendiary language. On Veale's side were two other fine attorneys, one of whom, Dennis Cunningham, is a strong writer. In discussing Chin's logic, Cunningham used a deft mix of empathy and passionate appeal for reason beyond prejudice. He often conceded to the court that the underlying presumptions of its case were "indeed shocking" and "outrageous" but also "substantial, and serious" and based on "an elemental knowledge of human history"—i.e., "evil is attracted to power."

Power, by this radical logic, is therefore naturally a primary suspect when it comes to the highest crimes and cover-ups. Of course, this kind of radical, populist logic is not Chin's federal court's cup of tea. Chin was rather lazy, according to the plaintiffs, and content to make a "blanket determination, not based on the factual allegations it was faced with but on the Court's [read: Chin's] subjective, personal reaction to the horror of the very thought of the wrongdoing alleged," and therefore, "the plaintiffs' claims were absolutely implausible—as a matter of law, as it were, emanating from the depth of the Court's gut—and therefore frivolous, and to be quashed without recourse."

Veale and company appealed. One year later, they were promised "five minutes" at a three-judge appeals court hearing in New Haven, Connecticut. One of the judges scheduled to preside was none other than president George H. Walker Bush's first cousin judge Scott Walker. Walker refused to recuse himself, despite a motion from the plaintiffs. It went downhill from there.

SHOWDOWN IN NEW HAVEN

On April 4, 2011, I traveled with one of the junior attorneys on the case, Mr. Mustapha Ndusa, from New York City to New Haven to attend the appellate hearing of April Gallop.

Having attended the appeals hearing of FBI agent Richard Taus years earlier, I was reminded that a three-judge courtroom looks like a triumvirate, a gang. Three judges instead of one means three huddled together in collusion, whispering loudly and talking over each other, talking over attorneys. In New Haven, they interrupted each other as much as they interrupted Veale. The *spirit* of an appellate court is already one of an intensely adversarial nature, so it's especially chaotic and bitter when your cause is asking questions about 9/11.

Attorney Bill Veale was heroic, leaning over and vociferously defending the cause. When he was hot, he was white hot. "Evil does exist. Power is attracted to it." He was a poetic prophet against a new devil.

In his twenty years of hard labor as a public defender, Veale served the battered proletariat. As court-appointed defense counsel, he tried to get poor crooks and accused crooks good deals and reduced time. This day was his first appearance in federal court.

Veale got about twenty minutes to make his case. Some of the judges did show some humanity, like the time they let Veale have a final two minutes to catch his breath and make his final points. But then when

Veale began to speak, Judge Walker would interrupt with an idle, long-winded request that they go through a list, vocally, of who the defendants were in this case: vice president Dick Cheney, former secretary of defense Donald Rumsfeld, JTOS Meyers, and John Does #1-X.

At one point, Bush cousin Judge Walker also made an "out of the blue" comment of his own. He did acknowledge that "there is a lot of controversy about this topic." He looked out directly at the galley, where we fifteen Truthers sat among the day's usual gaggle of fidgety lawyers and heiresses appealing estate matters of decaying Connecticut wealth. In the jury box sat twelve or fifteen bored-looking kids in blue suits and dresses, a distracted field trip from Yale Law School. But when the case was over, all fifteen Truthers stood up at once. The judges noticed it: There *is* a public with a bunch of questions and sharp suspicions about the Bush-Cheney 9/11 story. We were hoping the judges would keep that in mind when considering the evidence and arguments levied by Veale, April Gallop, and the Center. After all, it looked like even Judge Walker knew some of the questions people had, by acknowledging the widespread skepticism.

TWO $15,000 HAMMERS SLAM DOWN ON VEALE: "JUSTICE DENIED"

Judge Walker, of course, was not picked to write the inevitable denial that came from the Second Court of Appeals. Judge Calabrese did, and stuck to the script Judge Chin had used: Huff and puff about how outrageous the claim is, but don't actually respond to the evidence presented.

So, sixty-five pages of evidence, from sources such as the Bush White House's own officials Clarke and Mineta, can be tossed away as nothing but "pure speculation and conjecture." The three-judge appellate court stepped on the gas and added an aggressive layer of bile and mockery to its denial, which opens with:

> As the sentient world well recalls, on the morning of September 11, 2001, agents of the Al Qaeda terrorist organization hijacked commercial airplanes and attacked the World Trade Center in

*New York City and the national head quarters of the Depart-
ment of Defense in Arlington, Virginia.*

Calabrese pointed out that Gallop's case could be thrown out on the basis of "estoppel"; i.e., she had sued someone else before on similar grounds. However, she lost before, and according to the legal definition of "estoppel" cases, "estoppel" stops you only if you won something, using a different argument, in an earlier case. "Absent success in a prior proceeding," argued the Supreme Court in *New Hampshire v. Maine*, the courts are not supposed to deny appeals by citing estoppel.

In court that day in New Haven, Veale pointed out that new evidence about 9/11 factual data "is coming out all the time." Therefore, Gallop's prior suits were irrelevant. The nature of her claims changed based on new evidence.

In the denial, Calabrese then made the harsh claim that Veale "failed to provide" any of this new evidence. That's rather unfair, given that Veale was already over his five-minute time limit and was constantly being interrupted with asinine points of clarification from the bench. All of the evidence was outlined and prepared for court. It was described in summary form in sixty-five-page documents.

If Veale had been asked about what new evidence has come out recently, we know from the Center's various briefs on behalf of Gallop that Veale and company would not have been shy about talking about the evidence of the sophisticated demolition explosive nano-thermite at the WTC. The peer-reviewed Bentham.org study found evidence of nano-thermite in four out of four samples of WTC dust.

But in their denial (a good word for it), Judge Calabrese called this case an unnecessary imposition "on the government, which is forced to defend against the appeal, and on the taxpayers, who must pay for that defense. Accordingly, Gallop and her counsel are hereby ordered to show cause in writing within thirty days from the date of entry of this order why they should not pay double costs and damages in the amount of $15,000, for which they would be jointly and severally liable."

That's right. The judges just threatened to fine Veale $30,000. Imagine mobsters killing someone who won't pay protection money in order to send a message to the world. The threat of serious fines here shows that the judges didn't actually believe this case from Veale was lightweight "pure speculation," but thought it a very serious threat to a way of doing business.

Veale protested this sanction and made a motion to have the three judges removed from further involvement in this case. They were victims of 9/11's shock and awe, he argued, "unable to conceive that their own government did that to them. And that means that when they hear these allegations, they disregard them. They think they are the product of lunacy, or delusion . . . [They imagine], 'oh that couldn't possibly be true' . . . And that is the existence of a prejudgment or a bias."[7]

The judges responded to these motions with further denials and another set of sanctions, this time personally targeted at William Veale.

The American Bar Association did a terse article for the *ABA Journal*. The best part of the article was an online comment from one John Flynn:

> "Not content with being simply moderately corrupt and dismissing the complaint before the Plaintiff can hale these Defendants into Court and, I presume, even engage in discovery [the period when both sides in a court case examine evidence], the 2nd Circuit sees fit to try and chill other attorneys who may be considering similar lawsuits by issuing an OSC (Order to Show Cause) on the plaintiffs attorney, which I can only assume will result in over-the-top, severe sanctions, even though anyone who has looked at 9/11 in any detail knows there is at least sufficient evidence of the plaintiff's theory to defeat an MSJ (Motion for Summary Judgment) and get to trial."[8]

3 SUPREME REPRESSION RESULTS IN SUPREME RESISTANCE: FROM 9/11 TRUTH TO OCCUPY WALL STREET

In the preceding chapter, we saw a pattern. The court system consistently would not look at evidence in three separate legal cases regarding questions around 9/11. All three plaintiffs suffered as a result. NYC CAN saw all of our fundraising and efforts result in nothing. Meserlian lost his case without serious penalty, but could not get justice. Attorney William Veale, on the other hand, was levied with two $15,000 "sanctions" by the judges, as a punishment for filing a serious lawsuit.

This same pattern shows up in the life of the average 9/11 Truth activist. In 2010, when fellow truth activist Matt Meyer and others asked *Daily Show* executive producer Rory Albanese a few questions about his show's reluctance to look into 9/11, the discussion turned into a quarrel. Eventually Albanese threw a punch and caught Meyer in the eye. The police were called, and Albanese was arrested.

Sometimes the response from the powers that be is more subtle. Albanese's raw violence shows what a lot of the media elite do to Truthers, Occupiers, patriots, and revolutionaries who stand up against the juggernaut. But the violence and repression are often much more subtle than a punch to the face.

The system that won't answer us in the courts would rather fight dirty. I saw a striking example of this trend in March 2010. On the same weekend of the Treason in America conference, a "crazed lone gunman" decided to unload a pistol, shooting at the Pentagon. He was then mowed down by police, who said he "made no statements." But within a couple days, the media began to report that this mad gunman, John Patrick Bedell, was a "9/11 Truther." Never mind the lack of evidence—someone fed the media an angle, and they ate it up. That is how far we have come from logic. The 9/11 Truth issue is so taboo that there are forces at work behind the curtain of media/government power seeking to discredit 9/11 Truth by any means necessary. They fight with their fists and with their close connections to television producers. But their desperation to twist the truth is so blatant, we begin to see a pattern.

Perhaps it was just coincidental, but why did this incident happen the same weekend as the Treason in America conference? A full spectrum of lefty and libertarian activists, like Cindy Sheehan, Lt. Col. Shaffer, William Veale et al., and I, were speaking in historic Valley Forge.

ABC's *Nightline* showed up, and on camera, host Chris Bury asked me about the Pentagon shooter's "being a 9/11 Truther." That was especially weird because I had heard about the Pentagon shooter but hadn't heard that he was being painted as a "9/11 Truther." I stated right away that the allegation might in fact be disinformation. Chris Bury went on to run a clearly biased piece about the conference. *Time* magazine Woman of the Year Colleen Rowley also happened to be there, and she vociferously took Bury to task for slanting his reporting against the subject at hand.

So when Jared Loughner shot judge John Roll and then congresswoman Gabrielle Giffords, and others, I made a rare prediction: Loughner would soon be labeled a 9/11 Truther. Just a couple days later, in the *New York Times* article and on ABC News, we learned that Loughner supposedly questioned the Bush-Cheney account of 9/11. ABC News reported, via Loughner's best friend, that Loughner supposedly was a fan of the *Zeitgeist* 9/11 Truth movie. Yet the YouTube videos Loughner left behind were deranged manifestos about grammar and currency. Nothing about 9/11 Truth. He made no statements on that topic.

IT GETS PERSONAL

9/11 Truth is a social taboo. It goes to the heart of who we are, as Americans, what we do, on a daily basis, invading others' countries, killing the leaders of sovereign nations, in the name of an official story that most residents in foreign nations reject flat-out. So, of course, the growing skepticism at home will be clamped down on, hard.

Back in October 2009, as we awaited a verdict in the NYC CAN New York Supreme Court hearing, I was attacked by a stranger on the subway, "at random." This person got up and, just out of the blue, calmly slapped the shit out of me, then sat down across from me. The timing was odd: I was an employee of NYC CAN in the middle of a high-profile ballot referendum for a new 9/11 investigation. We had eighty thousand signatures; we were going strong.

I'm six-foot-three and two hundred pounds. I don't tend to lose street fights. So, after that October 2009 "random" attack on the train, over the Williamsburg Bridge, I called 911. Then, when the guy wanted to leave the subway at Marcy Avenue, I chased him down. He seemed like he might be just crazy, but he wasn't too crazy to try to dissuade me from chasing him. He kicked at me and tried to slip out the subway doors as they were closing. But I blocked the doors and got them to let me out as the guy took off down the platform.

A couple members of the NYPD and I had the guy, whose name was "Clifford Jordan," arrested. When I was called in to the Brooklyn DA's office later, I spoke with a young, rookie Kings County prosecutor named Andrew Sullivan.

I asked Andrew Sullivan what he thought about the 9/11 attacks.

"I was against them," he said, tongue in cheek.

"But what did you think about the *9/11 Commission Report?*"

He said that fundamentally, they got it right. But it turned out that Sullivan hadn't actually read the report.

I was curious about the background and motivation of the assailant, Clifford Jordan, so I put questions in writing:

> *Do you have access to his criminal file? Does he have prior arrests? Does he have a military background? ROTC? Any relationship to law enforcement?*

> *I know it's a controversial topic, but I am an activist in the 9/11 Truth Movement. This MAY have been a motive in the attack from Clifford Jordan ...*

I never got a response from Mr. Sullivan. The case against Jordan went to trial, and he was given a restraining order to stay away from me. But I wasn't allowed to know anything more about him.

REPRISALS FOR INVESTIGATING THE FBI MURDER OF DR. GRAHAM

In the next chapter, I will explain the life and death of 9/11 whistle-blower Dr. David Graham. I know there's a huge story here because on the same day I confronted the FBI in Shreveport, Louisiana, my café business back in Brooklyn was burglarized.

Imagine building a place by hand, putting in the oak floor yourself, and going up from there. Vox Pop meant a lot to me. It was a business I dreamed up during a year in Taos, New Mexico, with my girlfriend and our investors. We moved to New York City to create Vox Pop.

The idea behind Vox Pop was to create a more ethical, politically empowering take on the classic coffeehouse. We would choose a neighborhood that had no Starbucks and show the world, and ourselves, that a community-empowering, ideas-focused business, with fair-trade coffee, food, beer, and a ton of exciting live events, could, in fact, transform the neighborhood. In the end, we took a crime-ridden, economically depressed place, Ditmas Park, Flatbush, Brooklyn, and helped lead a wave of revitalization. But none of that could help Vox Pop when all kinds of federal and state agencies started harassing it.

After investigating the Graham death in Shreveport, I wrote a report to the inspector general of the Department of Justice. I was promised a response within six months. I never got any response within those six months, or at any point.

The Obama administration promised "hope" and "change," but the harassment of 9/11 Truth activists has worsened steadily, especially in 2010 and 2011, during which White House official Cass Sunstein published papers calling on the U.S. government to "infiltrate" and "disrupt" the "real space political organizing" of the 9/11 Truth Movement. In Los Angeles, local We Are Change activist Bruno Bruwhiller faced three charges, including charges related to "terrorism," all for making facial expressions of disbelief in a courtroom. Clearly, the judge knew and didn't appreciate Bruno's 9/11 Truth advocacy work, or his local outreach to befriend and educate the Los Angeles Police Department. Eventually the charges were dropped, but not before sending chills of real terror into the hearts of all local California Truth activists. We knew Bruno was being targeted for being a cofacilitator in one of the nation's most active We Are Change groups.

Back in NYC, the town is supposedly full of intellectuals and professional journalists, yet no one apparently thinks it's a prudent line of thinking to question the Bush-Cheney 9/11 official story.

9/11 is a sensitive, infected wound that needs to be drained. Someone has to stand up and say that in this moment, the United States is the global leader in violence, secrecy, torture, and war. The Occupy Wall Street movement is huge because the crimes of the United States are so huge. You will see 9/11 Truth and We Are Change people there, because the Truthers and Occupiers agree: In the USA, financial power and political power have morphed into each other. The results are demonic.

What a joy it is to sleep and eat together in the streets, to come out and play music, be together, talk to new people, feel this electric energy. To see the Occupy Wall Street movement happening in Denver, Omaha, Oakland, L.A., and NYC as I do the final revisions on this book is, in a word, simply perfect. There is a Spirit of Truth; it loves revolution and peace, and it wants us to look inside and see our true natures. We all have this Spirit of Truth inside us, and it's time for us to live a little, to let a lot more of it *out*.

It's time for a new philosophy, but more than that, it's time for a new practice. Instead of preaching about feeding the poor, inside the Occupy movements, we feed the poor, we eat together, we practice and make real a new world right now. They ask us, "What is your goal?" but I think what they mean is, "What is your lust for power?" We have no lust for power; we want to live out love and peace and truth right now, and that's not so crazy, is it?

The Occupy experiences have been similar to other gatherings and conferences about peace and truth that I have produced. In 2010, I produced something called the Truth Gathering. It not only looked into crimes and cover-ups, but also advanced a vision of the United States's becoming a country of "peace leadership."

The truth makes people strong. It calls us back to the Bill of Rights, to our first principles, to a country based on free expression, free inquiry, and government transparency.

The final section of this book is about the healing process, for NYC and the United States. We must summon the courage to leave behind the era of the War on Terror, and enter an "era of truth." Nothing could be more human, more American, or more necessary right now.

At Occupy Wall Street, I volunteered to build an altar for the "shared sacred space." Everyone contributed something from their own sense of devotion, until the maple-and-cherry altar was covered in articles of faith from the world's great religions.

Here's a picture of it:

That's when I knew that this movement is unstoppable—it is not "leaderless"; it's "leader-full." The leadership is the inner light, the Spirit of Truth that is already in everyone. We all have a Buddha, a Jesus, a punk-rock angel inside us, and somehow, a lot of us at once have decided that *now* is the moment—it's time for us to bring her out!

This movement isn't the same old didactic left-wing, super-rational, antireligion, lockstep, antiwar march on a weekend. It's a step up for a daily revolutionary practice. The game has changed. Somewhere in the machinery of history some gear just started turning, or some demon was just expelled, so that from now on, it's going to be just a little bit easier for more Davids to win against more Goliaths.

In time, very soon, starting now, it will be much harder for the CIA or the U.S. war machine to kill a 9/11 whistle-blower, even if he's a just a small-town dentist in the Deep South. This David died to inspire us to a new kind of life, and we'll meet him in the next chapter.

PART TWO

THE TRUTH OF
THE LIVING AND THE
TRUTH OF THE DEAD

4 WHO KILLED DAVID GRAHAM?

David Graham

Dr. David Graham was a dentist in the small city of Shreveport, in northwest Louisiana. He was a patriotic Christian who had volunteered to do medical work in Vietnam. There, he volunteered for MEDCAP missions, the U.S. Army's efforts to win over the hearts and minds of the Vietnamese people by fixing their teeth. Graham pulled peasants' aching molars out, even under enemy fire in the combat zone. MEDCAP had a second purpose, too: Once you have alleviated someone's throbbing toothache, they are much more inclined to help you out with information. Graham learned a few things about military intelligence work.

Graham returned home to Shreveport and set up a dental practice. He was never a hard-nosed businessman. He gave away dental care to former addicts and the poor. He was a Christian, but even that term seems weak. He was a Christian on fire. He didn't limit his service work to dentistry. He used his experience in Vietnam to seek out the truth about this corrupt world.

KEEL, a fifty-thousand-watt AM radio station, gave Graham his own show. There was plenty of strange corruption to tackle in Louisiana. For starters, the local parish DA was rumored to be running narcotics. In 1986, a local Air Force man named James Monds was sent to prison for murder. But many callers to Graham's radio show, and eventually Graham himself, came to believe that Monds had been framed by the parish DA. Working with local attorney John Milkovich, Graham helped get Monds's case reopened. Eight years later, the Louisiana Court of Appeals reversed Monds's life sentence. Graham was like Jesus: He came to set the captives free.

Attorney John Milkovich became a friend of David Graham's. A fellow Christian, Milkovich worked the Monds case pro bono. In return, Milkovich was attacked in a courtroom hallway by a local cop.

In 2000, when his friend David Graham met two of the "9/11 hijackers" and sent warnings to the FBI and Secret Service, the reaction in Louisiana was much the same, amplified a hundredfold. Only this time, it wasn't a courtroom scuffle. And Graham didn't live to tell his story.

Graham reported his experiences meeting two of the "9/11 hijackers" with a scientist's rigor, a spiritual man's passion, and a pit bull's tenacity. He just would not let go. His life was threatened numerous times, sometimes by his local FBI. He held the truth in higher regard than his own life.

Dr. Graham's brush with evil began with an act of compassion, the sort of service to his community that was typical of the man. After Graham donated some dental work, helping a depressed friend "fix his smile," the friend agreed to help Graham seek out investors for Graham's natural-toothpaste start-up business. The friend found a flamboyant albino Pakistani "businessman," who introduced himself as "Mohammad Jamal Khan." Graham started falling down a rabbit hole.

Khan had been hanging out a lot at the local "USA CASH" outlet, emailing his "important" contacts "around the world." In person, Khan was all over the place, bragging to Graham about family connections to

Osama bin Laden. He boasted he was connected to the Pakistani ambassador and had "many friends in Washington."

But it wasn't all talk. Khan had juice. Graham stayed friendly with Khan and took him to college football games, in order to observe him up close. Graham was alarmed that Khan had special access to Barksdale Air Force Base, a high-security, nuclear-armed facility that is a part of the Strategic Air Command. Graham later recorded on video that Khan regularly set up romantic encounters for U.S. Air Force men off base, with various military women Khan himself at times dated on base.

When Khan breezed onto the base, Graham felt protective. In Vietnam, Graham had won a Bronze Star for exposing a Viet Cong plan to blow up aircraft at Bien Hoa Air Base. Driving around with the jabbermouth Khan, Graham began to suspect that this exuberant Pakistani "friend of bin Laden" was plotting to damage the "mighty B-52s" at Barksdale.

In October 2000, in Khan's rented townhouse, David Graham met two "medical students." In his pushy, loud way, Khan explained that these timid, quiet Arabs were good and nice young men, "doctors" studying medicine in America. However, neither of the good and nice young men spoke English. Graham saw boxes in Khan's kitchen and wrote down the names of the young "doctors."

Graham called the FBI. The FBI was hostile, later reporting that a "crank caller" had warned them that someone would "get whoever ratted out MJ Khan." A week later, Graham called the Secret Service.

After 9/11, Graham was horrified to realize that that day in Khan's townhouse, he had met Nawaf al-Hazmi and Fayez Banihamad, both of whom were allegedly aboard Flights 77 and 175, respectively. Immediately after 9/11, the FBI began to treat Graham's calls seriously. But for some reason, their hostility rapidly returned and grew severe.

Before and after 9/11, Graham met with FBI special agents Ray Spoon and Steve Hayes at the local FBI office and hosted meetings with them in his own dental offices. The FBI hostility grew almost maddening as Graham became determined to write a book. According to friend Milkovich, the FBI would ask Graham, in face-to-face meetings, "How's your *health*, Dr. Graham? No, I don't think you understand—how's your *health*?"

Graham ignored the FBI's warnings not to publish said book. Before he could publish his work, however, Graham was poisoned mysteriously, in a small town in East Texas. He died after a painful struggle with paralysis and organ failure, from a lethal dose of ethylene glycol, sixteen months later. Ethylene glycol is the toxin in antifreeze, which was spread all around Graham's car and office back in Shreveport, as Graham checked into a hospital a hundred miles away in Texas.

Someone in Boise, Idaho, sent me the late Dr. Graham's unpublished book. The bright green metallic bubble envelope it came in glowed with an eerie power. It was a portal, a rabbit hole with no bottom in sight. A year after Graham died, in September 2007, I drove to Shreveport to investigate.

When I started turning over rocks, I brought along a reporter, an old friend of mine named Jordan Green, who ended up writing a fine piece of long-form journalism for *Yes Weekly* of North Carolina.[9] Graham's death was eerily similar to that of Bush biographer Jim Hatfield, five years earlier, in nearby Arkansas. I knew I should not go it alone.

Every single friend of Graham's we met in Louisiana and Texas felt that his death had involved foul play. The Shreveport and Texas FBI were the only ones who implied that Graham may have committed suicide, and the case the FBI made was rather halfhearted, only casting further suspicions on itself. Perhaps the FBI hoped that the 9/11 official story would remain an impregnable narrative, that controlling that "official story" was more important than controlling the facts.

Often, facts alone aren't enough to persuade, though. For instance, inside the 9/11 Truth Movement lies a wealth of scientific data, but all the compelling evidence competes for your attention. There's so much data, it competes with itself. It's hard to figure out just which bit is *the* smoking gun that can shake the monstrous hold of a powerful, problematic official story.

Graham's life and death help solve this problem. His story builds a bridge between the official story and the valid parts of the Truth movement.

Let me illustrate what I mean. I personally am open to the theory that the WTC towers may have been brought down by means that official investigators ignored. But some people are not. Some people won't even consider the suspicious presence of molten steel at Ground Zero for over three months after the attacks, or the fact that top international scientists published that they found residue from controlled demolition explosives in four samples of WTC dust. Some people just aren't persuaded by the stubborn realities of physics, chemistry, or engineering.

Science is all about proof. But some Americans are willing to ignore scientific evidence. Perhaps a different kind of proof will help open minds. I propose that the death of a man, the story of a hero, the self-sacrifice of a great U.S. citizen, is a new form of evidence. The life and death of a great hero is the model story we know and love. Graham's life and death present a new narrative, an emotional story, of a hero who lived, struggled, and sacrificed. Look closely at this man: an average American, a good man close to a cover-up. He gets crushed. To me, that proves not only that something is terribly wrong with the 9/11 official story, but also that the story is vulnerable. It's inferior to the truth.

When Graham met a couple of the 9/11 terrorists in November 2000, he grabbed hold of the experience, like a man grabbing on to the tip of an iceberg. What he didn't know, until too late, was that the iceberg was 98 percent invisible, lethal. The iceberg is in fact the cold-hearted U.S. military/intelligence juggernaut that Graham himself had volunteered to serve in Vietnam.

I knew that to get David Graham's story right, I'd have to understand what happened between him and the FBI. Of course, there's the obvious problem: The FBI does not talk. In my previous book and articles, I have never been able to get an FBI agent to speak to me, or to get an official spokesman to say anything of substance. This is an agency that has effectively become the American gestapo, a political police force that in past decades took it upon itself to destroy the Black Panthers and Martin Luther King, Jr. A memo from J. Edgar Hoover stated the FBI's "GOALS" were to include "Prevent[ing] the RISE OF A MESSIAH who could unify, and electrify, the militant black nationalist movement."[10]

Suppressing freedom movements has always been a core function of this federal police force. The FBI's COINTELPRO organization engaged in large-scale suppression of political dissent, including assassination. (For example, the FBI is widely believed to have been involved in the late-'60s killing of Black Panther Fred Hampton in Chicago.) Two congressional committees in the late '70s attempted to reform the bureau. Most of those reforms were swept away by the United States PATRIOT Act in the wake of 9/11.

I have never been able to get an FBI spokesman to comment on or explain any of the bureau's strange behavior around 9/11. But then, one day in 2007, a miracle of sorts took place. Jordan Green and I walked into the Shreveport FBI office. Dr. Graham had passed away a year earlier. But somebody was opening doors for us. We walked in at just the right time.

The receptionist at first tried to get rid of us, but we insisted that we needed to speak to the supervisor. When she demurred, I said it was "a matter of national security." This last line created a bit of a stir, and from behind the scenes, a stocky, mustachioed FBI special agent came to the plexiglass window. It was our man, special agent Stephen Hayes, the one Graham himself had met with.

He didn't identify himself, but the chain around his neck told us who he was. Just a few hours earlier, his boss, special agent in charge Mike Kinder, had sworn to Jordan vehemently on the phone that we would never be allowed to talk to Hayes.

In person now, we could see why. Special Agent Hayes clearly had a lot on his mind. As our conversation kicked into gear, he grew agitated with the questions I asked him. He was clearly under duress, wanting to speak to us even though it went against his training and instinct for self-preservation. He seemed deeply conflicted, and, in a way, he spilled his guts. In the final moments of our talk, perhaps he thought he had said too much. He barked out to his receptionist, "Call security!"—not the sign of a man who feels secure.

The FBI had claimed, when Graham was poisoned, that they had never met with Graham *before* 9/11. Hayes said otherwise. In the midst of our talk, I asked him, "Did you visit Dr. Graham in his office?"

> **Hayes:** *Yes, I did.*
> **Hicks:** *Did you visit him before 9/11?*
> **Hayes:** *Yes.*

Hicks: Was it to discuss young Arabs?
Hayes: It was to discuss a $10,000 investment in a textile operation.

With that, Hayes himself proved that the FBI had been lying when it claimed it had not met with Graham before 9/11. Graham's friend Richard Wilkes waited for us outside in the car, and we shared this news with him as soon as we left. He also noted its importance.

Hayes in person had blurted out that he had shown some interest in Graham and the man Graham suspected of being a terrorist handler, Mohammad Jamal Khan. Khan had tried to entice Graham to invest his money in a textile company, after Graham had pitched *him* on investing in the natural-toothpaste idea.

Khan was a blond, albino Pakistani. He was impossible to forget. Not exactly "low profile," he was a poor choice for a terrorist handler—unless perhaps he *wanted* to be noticed. Graham records in his book that at one point, Khan made the papers for jumping off a bridge in the Red River and swimming ashore.

In the videos that Graham made clandestinely of himself and Khan in 2003, Khan is clearly in his mid-fifties. Yet his police files in Houston and Shreveport show a date of birth of March 1, 1967. He consistently claimed to have arrived in the United States in 1995, but we later got Houston police arrest records of Khan for assault and battery in 1993. That mug shot from 1993 has some red flags for a case of stolen identity: The Khan in that picture has no chin dimple, a different nose, dark hair, and no blond eyelashes. Somehow MJ Khan wasn't an albino in 1993. The "Mohammad Jamal Khan" we are dealing with in this story seems to have enough juice to have stolen someone else's identity.

So who was this guy? And how did he have such carte blanche at Barksdale Air Force Base? Khan was so "connected" and so cocky about it. I had to ask FBI agent Hayes, "Was Mohammad Jamal Khan an informant?"

There was a five-second pause. Hayes's eyes burned into me, his anger focused like a laser. He glared at me so hard, there was a tic in his eye, a tremor in his neck muscles. After five long moments in time, he stammered out one of the greatest lines of our dialogue.

"We don't discuss informants." Pause. "But to my knowledge, no."

That was two answers. The first part was a tacit admission that Khan *was* an informant, or something like it. Someone well known, someone off limits.

The second part of the answer, though, seemed to be an instantaneous attempt to retract the first part. So I borrowed a line from Michael Moore's *Fahrenheit 911* and, with a bit of cockiness, said, "I'll take that as a 'yes.'"

Hayes grew just a bit angrier and louder, and he retorted right away with, "You can take it any way you want."

Graham was first poisoned over Memorial Day weekend 2004. In early May of that year, he had been putting the final touches on his book. Just a few weeks later, the local Texas FBI showed up at the small-town hospital where Graham was fighting for his life and asked doctors in the ER why they were trying to save a "crazy" man who had just tried to kill himself. The cardiac surgeon there stopped trying to save Graham, crumpling under the FBI's pressure. Meanwhile, back in Graham's hometown, the FBI's comments to the local TV station implied that Graham had attempted suicide. Local FBI told Shreveport TV Channel 3 that they did not know "if there is anything sinister to Graham's illness, or if it was a suicide attempt or connected to Graham's personal or business life."

Indeed, when I asked Hayes about all this, he didn't exactly exonerate himself.

"Why" I asked, "did Shreveport FBI imply that Graham may have committed suicide? Or that he was crazy?"

Hayes retorted, "Did you know that Graham lived above his office? Did you talk to his secretary? Did you know that Graham had to be reminded to lock up the office at night?"

What?

Hayes was really grasping here to claim that Graham was "crazy." But when we spent a week in Shreveport and New Orleans, we got a picture of who Graham really was. When a homeless man moved into an old trailer on his property, Dr. David Graham didn't call the cops; he brought out hot soup and clean clothes. He brought a spirit of healing. He struck up a conversation. In time, the homeless guy got back on his feet.

Graham wasn't some isolated crank; he was part of a community of intelligent, hardworking citizens. Unlike Graham's immediate family, his friends all spoke out and thought his death suspicious. In Shreveport, Jordan and I stayed with Richard Wilkes, who ran the twelve-step program at the Shreveport Community Church. He and his wife had helped do some of the layout for Graham's book, and both were convinced that Graham had suffered foul play.

Local private investigator Rick Turner was also happy to meet with us. Turner had helped Graham make hidden-camera videotapes of meetings between Graham and MJ Khan when Khan got out of jail in 2003. In those tapes, Khan corroborates the year-2000 meetings Graham had with the 9/11 hijackers. Turner was certain that Graham had not committed suicide. We also met with attorney John Milkovich, Graham's friend and kindred spirit, who delivered a blistering eulogy at Graham's funeral. It concluded with these words:

> *David had a message he wanted to give to his son. Not a simple message of words, you see, because the messages we express with our actions and our lives are so much more eloquent than the mere words that we speak.*
>
> *The message went something like this: "I have kept the faith, the faith of Christ. In the most trying ordeal of my life. Satan has set out to destroy my body and my soul; still, I have kept the faith. Not with cheap lip service, not with empty words, but with my life, my sacrifice, and my tears.*

But for all his writing, Graham never learned the whole story of 9/11. After all, Graham was working in isolation. Not only is there no 9/11 Truth movement in Shreveport, but when we asked Richard and Tanya Wilkes about getting in touch with the peace and social justice people in town, they said, "There are none."

Graham's sacrifice helps us focus on a crucial question: Just who were the "9/11 terrorists," and who were their friends? Right after 9/11, mainstream U.S. media briefly did some stories about the impending "9/11 trials" of the many accomplices to the "nineteen hijackers." In fact, John Ashcroft announced that since the terrorists had to have had help, the Department of Justice had detained "nearly one thousand individuals" for aiding and abetting the hijackers. Yet almost all these one thousand people were quietly and individually released.[11] The widows and grieving parents of the 9/11 victims are still waiting for the promised "9/11 trials" of the accomplices.

On the videotapes he made before he died, Graham referred to the terrorist handlers he had met as "unindicted coconspirators." They were unindicted despite Ashcroft's grandiose promise to soon commence the grand "9/11 trials" of those coconspirators. Graham was left to research the 9/11 attacks by himself, using mainstream news as his sources. He tried in vain to figure out why the FBI had ignored his warnings. Graham wanted to do the right thing, but he was naive about what he was up against—he even thanked the FBI in his book.

If Graham's story were a play, his fatal flaw would be that he was too trusting. He not only warned the FBI but also traveled to Washington, where he sent his "9/11 Graham Report" to the Bush White House, and to his congressmen. He met with representatives of the Joint Inquiry and stayed in touch with the 9/11 Commission.

Graham was poisoned just before he published his book. On Graham's deathbed, when Richard Wilkes asked him, "Who did this to you?" Graham said, "I don't know. Maybe the FBI."

The reason the U.S. government never indicted these "unindicted coconspirators" is that the U.S. government was controlling them. Bad things happen to people whenever an individual gets in the way of the U.S. military juggernaut. Graham's story, and this book, consistently make that case.

During our short visit to the FBI's tiny white lobby, agent Steve Hayes talked too much. But God bless him for letting the truth come out.

It's ironic that Hayes was still there at all. The other FBI agent Graham interacted with, Ray Spoon, was much more combative. Graham himself notes this in the acknowledgments of his book. It was Spoon who passed along the "crank caller's" death threat when Graham first reported suspicions about Khan. And today, it's Spoon who has quit the FBI. Perhaps he, too, is trying to find a way to deal with the blood stains on his hands.

When Hayes was glaring at me, it was as if he were trying to burn through the plexiglass with just his eyes. But he was shaking a little. *This story is big*, his body language seemed to plead. *It's bigger than me, and it's bigger than you.* When we locked eyes, it was as if he had a ton of suppressed emotional energy, be it guilt or shame. Here's the last part of what we said to each other:

> **Hayes:** *Are you saying [Graham] knew all about 9/11 before it happened? I mean, I haven't read all of his book.*
> **Hicks:** *Why not? You're a paid federal agent.*
> **Hayes:** *Did he ever get it published?*
> **Hicks:** *Special Agent Hayes, he was poisoned on the verge of publishing his book. You cannot argue that—*
> **Hayes:** *You and Graham would have gotten along real well . . .*
> **Hicks:** *What are you saying, that—*
> **Hayes:** *You and Graham would have gotten along real well together.*
> **Hicks:** *Yeah, I believe so, too.*
> **Hayes:** *We're done.*
> **Hicks:** *Why are we done?*
> **Hayes [turning to the receptionist]:** *Call security.*

With our adrenaline gushing, Jordan and I hit the stairs. Earlier, we had joked about ending up in a "black site," being tortured for poking around this story. Suddenly, it seemed a draconian imprisonment was not out of the question. With Graham, the gloves had come off. Jordan pointed out that we couldn't be arrested for "trespassing," as we had never been asked to leave.

"THE PROBLEM WITH KHAN"

It's unfortunate that the story of Graham's life isn't yet widely known. But we can honor his memory by publishing the truths he was fighting to expose, the story he had stumbled into.

Let's look more closely at MJ Khan, whom Graham met with several times. He was a "cutout," a go-between, a part of the puppet strings that connect the "9/11 hijackers" to the U.S. government.

When 9/11 happened, Khan's "medical student" friend, Nawaf al-Hazmi, was accused of being one of bin Laden's right-hand men. That's strange, because al-Hazmi and his cohort Khalid al-Mihdhar had been protected by various agencies of the federal government, and by the Saudi consulate in L.A., multiple times.

After 9/11, Graham set up a sort of sting operation. He lured Mohammad Jamal Khan back to his office, after setting up a hidden video camera. On a separate occasion, he also talked a medical associate, Dr. Mohammed "Habeeb" Ahmed, who had also been in Khan's townhouse that day with the terrorists, to come back and talk over what had happened. Graham got it all on tape; his forensic-evidence gathering made him a formidable opponent. The entire juggernaut of the U.S. government couldn't really fight fair against this David, so they had to fight dirty.

On camera today, we can see Dr. Graham speaking about the terrorist meetings with the handlers who had introduced him to two of the infamous "nineteen hijackers." The videotapes, available online at Sander-Hicks.com, prove Graham's credibility and wiles.[12]

The two handlers are very different sorts of people. Dr. Ahmed claims to not really know MJ Khan, and wonders aloud why he "gave him money." Ahmed observes that "the problem with Khan is that he talks a lot."

So true, Dr. Ahmed. On tape, we see that Khan just can't stop talking. When asked about the legality of being married in both Texas and Pakistan, to two different women, Khan unctuously tries to give Graham a high five.

He brags, "FBI tried to convict of me that one, but he had no chance to convict me, because I have a lot of people, backup, in Washington. I have that, I already told you ... If something comes up ..." Khan bragged about help from "political friends, American friends, my ambassador there."

Khan's connections to the 9/11 hijackers and to Washington, D.C., are beyond dispute. But Graham's paper trail is not the only one out there.

Right after 9/11, in October 2001, Khan was picked up in East Texas for "possession of a firearm by a prohibited person." Prosecutors alleged that Khan "was in the country unlawfully after his visa expired in 1998." (Yet somehow, that "expired Visa" didn't stop Khan in 2000 from freely moving on and off Barksdale Air Force Base.)

Suddenly, someone wanted Khan out of the country. Recall the timing, October 2001, and the strange charge, "possession of a firearm by a prohibited person." It seems that in the wake of 9/11, the powers that be needed to get the "1,000 accomplices" and everyone like Khan off the streets, in custody, and eventually disappeared, liquidated, or sanitized.

But *not* tried in an open court of law. In February 2002, federal prosecutors added an indictment to Khan's charges: wire fraud, for illegally wiring $9,999 to Pakistan. That April, in exchange for Khan's guilty plea, the government agreed to dismiss charges. Khan was fined $100 and sentenced to time served.

Here's the kicker. Look at the fine print of his plea agreement, a public document accessible to anyone:

> *In no case does the [government] agree that there will be no prosecution of the defendant for any crimes concerning the hijacking of any airline or attack on any building or deaths that occurred on or about September 11, 2001. The United States Attorney for the Western District of Louisiana is simply not aware of the involvement of the defendant in these crimes at this time.*

When my fellow reporter Jordan Green called the U.S. attorney's office in Louisiana to inquire about their reason for insisting on the inclusion of the curious statement, calls were not returned. For some reason, federal prosecutors wanted to reserve their right to prosecute Khan for crimes related to 9/11 … but not actually *do* so, or ever talk about it. Khan later skipped town (or was helped out of the country) rather than face another extradition hearing for soliciting a prostitute.

Before he was killed, David Graham traveled to Washington, D.C., with a rough draft of the book he was writing. On June 4, 2002, he met Steven A. Cash, counsel for the Joint Select Intelligence Committee. After a thirty-minute conversation, Cash accepted the report. But today Cash will not speak on the record about meeting Graham. Why?

The answer opens up if you know a few basics about the joint House/Senate 9/11 inquiry. In my previous research on 9/11, I have reported that the streetwise Florida FBI informant Randy Glass also testified in a closed-door hearing to the joint inquiry. State Department top brass had allegedly told him in July 2001, "Randy, we know all about planes being flown into the World Trade Center." Glass had originally heard of the plot through his connections to Pakistani and Egyptian arms dealers on the black market. Glass had very combative experiences with the joint inquiry, in which he denounced them from the stand, claiming, "None of you are here to hear the truth, okay? All of you are here to watch over the truth."

Glass claimed that joint inquiry officials Kay Holt and Rick Cinquegrana were in fact CIA agents. It's a sensational claim, but one that I always found difficult to prove. Could the CIA really control Congress's own 9/11 joint inquiry?

When Graham handed the joint inquiry's Steven Cash his "9/11 Graham Report," the effect was the same as if Graham dropped it down a deep, dark well. We later dug up Cash's resume. The document is astonishing, and it's clearly not meant for public consumption.

The joint inquiry had hired Cash fresh from work at—you guessed it—the CIA. There, he was an "Intelligence Officer, Directorate of Operations (1996-2001)"; among his duties was his role as an "Acting Branch Chief in unit assigned to high-value Middle-Eastern terrorist group."

Even as Dr. Graham's memory dissolves into American history, the names of those two young Saudis he met, Nawaf al-Hazmi and Khalid al-Mihdhar, keep on coming back up. In 2011, a big *Vanity Fair* article detailed their connection to the Saudi ruling class. But that tells only half the story. A bright and shining aegis of U.S. federal protection was always hovering over those two. Supposed 9/11 "mastermind" Khalid Sheikh Mohammed said they were "bin Laden's right-hand men," but that's true only if you believe bin Laden was the mastermind of 9/11. (If he was, then why did the CIA tightly control both 9/11 investigations?) These terrorists Graham met were clearly part of *someone's* "high-value terrorist group." But that someone was not bin Laden.

Perhaps al-Hazmi and al-Mihdhar were not aware of whom they were working for. Graham reports that on occasion they seemed drugged or hypnotized. But their consistent, multiple ties to the CIA and the Pentagon are indisputable.

Back in Shreveport, there has never been an investigation of David Graham's death. Corruption seems to be as common as the casinos, churches, and Southern-fried dive bars. Yet everyone seems to know the deal on this story. It's not in the papers. It's the word on the street.

After the 2007 trip, I went back to Shreveport for a one-day stop in January 2009. I wanted to stimulate a response from the local federal prosecutor, U.S. attorney Robert Gillespie, who had ignored my letter and my request for oversight. So I called for a protest outside the U.S. courthouse in downtown Shreveport.

I couldn't get any locals to help protest on short notice. Yet another "only in Shreveport" kind of miracle took place: My one-man protest at the courtroom made the evening news on KSLA TV Channel 3.

To those with their eyes open, Graham's death is Shreveport's lively open wound.

5 ABLE DANGER: THE STORY OF LT. COL. ANTHONY SHAFFER, THE GOOD SOLDIER, SILENCED

The author, (left) with Lt. Col. Anthony Shaffer, former Defense Intelligence Agency agent, at the Wayne Theatre, Wayne, PA.

Who *were* the 9/11 terrorists?

This question gets more curious as we look into the story of defense intelligence agent Lieutenant Colonel Anthony Shaffer.

Shaffer was a CIA-trained defense intelligence analyst, part of the U.S. military's "best and brightest" who used the power of new technologies to "data-mine" and expose social networks. Named Operation Able Danger, they were tasked in early 2000 with figuring out what this new "Al Qaeda" thing really was. Able Danger's mission was to find out if "Al Qaeda" were already in the United States, and if so, who was financing them.

The problem is that someone else high up in government already knew all the answers. The simple life of a good soldier got intensely complicated. Lt. Col. Shaffer today is a frequent guest on cable news shows, but the book he tried to publish was seized by military censors. As with Graham, I'm not sure he sees the entire picture yet.

Remember, back in the year 2000, Al Qaeda was not a household name. It was only a couple of years old; it was the moniker of a mysterious, undefined new enemy. The word had not been used in the media until the 1998 African embassy bombings.

Remember, too, the names of the alleged young Saudi "Al Qaeda" agents whom Dr. Graham had experiences with: Nawaf al-Hazmi and Khalid al-Mihdhar. These same names pop up in the story of Lt. Col. Shaffer.

At some point in 2000, Shaffer had those same Saudi names, as well as the name of eventual lead terrorist, Mohamed Atta. Shaffer and his team were about to do a presentation and spread the word on these guys to fellow Pentagon intelligence workers. Shaffer put the names and faces up on a flowchart of Al Qaeda operatives at work in sleeper cells inside the United States. But before the meeting got under way, Pentagon top brass came into the room and covered up the faces of all of those guys with yellow sticky notes. The Pentagon's excuse? They were "U.S. persons" or were in the country legally, and therefore should be given the same privacy protections as U.S. citizens. In other words, Shaffer had run into the special shield of federal protection around certain "Al Qaeda" members. Somehow these "Al Qaeda terrorists" seemed to enjoy some kind of "national security override." They were a part of something the CIA calls a "high-value terrorist group."

Shaffer wanted help. He tried to reach outside the Pentagon. Three different times in September 2000, he tried to schedule meetings with contacts at the FBI's Counterterrorism Division. But each time, Pentagon lawyers from the United States Special Operations Command (US-SOCOM) canceled those meetings. Later that same month, Shaffer and Able Danger warned about an impending Al Qaeda attack on the USS

Cole, but they were ignored. Nine U.S. soldiers died when a small boat blew a huge hole in the side of the USS *Cole*. No "Al Qaeda" operatives were ever arrested for that attack. In fact, every suspect was allowed to slip away, back into the wilds of Yemen. One of the suspects was Khalid al-Mihdhar himself.

Late in 2000, Able Danger was forced to destroy four terabytes of financial data tracking just who was backing the Al Qaeda "terrorists."

This is not just one soldier's story; Lt. Col. Tony Shaffer was among a team of eighty operatives inside the Pentagon. Some were military, some civilian contractors. Some turned whistle-blowers with Shaffer, including captain Scott Philpott, who also gave sworn testimony on Able Danger to a U.S. congressional committee. But Shaffer was the most outspoken and articulate. He's the only one of the eighty who wrote a book. Or tried to.

Although 9/11 Commission executive director Philip Zelikow flew to Afghanistan to interview Shaffer, ultimately the 9/11 Commission suppressed all mention of Able Danger from its final report. Later, Shaffer told me personally that there was something *else* interfering with the 9/11 Commission's objectivity: the CIA. As with the joint inquiry, they were the controlling mechanisms: "Frankly, CIA held the high ground there. CIA attached people to that investigation that I don't think should have been on that investigative team." Because Shaffer had been trained by the CIA as a DIA agent, he knew what he was talking about.

After the 9/11 Commission report was published, Lt. Col. Shaffer happened to meet with Rep. Curt Weldon (R-PA) on Capitol Hill, while working for the U.S. Navy. Shaffer touched upon the topic of Able Danger. When Congressman Weldon heard that Pentagon intelligence was blocked from interfering with key 9/11 "ringleaders" in 2000, he became piqued. When he understood that the 9/11 Commission had interviewed Shaffer but censored him from its report, Weldon promptly called for hearings. Those hearings took place in early 2006, shortly after the 9/11 Commission Report had become a bestseller, nominated for the prestigious National Book Award.

The Able Danger hearings did receive a good week's worth of media attention, and then the topic sank out of sight.[13] The "master narrative" of the 9/11 Commission Report was to become the dominant "reality," the "official story" a big-budget production pasted together with weak myths. The masters of propaganda packed a punch. They were connected and ready to attack people like Shaffer, Weldon, and Graham if they stood up.

Compared with the big money behind the 9/11 official story, Able Danger was just one "media moment" the size of a mosquito. After the Able Danger hearings' week in the news cycle, the blame-free insouciance of the 9/11 Commission Report returned to dominate the airwaves, despite the glaring errors of omission available to anyone who actually read it.

THE WELDON TAKEDOWN

Rep. Curt Weldon stood up to one of the most glaring cover-ups of 9/11 and, as a result, lost reelection immediately thereafter. Weldon's public excoriation showed that the Able Danger topic was such a political live wire, it would "destroy the life" of this maverick member of Congress.

He was a shoo-in for reelection, but all that changed when Weldon's daughter's office was suddenly raided by FBI agents, the same year Weldon had held hearings into Able Danger. The raid was leaked to the media as it happened. Weldon's daughter, Karen, had been working as a lobbyist. Despite insinuations of improper influence, no charges were ever levied against her. Yet, at the time of the raid, the media coverage was colorful, splashy, and thick. The oddly timed raid became a "scandal" that cost Weldon dearly at the polls.

FBI director Robert Mueller is a longtime D.C. insider. He knows where the bodies are buried, going back to the Iran-Contra/BCCI scandal. Yet even *Mueller* was compelled to shake off his lifelong lethargy after this raid on the Weldons. Mueller complained publicly that Weldon's upset at the polls shortly after the Able Danger hearings was due to political intrigue. It didn't help that Rep. Weldon had been an outspoken critic of the CIA, or had investigated the more corrupt parts of the Democratic Party establishment (Sandy Berger and Clinton's 1996 sale of missiles to China, etc.).

During the Left Forum 2010 panel, "Going Undercover: The Yes Men and Gumshoe Journalists Discuss Subterfuge and Satire in Activism and Investigative Journalism," Ken Silverstein, D.C. editor of *Harper's*, told with enthusiasm the story of "one example of journalism really having an effect." He went on to describe the time that he "destroyed a man's life" and "really enjoyed doing it." That man was congressman Curt Weldon.

Ken Silverstein had been working the Weldon daughter story for years, starting at the *Los Angeles Times*. Yet for all his expertise, Silverstein refused to discuss the larger story around Able Danger. After the panel, I introduced myself politely and asked Silverstein if he had ever read Anthony Shaffer's congressional testimony. He winced.

"Look" he said, "I don't believe the 9/11 Truth stuff."

"I'm not asking you about that. I'm just asking you about Able Danger. Have you read the congressional testimony about Able Danger?"

"Look, I may have," he said, an edge rising in his voice.

"I'll take that as a no," I said.

He began to walk briskly out of the auditorium. Keeping pace, I asked him something to the effect of, "You destroyed Weldon's life. Who tipped you off to the story?"

"I'm not going to tell *you* that." At that point, friends joined him at the door to the hallway. His voice dripping with sarcasm, he said, "You can go and write that the source of the Weldon story tipped me off to destroy Weldon for the Able Danger hearings—fine."

It wasn't I who looked crazy at that point. Silverstein's vibration of hate was the same frequency of weirdness of Shreveport FBI agent Steve Hayes. Something was not right. I was starting to see now that how you felt about 9/11 Truth didn't depend at all on your politics. It was more of a class thing: how much you had to lose, how much "status" you had.

ZELIKOW: ABLE DANGER "VERY IMPORTANT" (TO SUPPRESS)

In 2003, at Bagram Air Base, Philip Zelikow, of the 9/11 Commission, flew in from D.C. He found Shaffer's work back in year 2000, tracking Al Qaeda, "very important." What he meant was that it was very important to suppress.

Zelikow was making the rounds with active military intelligence, trying to find who, if anyone, had any "pre-9/11 intelligence" on Al Qaeda. Shaffer related his story about the hot water he got in, the suppression, and the yellow sticky notes, around certain "Al Qaeda" terrorists. Zelikow handed him a business card, instructing him to come see him in Washington after his tour of duty.

In our interview in 2011, Shaffer agreed with the 9/11 victims' families who publicly stated that Zelikow should never have been allowed anywhere near the 9/11 Commission. The conflicts of interest were borderline criminal: Zelikow cowrote a book with Condoleezza Rice and served on the Bush White House's National Security Council. Zelikow, as an academic, had written a thesis about the power of "creating public myths." Three years before 9/11, he coauthored, in *Foreign Affairs* (mouthpiece of the influential and mysterious Council on Foreign Relations), an article entitled "Catastrophic Terrorism: Imagining the Transformative Event."

According to Philip Shenon's *The Commission*, most of the 9/11 Commission staff came to resent Zelikow for his arrogance. In the very first hearings at the 9/11 Commission, Zelikow called nutty right-wing militarists like Abraham Sofaer and Lauria Mylroie. Mylroie made unsubstantiated claims that Saddam Hussein was behind the 1993 WTC bombings and had worked with bin Laden. Sofaer used the bully pulpit to advocate for preemptive war, at a time when the Bush White House was preparing a fraudulent case for the Iraq invasion. Funny thing, that, because it was Zelikow himself who coauthored the White House's September 2002 "preemptive defense" offensive strategy. He communicated frequently with both Condi Rice and GOP master strategist Karl "Bush's Brain" Rove over the course of the 9/11 Commission's "independent" investigation.

So, when Zelikow met Lt. Col. Shaffer, he correctly observed that what Shaffer told him was "very important." Able Danger provided a wealth of data and documents to the 9/11 Commission. Team Zelikow in return deleted all mention of Able Danger from the final 9/11 Commission report. When congressman Curt Weldon demanded to know why Able Danger was omitted, Zelikow's people said, "We decided that that was not the story we wanted to tell." It wasn't a part of the public myth they were stitching together.

MY INTERVIEW WITH SHAFFER

The first time Lt. Col. Tony Shaffer addressed a 9/11 Truth gathering, he was scheduled to appear in person but for some reason couldn't make it. In a videotaped statement he sent to the Treason in America conference in 2008, in Valley Forge, Pennsylvania, he pissed off a lot of people, including me, by emphasizing, "I am not a Truther . . . and yet I do support a new investigation."

Despite all that, when he began addressing Truth Movement gatherings in person, during the ninth anniversary of 9/11, he spoke at a benefit for first responders—and again emphasized his message: *Not a Truther. But . . .*

It's hard to believe that Shaffer is *not* walking some kind of fine line between what he believes and what he can say publicly on MSNBC or Fox News. Perhaps the prize of media access is what keeps one controlled.

That said, there is something admirable and likable about this guy. I have been following Shaffer with keen interest since he went public in 2006. In preparation for this chapter, I traveled to Wayne, Pennsylvania, to see him speak. I learned a lot from our interview, which took place in January 2011.

Shaffer told an eager audience of forty citizens that even today, the full story on Able Danger has never been told. "During closed hearings in 2006, in front of the House Armed Services Committee, at the top-secret level, as I was starting to talk about that last 10 percent . . . of what Able Danger was about . . . I was told to stop—'people in this room are not cleared to hear about that.' To this day, even though I've offered to go testify, no one wants to hear about it. You got to ask yourself, 'Why?'"

Today, Shaffer has a new book, called *Operation Dark Heart*. Although the book was cleared by a U.S. Army auditor, the more sensitive DIA intervened at the last minute. In the fall of 2010, the DIA purchased the entire first printing of ten thousand copies and destroyed them.

The edition that was released was heavily redacted. As a lover of books, I personally want to scream at someone when trying to read *Operation Dark Heart*. It's impossible to read, since so much is blacked out. We Americans have been told all our lives that we are so lucky not to live under totalitarian censorship. But this book is a desecration of First Amendment freedoms. The most newsworthy material in this tome is about Able Danger, but it's the Able Danger material that seems to get blacked out most often.

This is a sample spread of pages from *Operation Dark Heart*:

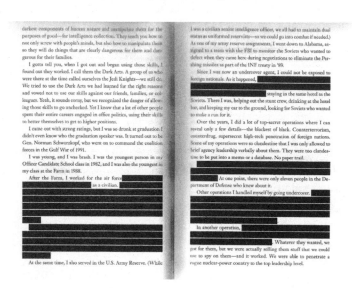

Shaffer's night in Wayne was a speech followed by a "book signing." But really, it was a chance to recognize a new form of censorship in "free America."

Shaffer identified as an old-school conservative—not a neocon, but a "smaller government is better" guy. He urged people to resist their natural urge to ignore corruption in high places. He said we were taxed too much. He earned applause for coming out against the war in Afghanistan and urged immediate withdrawal. For a veteran of defense intelligence who saw combat there, this was a groundbreaking declaration.

Shaffer was speaking to a room full of 9/11 Truthers, but he frustrated many with his same line: "I am not a Truther . . . but there is common ground between us. What we need is a new investigation." Most of the Truthers in the room wanted to scream at that point.

I love the 9/11 Truth movement. We are such a mixed bag. Every time the charismatic Tony Shaffer says, "I'm not a Truther, but . . . " it seems half the room gnashes their teeth while the other half line up to get their picture taken with him. We are both vindictive and forgiving. We are known for our passion. I like to joke with people on the political Left that either you are adamantly in the 9/11 Truth movement or you are pissed off because the passion of the 9/11 Truth movement is just too much to take.

We tend to be intense. We tend to be brainy and able to absorb and hold great amounts of data, but we're not always great at communicating it to others in condensed form. We've been set up and attacked so many times by the mainstream media (by the BBC, in a well-known article in *Popular Mechanics*, and by *Nightline*, to cite just a few examples) that an already paranoid movement seems at times driven to the brink of insanity.

Then there's the problem of how to reach a mass population with a message that a hostile, pampered professional media is staunchly against. That message is that the CIA and Pentagon pulled off 9/11. They stage-directed the show. You can see that in the pattern of protection and control around Nawaf al-Hazmi, Khalid al-Mihdhar, and Mohamed Atta.

During Lt. Col, Shaffer's book signing, I took the opportunity to run that basic Truther premise by him, and he winced. We were nearly alone in the red velvet lobby of the Anthony Wayne movie theater. The older, baby-boomer Truthers had left in disgust, but the younger, more conservative ones from Staten Island were sticking it out alongside me. I had my video camera running.

I relished the chance to knock heads with the lieutenant colonel about a pattern I was beginning to perceive. Shaffer ran into 9/11 terrorists, but then ran into some kind of aegis of protection around them. It was the same aegis that Graham had slammed into. (And then that blunt aegis slammed into him.)

What Shaffer found through open-source data mining, Graham had found in real-world run-ins. I asked Shaffer about fellow author/whistleblower Joe Trento, who wrote a book called *Unsafe at Any Altitude* that identified the "terrorists" Nawaf al-Hazmi and Khalid al-Mihdhar as "agents of Saudi intelligence."

"It's possible, but I don't know," Shaffer said. "That's not something I had direct knowledge of."

But were the "terrorists" protected?

"I still think the whole issue relates to incompetence, not necessarily a conspiracy." Shaffer's response was an argument that most serious researchers of 9/11 had abandoned around 2003, as the 9/11 Commission hearings began. Since then, we have seen the 9/11 Commission bend logic and ignore pertinent evidence, like Able Danger itself.

I then asked Shaffer about the fact that the same "Al Qaeda" terrorists that he himself and David Graham had found had also been living with an FBI informant in San Diego. (This story was broken in the mainstream news first, ironically enough, by *Newsweek*'s Michael Isikoff.) The same two terrorists living with FBI in San Diego, it turns out, had also been highly monitored, but not stopped, by the CIA in the 2000 Malaysian "terror summit." Heck, probable Saudi agent Khalid al-Mihdhar had been involved in the USS *Cole* bombing but wasn't even on the "terrorist watch list." All of these "anomalies" point to a pattern of CIA protection, no?

Shaffer's response: "I believe that there are conspiracies. I believe that that's a possibility, what you're mentioning. However, the only way we get to the bottom of it is to have a fair investigation, with competent people."

Shaffer could see the pattern I saw. He admitted it might be real. That might be the closest I will ever get to a blessing from a defense intelligence officer. Shaffer went on to talk about the many other anomalies in the 9/11 official story that bothered him, beyond the Able Danger subject. I asked him what keeps him up at night. We had the following dialogue:

"A lot of the individuals we are talking about, who were involved in the attack, have never been identified," he said.

"Right!" I said. "The coconspirators. Ashcroft said there were one thousand people."

"That's true," Shaffer nodded.

"And he never indicted a single one of them."

"That's true. And I think that that's something that needs to be looked at," said Shaffer, "because I know there are others out there that supported these guys."

For example, we could start with one of the alleged "unindicted co-conspirators" whom Dr. Graham accused in his premortem videotapes, Dr. Mohammed Habib. Habib is still in the country, practicing medicine in San Jose, California. When reporter Jordan Green contacted the doctor, Habeeb disavowed any involvement in this story whatsoever. However, he did so through an attorney.

Shaffer also said, later, "A lot of these guys are still out there . . . planning for the next 9/11." But that to me sounded like just more fearmongering, the kind we've heard ad nauseam since September 11, 2001.

I suggested a different theory: "But there could be black-ops divisions of the CIA that you don't even know about."

"I'm sure there are," Shaffer said with certainty.

"That could be running these guys."

Shaffer squirmed like he was back on the hot seat—he smiled, as if this is were something he might be able to talk about someday, but today would rather not. We had entered territory that could jeopardize the lieutenant colonel's continued appearances on Fox and MSNBC.

"Look, I know from my own experience, there are layers to the onion—there's always something else—but, to my knowledge, no."

At that point, the Truthers standing next to me let out a little sigh, our hopes dashed. But we broke out laughing at what Shaffer said next.

"And I don't believe that any sworn officer would engage in that sort of thing."

Danny Panzella, a young, amiable Truther and political candidate from Staten Island, laughed loudest: "*Now* you're losing *me*. What about al-Awlaki meeting with the Pentagon officials? Now he's the top Al Qaeda guy?"

Shaffer nodded with enthusiasm. "That is one of the issues I am trying to help resolve, believe it or not."

He explained that in his current work, with the U.S. Army, he's still trying to track which Al Qaeda members are working which side. But has it occurred to him that perhaps some are working both sides? Or that perhaps some are not working the terrorist side at all?

For instance, the guy in question, Anwar al-Awlaki, as reported on CBS and MSNBC, was the leading Al Qaeda man, with ties to the Fort

Hood shooter and the 9/11 attackers. *And he was hosted at a dinner at the Pentagon in the months after 9/11.*

"I do believe he was a part of the active support network before 9/11. And we tried to turn him. And it didn't work. He's still out there running around, doing things. Because we did in fact bring him into the Pentagon, which the Pentagon does not like talking about, to say, 'We really want you to be on our team,'" explained Shaffer.

What's curious is that Shaffer can see this, and say this. But at no point will he verbally consider anything more nefarious. It's as if there are possibilities he's not even allowed himself to imagine.

Shaffer is a man of integrity, a good soldier, who hasn't yet realized that he's surrounded by a system that is one big moral compromise. A good man cannot stay good surrounded by evil.

Shaffer shared a lesson from combat with us that night: If you are shot at, keep moving. To Shaffer, I would say, "Take your own advice. Come out there. The Pentagon betrayed you; they tried to silence you. Remember that when you testified for Congressman Weldon, the Pentagon revoked your security clearance, as nasty stories about you popped up in *The Washington Post.* As you tried to tell the truth, under oath, you were effectively shot at. So, keep moving."

The problem with Shaffer is that for all his rigor, his passion to stop Al Qaeda, he can't see, or is not willing to see, the bigger picture. Staying in the employ of the U.S. Army changes what you are willing to let yourself see. The simple truth is that the U.S. military is a sophisticated killing machine. The F-16 is a homicide bomber. The U.S. military is in the business of taking human life. It's likewise in the business of trying to create a "reality" that will justify its actions.

I would further advise Shaffer to look into the story of captain Brad Ayers, another military man caught between two worlds. I worked with Captain Ayers when I published his memoir, while I was head of the Vox Pop corporation, in Brooklyn. In early 1963, Ayers was a young paramilitary expert in the U.S. Army when the Pentagon tasked him to work with the CIA, down at the agency's domestic base in Miami. CIA deputy director Ted Shackley was training Cuban nationals in paramilitary exercises, for a possible second Bay of Pigs–style attack.

When JFK was shot and the "magic bullet" official story made no sense, Ayers's orderly, military-based life fell apart. He watched as the president's brother, RFK, was also gunned down by a "lone gunman" in 1968. Ayers was a man of integrity, just like Shaffer. After a period of deep reading and personal research, Ayers eventually realized that CIA personnel close to him were involved in the killing of both Kennedy brothers, a moderate sitting president and a more progressive presidential candidate. Ayers personally identified CIA agent Gordon Campbell and David Morales in photographs at the Ambassador Hotel taken the night RFK was taken out.

Lt. Col. Shaffer needs to know that the path he is on never ends with a "moment of truth" among his superior officers. Ayers was harassed by Pentagon and CIA black ops repeatedly, until he moved to a log cabin in the Wisconsin outback.

"If you are shot at, keep moving."

6 WOLFGANG BOHRINGER: MOHAMED ATTA'S CIA DRINKING BUDDY

Wolfgang Bohringer was a German-Swiss citizen who happened to move to Naples, Florida, to open a flight school in 1995. Around 2000–2001, he was part of an inner circle that allegedly partied wildly and snorted cocaine with future 9/11 terrorist Mohamed Atta. After 9/11, he moved on to the South Pacific, via his yacht, to open another flight school. In the tiny nation of Kiribati, members of the genteel boating class say that Bohringer stood out like a sore thumb. He was a bit rough, bragging that he hated Jews. He kept a big box of cash onboard, and he boasted of his close relationship to "lead 9/11 hijacker" Mohamed Atta. Although Kiribati was extremely remote, 1,200 miles south of Hawaii, Bohringer said he had the money and the connections to build a flight school and resort. He even got a meeting with the island nation's president.

The "yachties," especially Mr. Chuck Corbett of Fanning Island, warned the government of Kiribati of Bohringer's uncouth side. The Kiribati government in turn contacted the U.S. federals. In 2006, the Joint Terrorism Task Force declared Bohringer a "person of interest" in the 9/11 investigation and then promptly arrested him in international waters. However, Bohringer was able to pull strings. Today, he is a free man, although only a few people at the CIA know exactly where. His story provides further proof of a special layer of protection granted by the federal national security state to the key "nineteen hijackers."

Wolfgang Bohringer's name consistently came up in interviews with Mohamed Atta's short-term Florida girlfriend, Amanda Keller. Amanda claimed she was another coke buddy of Atta's. She dated him on the rebound from a broken heart. She called Atta and Wolfgang "inseparable" and described how they had been kicked out of the bar Hooters together. She said Atta called Wolfgang "brother," a name he reserved for particular white Europeans.

On the docks in Kiribati, Bohringer bragged, "Atta was a good friend of mine. I liked him. Too bad he had to die." He said that Atta wasn't such a bad guy.

Well, Atta wasn't such a good guy, either. According to Amanda, he had a foot fetish; was moody, jealous, and often depressed; and was a terrible lover. He dismembered a litter of kittens in her apartment when she dumped him. His inner darkness was a perfect way to create the needed story: that "9/11 was the product of heartless and hateful Muslim terrorists." Atta's picture speaks louder than words. It is an important part of the "Muslim hate" that the 9/11 official story claims is at the root of the spectacle.

But this one image is only that: an image. It stands as a grand substitute for an official story that has never actually been proven.

Behind this simple image, a whole other reality about Mohamed Atta exists for those willing to venture outside the confines of the official narrative. One pathway here is the story of Amanda Keller. She was a colorful, ex-stripper paramour whom Atta lived with, for a time, in Venice, Florida. Her relationship with Atta ended with her throwing all of his clothes out the door and two stories down, into the apartment parking lot.

Florida's top guerrilla reporter, Daniel Hopsicker, tracked Keller down and through her discovered that the FBI was doctoring many facts about Atta. He hadn't appeared in Florida in June 2000, as the FBI claimed, but had been in the state much earlier. He wasn't a devout Muslim—he actually enjoyed alcohol, cocaine, pork, and rap music. He had many passports and spoke many languages, including German and Hebrew. With his European friends, Wolfgang Bohringer, and another man named "Stephen," he went on weekend-long cocaine binges in Key West. Atta was quite the partier; he even appeared on GOP fundraiser Jack Abramoff's party yacht one week before 9/11.[14]

The FBI's claim that Atta came into the United States in June 2000 is problematic for a number of reasons. On videotapes that Hopsicker made, Amanda Keller speaks of living together with Atta before then.[15] Another source, Johnelle Bryant of the USDA, speaks of meeting Atta in "late April or May of 2000." Atta wanted the U.S. government to loan him $650,000 to buy an airplane to use as a crop duster, to be converted into a chemical-bomb plane. Atta admired a large aerial photograph of Washington, D.C., in Bryant's office and clumsily offered to buy the picture with a wad of cash.

Atta actually stated outright he only wanted room for one passenger and a giant tank for chemicals. He then made a scene whipping out a wad of big bills, as he tried to buy a large aerial photo of DC the loan officer had on her wall.

Atta spent plenty of time at the Venice Municipal Airport, although he already had a pilot's license when he arrived. Keller had lived with Atta in this tiny West Florida hamlet, across the street from Venice's little airstrip, which had been decommissioned from the U.S. military. When I traveled there, remnants of the U.S. Air Force still existed: Signs announced that you were on the former base of the 422nd Army Air Force Base Unit, USAF. According to Hopsicker, Keller alleged that when Atta wanted more cocaine, he would come to this small airstrip and pick it up at the "flight training center."

In fact, this insignificant airstrip has been a site of shady activity for decades. When captain Brad Ayers (who, remember, worked under CIA top brass Ted Shackley in Miami in 1963) became a DEA agent in the mid-'80s, he actively helped to shut down a CIA front company, Southern Air Transport, for trafficking narcotics. Ayers had plenty of experience with the Venice Municipal airstrip as well: "When things started to heat up in Miami, in Key West, more and more the agency shifted operations, particularly air operations, over onto the West Coast, and Venice was a hot spot, simply because it was so easy to operate out of."

THE BATTUELLO CONNECTION

Lois Ann Battuello is a good researcher, and she taught me a lot. An older woman living quietly with her mom in California, Battuello has a secret life as an investigator with all kinds of contacts, including at the CIA, the FBI, the SEC, and the NASD (that's the National Association of Securities Dealers). Some of these contacts are helpful; some work against the truth. I respected Battuello's request for anonymity in my last book, *The Big Wedding*, and referred to her as my "SEC contact," since she once worked on a blue-ribbon research panel at the SEC.

Lois was a behind-the-scenes investigator who ended up helping to expose the Riggs Bank–Saudi scandal in 2003. She taught Daniel Hopsicker and me a few techniques for real "gumshoe reporting": how to pull down publicly available corporate records.

However, back in 2004, I trusted her too much. Under her influence, I placed too much blame for 9/11 on the Muslim Brotherhood and the international "far Right," when so much of 9/11 came from a pragmatic wing of the CIA/U.S. military.

I see now there was a deliberate shifting of the blame on Lois's part, away from the CIA and onto an amorphous "international Reich movement" of Muslims and Nazis. We are no longer in touch.

In the mid-2000s, when we were still friends, Battuello often bragg\
that she was a financial researcher who had been trained inside a "CI\
bank." She had cut her teeth at the United California Bank (UCB), right
after former CIA director John McCone served as chairman.

"UCB had been on the brink of collapse, under the weight of highly
irregular loans," Battuello told me then. UCB had been known as John
McCone's "piggy bank," and, with businessman Myron DuBain on the
board, it allegedly "attempted to recover monies looted and missing" by
Saudi arms dealers, like Adnan Khashoggi and former CIA personnel.

Battuello's connections and interest in the Venice Municipal Airport
were somewhat personal. United California Bank was connected to Wally
Hilliard, the *owner* of the Venice Flight School where Atta "trained." One
of Hilliard's planes was busted with forty-three pounds of heroin aboard,
just before 9/11. Hilliard claimed the plane was rented out. He was not
criminally charged.

I do believe that Lois Ann Battuello is at heart a good person who at
first wanted to expose Wolfgang Bohringer. When Bohringer surfaced in
the South Pacific, residents first alerted the Hawaii FBI, who did nothing.
Then they contacted Daniel Hopsicker through his website. Hopsicker
contacted Battuello.

Battuello got on the horn to the Joint Terrorism Task Force. She pho-
tocopied and faxed the relevant passages from Hopsicker's book, *Welcome
to Terrorland: Mohamed Atta and the 9/11 Cover-Up in Florida*. She later
told me, "JTTF relied heavily on Daniel's research on Atta and Amanda
[Keller]."

The Joint Terrorism Task Force must have liked what it read. It was
Hopsicker's work that sparked the JTTF's "terror alert" for Wolfgang
Bohringer, on November 16, 2006.

It was an exciting moment for all of us. The five-year anniversary of 9/11
had just happened in NYC that fall. The Truth Movement was turning out
to be larger than anyone had expected. At the anniversary ceremonies at
Ground Zero, we showed up in force; it seemed like there were a thousand
or so folks, all in black INVESTIGATE 9/11 T-shirts. We saw ourselves as if
for the first time. The Internet movie *Loose Change* was breaking records
for online views. *Time* magazine that year called the Truth Movement

"a mainstream political reality." New media had helped feed a new consciousness: We were together realizing that the U.S. ruling class cared *nothing* for truth or peace. All bets were off. The two wars were illegal and were based on lies. The movement had to be new. It had to go beyond Left and Right. It had to become a revolution of truth. Anything was possible.

When the JTTF issued its "terror alert" for Bohringer, it felt like a light was breaking behind the thick cloak of the Bush-Cheney 9/11 cover-up. It was ironic that the JTTF used Daniel Hopsicker's work. He is the most maverick of researchers, a former '60s radical and ex–mainstream TV producer. With gonzo rage, he has lashed out and denounced the rest of the 9/11 Truth Movement.[16] Hopsicker seems to prefer to work in isolation. But his discoveries are among the best, documented by corporate records and gumshoe investigating. It seemed, for a moment, that the information he had found on Bohringer/Keller/Atta was too compelling to be ignored, even by tightly controlled federal law enforcement officials.

The JTTF swiftly descended on Wolfgang Bohringer, outside Fanning Island, in the South Pacific on November 17, 2006. When Bohringer was collared, the "first thing out of his mouth," according to arresting officers, "made him go from a 5 to an 8 on a scale of importance."

Bohringer claimed, "You can't arrest me—I'm working for the CIA."

Lois Ann Battuello told me that personally. She had traveled that next day, November 18, 2006, to my place of business, the Vox Pop café, in Brooklyn. We had together produced a big author event for Joe and Susan Trento, for their new book, *Unsafe at Any Altitude: Failed Terrorism Investigations, Scapegoating 9/11, and the Shocking Truth about Aviation Security Today.*

Battuello had really pulled out all the stops that week for her friends the Trentos. She invited all of her U.S. intelligence and police connections to come out for the book party. *She even invited former Bush terrorism czar Richard Clarke.* (I had no idea she even knew him.) In a complimentary guest list from her that I saved in my files, she noted regretfully, "I don't think Dick Clarke will make it."

Also on the Battuello guest list were the authors and financial researchers Dr. Rachel Ehrenfeld and Alyssa Lappen. Ehrenfeld wrote a 2003 book on terrorist funding but is hardly objective about 9/11. She is a member of the board of directors of the Committee on the Present Danger,[17] alongside former secretary of state George Shultz and former CIA director James Woolsey. Ehrenfeld and Lappen are both pro-Zionist and pro-Israel, often taking things to extremes in David Horowitz's *Frontpage Magazine*. Lappen went so far as to claim that the 2000 on-camera killing of Palestinian child Muhammad al-Durrah was just a hoax perpetrated by the French media. The twelve-year-old was shot in a crossfire between Israeli and Palestinian forces while cowering under his father at the outset of the Second Intifada.

Lois also asked me to personally invite two New York FBI special agents, Andy Arena and Richard McCarthy. None of the FBI personnel or pro-Zionist researchers showed up. After all, my café was already branded as a "conspiracy café" in the media. The right-leaning *New York Post* had branded me the "9/11 JAVA JACKASS" in 2005 when my first book[18] on 9/11 came out.

Yet I was personally very excited for this event. Joe Trento was author of *The Secret History of the CIA*, which relied in part on his personal, deathbed confessions/interviews with CIA heavyweight James Jesus Angleton. His 2005 book, *Prelude to Terror*, was an excellent critique of the privatization, corruption, and black ops that the CIA had engaged in for twenty years before 9/11. It helped lay the historical background for understanding how and *why* 9/11 happened. It explained that ever since the Iran-Contra operation, rogue CIA elements had had carte blanche to engage in illegal arms trading and secret wars. In this world, "Al Qaeda flourished under Saudi and CIA protection."

After Trento's masterful *Prelude to Terror*, I was expecting a huge 9/11 exposé, so I was a bit disappointed in the book on aviation safety. However, it was Lois Battuello who pointed out that buried inside the critique of airline security was a little nugget of golden info. The Trentos wrote that Nawaf al-Hazmi and Khalid al-Mihdhar were agents of the Saudi CIA, the "General Intelligence Directorate." Trento later told me he knew this from "sources inside Western and U.S. intelligence."

Lois arrived at the event breathless. She came with a short, perky, gray-haired guy named Wally Zeins. We got Wally some fair-trade coffee, and Lois took me aside. She told me she was energized by incredible good news: In the car ride over to our place, Wally Zeins, a former NYPD intelligence officer, had had a conversation on speakerphone.

Lois overheard that an important arrest had been made. Wolfgang Bohringer had been collared.

Let's take another look at Bohringer's memorable statement "You can't arrest me—I'm working for the CIA." At the time, I thought it was a rather desperate thing to say. Those with real juice don't have to panic and invoke said connections. But as I would soon see, this confessed smuggler was certainly well connected.

I had a photograph of all of us taken that day, just in case I would someday need to document what had happened.

Left to right: 9/11 widow Monica Gabrielle, the author, Lois Ann Battuello, Susan Trento, unknown, Joe Trento

BASEMENT BRIEFING

The next day, November 19, 2006, Lois Battuello sat down with me in my basement office underneath Vox Pop and gave me a kind of guerrilla "intelligence briefing." I took five pages of notes and kept the file. She tied Bohringer to a powerful international smuggler, the "Pirate of Prague" Viktor Kozeny. Kozeny is tied to some very powerful figures in the United States. It turns out that Andy Arena, at the New York FBI, was the "expert" on Kozeny. The FBI's Richard McCarthy and an agent named Bennett (first name maybe John) were the so-called "lead men" on Atta (for what that's worth).

But for all their "expertise," the tragedy here is that Wolfgang Bohringer was right—the JTTF and FBI could grab him, but they couldn't detain him. Because it looks like he *was* working for the CIA. Or perhaps, as Lois claimed, not the CIA, per se, but "rogue elements" of "former CIA people" who were working as private contractors. Either way, Bohringer was clearly working confidently for someone with the juice to spring him. CIA or quasi CIA. Bad or worse. Wherever his connections are, they are powerful.

The day after my "briefing," Lois Ann Battuello herself was forced to do an about-face. She told me I could not write this story. With a mix of vague threats and desperate attempts at persuasion, she claimed that an error had been made: It was not Bohringer who had been arrested. It was someone else.

I asked whom. She could not say. That identity was secret.

I was ordered not to report on Wolfgang Bohringer online, or in the Vox Pop newspaper, *New York Megaphone*. If I did, the consequences would be grave. Lois would cut me off.

I figured, *This is one hell of a story. My job is to raise hell.* There were people in the 9/11 Truth Movement who had claimed my first book didn't go far enough, didn't see the forest for the trees, was not rigorous enough, or comprehensive. I was eager to prove them wrong and to be a better Truther, to better serve this movement we were trying to create.

I printed forty thousand newspapers. I ran the Wolfgang story on the front cover. I disguised Lois's quotes as being from an "anonymous source close to JTTF" to protect her identity. But it was no use. I have not heard from Lois since, nor have I contacted her. At one point, her lawyer wanted to threaten me about something on a website. Daniel Hopsicker also felt betrayed by Lois and the JTTF. His bitter comment for the press was "Please pass on my cordial 'fuck you' to all involved."

Before the story ran, though, I felt compelled to take a different tack, be more of a "straight" journalist. Most editors follow the rule that a story is printable if you can get *two* good sources. I dialed up Randy Glass, who was a former JTTF informant and undercover operative for the antiterrorist Operation Diamondback. Glass, also in Florida, was the arms dealer and undercover operative I referenced back in the Dr. Graham chapter. Glass had been close to people who knew about 9/11 in advance, first in contacts at Pakistani intelligence and then at the U.S. State Department.[19] I left him a voice mail about Bohringer, explained the situation. He phoned my office on December 11, 2006, and left a pithy message. Wolfgang Bohringer *was* arrested on November 17, 2006, he confirmed. *"The answer is yes, and he's working. Can't talk about it."* Click.

Combine this story with the Able Danger story of top-brass protection of Atta and others, and this might be the closest anyone has come to "proof" that Atta and the key 9/11 "hijackers" were actually pawns being played by the CIA/U.S. military/Bush-Cheney White House. I am not basing this on an opinion or a single source. If Bohringer was CIA, Atta was CIA. All the sources lead to one conclusion.

The CIA-controlled 9/11 Commission Report, with a sterile tone, claims, "The FBI and CIA have uncovered no evidence that Atta held any fraudulent passports." But Amanda Keller says Atta had passports from Egypt, the United Arab Emirates, and Saudi Arabia. Some were his face with a different name. Like Mohammad Jamal Khan, Atta had the ability to change his identity.

Atta had a locked briefcase he kept with him at all times. Once, Keller saw inside it when Atta was nearby. She saw multiple pilot's licenses from various countries. One of the photos "didn't look anything like" Atta. Atta spoke English, Arabic, German, and French, and read Hebrew to her.

While Atta was in Hamburg, the CIA has admitted it had Atta "under surveillance." Perhaps that is a euphemism for "under control" or "on the payroll." This guy went to Hamburg, Germany, and spent seven years in a one-year program, a "grad school" paid for by U.S. tax dollars via the Congress-Bundestag Youth Exchange program. (The organization's website chirps that one of the program's top benefits is that it can "connect" youth "to an elite network of U.S. Department of State program alumni.") According to the German intelligence magazine *FOCUS*,[20] the CIA began surveillance of Atta, which lasted to May 2000. "U.S. agents followed [Atta] mainly in the area around Frankfurt am Main and noted that Atta bought large quantities of chemicals for the possible production of explosives . . . On May 18, 2000, the U.S. Embassy in Berlin gave [Atta] a visa . . . Strange that the visa application and granting it happened in the period when the [CIA] was still observing the suspicious buying of chemicals by the person [Atta] concerned." German intelligence sources told *FOCUS*, "We can no longer exclude the possibility that the Americans wanted to keep an eye on Atta after his entry in the United States."

Mohamed Atta graduated from International Officers School at Maxwell Air Force Base, Alabama, according to multiple sources in the mainstream media.[21] The FBI claimed this was just a case of mistaken identity, and the media dropped the story. The Air Force wasn't sure; it said that there were *probably* two different Mohamed Attas. Daniel Hopsicker called up the Air Force and requested the other Atta's birthday, but he was refused that information. The Maxwell records department bluntly discouraged him from further curiosity.

Atta did seem to have some contacts inside the U.S. military, Air Force, and military airline industries. His email list included aviation and defense contractor personnel, including the Canadian firm Virtual Prototypes, which helped develop the avionics for the F-15 and F/A-22 fighter planes and the B-2 bomber.

Four of the other hijackers also enjoyed high-level training at U.S. military bases; for example, Abdulaziz al-Omari attended the Aerospace Medical School at Brooks Air Force Base in Texas, and Saeed al-Ghamdi was at the Defense Language Institute at the Presidio in Monterey, California. The Defense Language Institute is noteworthy because its vice chancellor, lieutenant colonel Steve Butler, was suspended for a 2002 letter that claimed, "Bush knew about the impending attacks on America. He did nothing to warn the American people because he needed this war on terrorism."

But Atta wasn't the only one with a complicated history with the CIA. Back at Vox Pop, Lois told me that the special agent in charge of the Joint Terrorism Task Force was Will Nattinger, who spoke to her about Wolfgang Bohringer on September 5, 2006. Bohringer, he told her, was a confessed smuggler who worked for Viktor Kozeny, the Pirate of Prague. Viktor Kozeny was a wanted man in several countries for scamming investors out of billions of dollars, both in his native Czech Republic and in Azerbaijan.

Lois's sources reported Bohringer said about Kozeny, "I was his double. I smuggled planeloads of cash for Viktor, from the Bahamas into the U.S. . . . If you like arms, I can get you any kinds of arms."

Some of the truth about Viktor Kozeny came out in the 2009 trial of his former partner, Frederic Bourke, a Greenwich, Connecticut, entrepreneur. Bourke, a onetime member of the Ford family, had in turn convinced his friend, the former Senate majority leader George Mitchell, to invest $200,000 with Kozeny. When Mitchell flew to the peace negotiations in northern Ireland in the late '90s, he on occasion flew on Kozeny's private Lear jet.

Today, Viktor Kozeny is a free man, living in the Bahamas. The Bahamians refused to extradite Kozeny to courts in the United States or the Czech Republic.

After I disobeyed Lois Battuello's order not to write about Bohringer, she dropped me from her list of people she communicates with. I have come to believe that this is just as well; I am in fact grateful for her exclusion.

When you stop and think about it, the thing we know most about Atta is that he looked terribly sad and murderous in a photo. We assume he was on Flight 11, the first plane to hit a WTC Tower on 9/11, because we have been told so. But there has never been any proof. There is one blurry photo of Atta making a connecting flight in Portland, Maine. There is a bag he "accidentally left" in a rental car, with flight manuals and a "last will and testament." To assume that any of the official story is true, when so much of it is not, is to risk perpetuating a toxic illusion—and illusions are indicative of a great spiritual malady.

With these chapters on Graham, Shaffer, and Bohringer, we have three compelling stories that show that 9/11 was a monster that didn't come from Muslims, from bin Laden, or from the so-called "Al Qaeda" network. It came from the U.S. military–CIA–black-ops world. On 9/11, that world was under the control of the Bush-Cheney White House.

But before we consider political solutions to the problem, let's dive a bit deeper into analyzing it. Let me take you "home" to a place I've lived for most of the last twenty years, New York City, and show you some New York stories up close. These stories further examine the political corruption we the people must overcome before we can create a new world. And since we're talking about my hometown of twenty years, the place I have such intense love and loathing for, these New York stories will continue on the path we are on: to truly report 9/11, in an intimate, personal way, yet always grounded in hard facts.

PART THREE

NEW YORK STORIES

POLICE STATE NEW YORK

This is a eulogy for the dying spirit of freedom. For the past ten years, I have seen the spirit of New York City crushed, in the name of 9/11. You can't go anywhere in this city without seeing a mural, or a bumper sticker, or a decal on a fire truck that memorializes 9/11. It's usually followed by the inscription NEVER FORGET. But how can you forget what you never knew?

The City of New York has a police force bigger than the armies of most countries. But the city has never investigated 9/11. The city has always ceded that task to apathetic federal officials. The city of New York is serious about 9/11 only when there's an opportunity to increase police power. The city is tough and sentimental and morbid about 9/11 but lacks the emotional strength to look under the hood.

The 9/11 events transformed a city of free-spirited creativity into a metropolis of paranoid checkpoints. In the past couple years, the NYPD has started the Container Inspection Program, in which the NYPD sets up a plastic table in a busy subway station, stops every seventh person, and does a search of their purse or backpack. This, of course, strips the searched person of an important constitutional freedom—the Fourth Amendment's protection against "unreasonable search and seizure" and the Fourteenth Amendment's "due process" rights. Supreme Court justice Louis Brandeis once wrote that the spirit of the Fourth Amendment protects our unspoken, universal "right to be left alone." We are supposed to be "innocent until proven guilty," but NYC law enforcement treats everyone like a suspect. Their actions have long-term effects.

Am I "the only living boy in New York" who has read the Bill of Rights? I watch the people of this city give in quietly and let their bags get searched. They don't realize that you don't have to consent. It's just as easy to get into the subway through a different entrance—which shows that this policy is not about security; it's psychological. It isn't actually about finding a real bomb in a backpack. There is none. Not one has been found.

In a little-known court case in 2005, the NYCLU organized five plaintiffs to sue the city over the Container Inspection Program, on the grounds that the program is unconstitutional. The NYPD argued that the program should be allowed to continue, because it "reinforces the awareness of . . . the public of the need to be alert." Heck, if more alertness is what you want, maybe we should have more random Tasings?

Sounds like what they want to "reinforce" and "never forget" is the fear of 9/11, without examining the gross anomalies that just will not go away.

To the people of New York City, I say: Read the Constitution and fall in love again with your rights, your freedoms. It's exciting to break out of your routine, smile at the cops, and politely say something chipper, like, *Hey, guys, aren't you worried these searches might be illegal? Didn't you swear an oath to protect my constitutional rights?* This usually leads to an interesting conversation, usually about 9/11. A couple of times, I have been surprised to learn how many New York cops have seen the 9/11 Truth movie *Loose Change.*

The cops, my experience shows, usually claim that the subway is private property. It's a flimsy argument. Technically, the subway is administered by the Metropolitan Transit Authority (MTA), which is a "public benefit corporation" chartered by the State of New York. But even if the MTA were a for-profit, private corporation, say, like McDonald's, it wouldn't matter—my constitutional rights don't get suspended when I walk into a restaurant or when I hop on a train.

It seems the illegal subway searches are part of an agenda to spread fear throughout the media capital of the world. The NYCLU's court case was swiftly smacked down by a federal judge, who argued that the threat of terror was so great that privacy was worth sacrificing. The court found "credible and persuasive" testimony from "experts" like former CIA officer David Cohen (now top brass at NYPD) and ex–terror czar Richard Clarke. In a leap of logic, the court argued that it was okay to "defer" to the law enforcement authorities. Instead of standing up for constitutional liberties, the court caved and wrote in its decision that "the risk to public safety of a terrorist bombing in New York City's subway system is substantial and real." Of course, the "real" here is defined by Cohen and Clarke—the same people who claim that the Bush-Cheney 9/11 official story is "real."

I just looked back on the city's recent history by watching the Bronx hip-hop documentaries of British filmmaker Dick Fontaine. I saw a city brimming with creativity. The subways were covered in art, bursting with color, richly painted. The city could not contain the graffiti writers, because there were just too many, protesting against the powers that be. What happened to that city?

Today, the subway cars are sterile, inside and out. The stations themselves are decrepit, full of leaks, filth, and mold. (A young visitor from Sweden told me she was shocked the subway has been allowed to become so run-down.) But the subway cars themselves are blanketed in clean chrome and corporate advertisements. A new public address system broadcasts automatic recordings barked out in a classic 1950s-style, paternal radio-announcer voice. This "voice of authority" urges you to fear those around you. New Yorkers hear this announcement once every five to ten minutes:

> *Ladies and gentlemen, this is an important message from the New York City Police Department. Keep your belongings in your sight at all times. Protect yourself! If you see a suspicious package or activity on the platform or trains, do not keep it to yourself. Tell a police officer or an MTA employee. Be alert. And have a safe day.*

I realize that plenty of New Yorkers ignore these announcements more often than not. But what would happen if we really listened and analyzed its text? Usually everyone is zoned out, tired from work, wearing black, the volume cranked on earbuds jammed into their heads.

But let's wake up, and really listen to what the message claim.

"Ladies and gentlemen, this is an important message from the New York City Police Department. Keep your belongings in your sight at all times."

Wait, petty crime is down in NYC and the subways are covered in cops, some with German shepherds, Kevlar, combat gear, and assault rifles. Is it really mandatory that I feel afraid of getting robbed now, too? Is this just a scare tactic to grab my attention for what comes next?

"Protect yourself!"

Whoa! I thought all of these police in the subway were here to protect me and my kid. Are we truly on our own against the evils of the world?

"If you see a suspicious package or activity on the platform or trains, do not keep it to yourself. Tell a police officer or an MTA employee."

These announcements came into the New York subway around 2004–2005. Those were the years of the Madrid train bombings and the London subway bombings. However, even though the Madrid bombings were instantly blamed on "Al Qaeda," they happened right before a hotly contested election of right-wing candidate Jose Aznar. Aznar, of course, blamed Al Qaeda, despite evidence. The people of Spain didn't buy it. Despite a lead in the polls, Aznar lost the election. The incoming president immediately withdrew Spanish forces from the United States's Iraq War. No Al Qaeda link to the bombings was ever proven. Political experts across the board blamed Aznar's misrepresentation of the train tragedy for his defeat.

The London subway bombings on July 7, 2005, are an even grosser hoax. Like 9/11, in the UK, they have become iconic, an emotional controversy referred to by the date 7/7. The similarities to 9/11 are alarming. Three young Arabs and a Jamaican were blamed, accused of setting off bombs in backpacks. However, a good deal of physical evidence in the wreckage showed that the blast holes showed an explosion coming *up* from explosions that occurred *underneath* the bus and subway cars.[22]

It gets even creepier when you learn that there was a drill, by the UK government and security services, scheduled for that day, *in those same sta-*

tions. This is strange because the Twin Tower attacks also happened on a day when several different drills were being run. Air defense fighter jets were in the sky, imagining a terror attack (Operation Vigilant Guardian, et al.), and bioterrorism experts from Mayor Giuliani's office were doing the Tripod II drill down at Ground Zero.

The drill in London that day was run by Visor Consultants security company, headed by former Scotland Yard official Peter Power. Power is quite a contradiction. On July 7, 2005, he simultaneously described how strange and eerie the coincidence was; it made the "hairs stand up on the back of his neck," he told the BBC. Former NYC mayor Rudy Giuliani happened to also be in London that day. Running mock terror drills has become a specialty of Giuliani Partners LLC since Rudy left office. Rudy wasn't directly linked to the London bombings, at first glance, but he was staying nearby, and his company had connections to Visor Consultants.[23]

Shortly after the 7/7 bombings, it was reported that Anwar al-Awlaki had inspired the bombers. Yes, that Anwar al-Awlaki, the same one who had dined at the Pentagon after 9/11. The same al-Awlaki who was of grave concern to Lt. Col. Shaffer.

So, if you know just a few basic facts about 9/11, the Madrid hoax, and the London subway bombings, the NYC subway announcements are beyond annoying. They should cause you to writhe and take action. They repeat an already banal call for more fear, for less freedom, for paranoia about an undefined and unproven enemy.

Other shorter announcements include "Do not display cell phones or other electronic devices," as if the subway were full of thieves who are brazen enough to grab your phone or iPod. Or listen to this one: "Ladies and gentlemen! Soliciting money on the subway is *illegal*. We ask you not to give. Thank you for helping us maintain an orderly subway."

Orderly? According to the above mentality, a poor person asking someone for money is "disorderly." The MTA can interrupt my ride with loud, bossy announcements preaching fear, but a poor man asking for money is not allowed.

In the Gospel of Matthew, Jesus says that when you give food to the hungry or drink to the thirsty, you are not a "disorderly" thing but a good thing, a *holy* thing. You are becoming more merciful, you are becoming more human, you are connecting to God. Empathizing with another's hunger connects us to our common humanity. But in cold NYC, empathy is illegal.

American genius poet Walt Whitman said, "This is what you shall do ... give alms to everyone who asks." The city Whitman lived in is now a train careening at top speed toward a Nazi-like police state.

Leave the subway and go outside. Ah, fresh air. But no, thirty NYPD cop cars are speeding by with their flashers on.

This is standard policy for the NYPD. They burn through tons of gas, parading through the streets. An outside observer might assume that they are clearing the way for a visiting dignitary. But if you ask, the cops say this is their new NYC procedure to "deter terrorism."

How is this police parade dissuading "terrorists"? Are you insinuating that we, the people of NYC, are all terrorists? Or is this an operation designed to raise the stress level of average people, to put us in a state of anxiety, always on the lookout for "suspicious activity," whether it be a bomb or a political idea, always ready to let the cops open up our bags and go through our books and papers with rubber gloves?

Ten years after 9/11, NYC has become a police state. But the trick for me has been to find a way to have the War on Terror make me *more* philosophical, not less so. As with a move in aikido, I have tried to allow "terror" to make me more compassionate. The path for me has been to detach from fear and seek to banish all illusions. Seeking the truth about 9/11 has run parallel in my life to seeking what's good in the story of Jesus, Christianity, and Zen. The trick for me is to not go crazy as the world goes mad. That has meant spending plenty of time outside the city.

I have moved out of New York City three times in the last ten years. The first time was September 10, 2001, ironically enough. Bush biographer Jim Hatfield had just died a month and a half earlier, and I was burnt out.

A wise old woman explained this to me during one of my trips: There's a higher power out there who is looking out for those who work for truth. The angels love the Davids.

After publishing all of the dirt on the Bush–bin Laden connection since 1999, it I would have found it especially traumatic to witness 9/11. Fate intervened when I moved to my aunt's house on Long Island on 9/10. I was a safe distance away when the world changed. I had the time and the space to begin to look critically at the "news" about bin Laden that people were desperately drinking in on cable television.

8 "CONSPIRACY THEORISTS ARE EVERYWHERE": CONFRONTING RUDY GIULIANI

When I came back from Shreveport in September 2007, the experience of Dr. Graham's murder changed me. His death gave me new life. I had published a book about 9/11 in 2005, and at that time had been careful not to appear too radical. But after Shreveport, the blinders fell from my eyes. I realized that my 2005 book, *The Big Wedding*, had at times been too cautious. But I had nothing to fear.

It became clearer to me that 9/11 had been stage-managed by the powers that be: federal law enforcement, military, and intelligence. It was time to go from research and reporting to direct action. One of those key confrontations happened in November 2007, when former NYC mayor Rudy Giuliani was running for president.

Giuliani had been a polarizing mayor, but suddenly, on 9/11, he filled a void. Covered in ash and soot, he seemed on television to be the kind of dependable person you need in a crisis. Despite his actions in the past, Rudy became known as "America's mayor."

Few remembered what a bastard he had been as NYC mayor: rounding up the homeless, sending an NYPD tank out against the Thirteenth Street squatters, fingerprinting and sending to prison everyone for even minor offenses, like jumping a subway turnstile. (And yes, I have done hard time for that, too.)

"America's mayor" constantly invoked 9/11 in speech after speech, and in November 2007, he was at the height of his influence as the front-runner for the GOP nomination.

I met Giuliani in Colorado at a campaign event. A fellow Truther flew me to Denver to do a speaking engagement about 9/11 and Dr. Graham. At that event, the local We Are Change activists, the Truth Alliance, the Christians, and the Ron Paul supporters invited me to travel north with them the next day. Giuliani himself was going to be in Loveland, Colorado, campaigning.

I tried to ask Giuliani a question about 9/11, but Colorado police forcefully stopped and cuffed me before I could get it out.

The question was, "You said you were told the World Trade Center was going to collapse. Who told who this, how did they know, and why were the firefighters not warned?" This question, to this day, *still* needs to be asked.

On 9/11, covered in soot, Giuliani told the following to Peter Jennings, as he staggered north from the site:

> *I went down to the scene and we set up headquarters at 75 Barclay Street, which was right there with the police commissioner, the fire commissioner, the head of emergency management, and we were operating out of there when we were told that the World Trade Center was going to collapse. And it did collapse . . .*

Giuliani now denies having said that, but it's archived, in his words, on YouTube. And Giuliani can't just say it was a lucky guess, because no steel-frame structure has *ever* collapsed because of fire. The original architects are on record explaining that the WTC towers were built to withstand the impact of a jetliner. No one should have "known" that the towers were going to collapse. It was not at all likely, if the laws of physics were still applicable that day. Giuliani let the truth slip out: He was given forewarning of an impossible event, because the collapse of the towers was controlled.

If you believe the official story about the collapse, you run into a number of thorny problems. A high-school physics teacher, David Chandler, can walk you through an online lecture about the "freefall speed" at which the towers came down. That's right, folks, freefall. No resistance. All of that steel support, all sixty-four columns, somehow were turned into dust simultaneously.

Giuliani should also be asked questions about the incredible amount of heat in the ruins of Ground Zero. America's mayor himself admitted that molten steel and intense fires were deep in the wreckage for over "one hundred days." Some may assume this is just the natural product of a structural collapse, but a structural failure would not create a lake of molten steel that lasted at Ground Zero for over one hundred days. Steel melts at over two thousand degrees Fahrenheit, but the burning jet fuel could reach a maximum temperature of only 750 degrees. The laws of physics beg for another source for all that heat.

Our ambush on Giuliani in Loveland was a huge success. We cleaned up well; we looked like good Republican youth. We got roughed up a bit, but we sent him running. I was one of the first to shake Giuliani's hand, and I held on as I tried to ask him about his foreknowledge of the towers' collapse. But he cut me off and said, "Why don't you let go of my hand?" He scurried off as I got a nasty look from a seven-foot-tall, overweight security guy.

Once inside the Loveland Coffee Roaster, the crowd chanted, "Rudy! Rudy!" as Giuliani signed autographs and shook hands. But then a few We Are Change Colorado members shouted out a few pertinent questions, along the lines of "Why did you export the steel?" Not a bad question—it referred to the mystery of why Giuliani, a former federal prosecutor, would have ignored "rules of evidence." Giuliani swiftly had the steel girders from the WTC packed off to India and China. Covered in human remains, the half-melted steel was evidence of an atypical collapse. Instead of protecting the crime scene, Giuliani had the evidence sold as scrap.

Instead of answering the heckler's question about the steel, Giuliani hunched his shoulders, leaned forward a bit, and cackled. Someone must have told him that laughter is the best medicine, but they forgot to tell him not to overdo it. It was peculiar, bordering on zany. Giuliani's version of lighthearted, "hey, this is nothing, I can laugh it off" behavior was a caricature of an evil scientist delighting in his plan to destroy the universe.

The crowd had a different response. As the Loveland police, mostly undercover in plainclothes and long hair, started to jerk the loud Truthers out of the coffee shop, the crowd chanted, "Tase him, bro!" And they, too, laughed with a Giuliani-like cackle. The Taser reference recalled the then-recent brutal electroshocking of student Andrew Meyer at a senator John Kerry speech at the University of Florida.

Meyer had attempted to ask Kerry a question about his membership in the Skull and Bones secret society at Yale, as part of an inquiry into why Kerry didn't protest the probable theft of the 2004 presidential election. Despite Kerry's mild call for tolerance, six police officers tackled Meyer, cuffed one hand, and then electrocuted him with a Taser when they couldn't get the other arm cuffed. "Don't Tase me, bro" became the official "most memorable quote of the year" in *The Yale Book of Quotations*.

Back in Loveland, this crowd showed that it was inclined to cower before power, but we Truthers kept coming at them. We kept popping up like Viet Cong. When one of us would get pulled out of the coffeehouse by the cops, another would rise up and speak out. Afterward, Giuliani did a little press conference for the media, and noted with regret, "The conspiracy theorists are everywhere."

I wasn't called on at the press conference. It was my fate to become like Andrew Meyer in Florida. It seemed like the "don't Tase me, bro" incident was on everyone's mind, a media memory that diminished how much freedom of speech would be allowed in daily life.

After the press conference, Giuliani made one last pass through the parking lot, still signing autographs. As he signed someone's red, white, and blue leather jacket, I was on my toes, nimbly avoiding pushing or being pushed by someone. I loudly asked, "Mayor Giuliani, on 9/11 you said you were told . . ."

Bam. Someone grabbed me and pulled me backward. It was the Loveland police. Before I could move, my wrist was turned up, my arm extended and held straight behind my back. I could tell I was in the hands of a professional because I could feel the painful effect of a submission hold. One second more, and my wrist could have easily been broken. This was communicated with the most direct and simple of languages: brute force. But I kept calling out my question, until the cops walked me away and cuffed me. They checked my ID. I was pissed off and said, "You just violated my fucking Bill of Rights." They claimed I was pushing people, although I was not.

Later, the Colorado ACLU was interested in possibly pursuing a case, but I wasn't focused on turning the situation into financial gain. In retrospect, it was a naive decision. I could have gone for the jugular and sued the Loveland police on constitutional grounds. But instead of a lawsuit, I wrote the chief of police in Loveland a letter. I simply asked how this could have happened. I asked if their officers were trained to respect the Bill of Rights. He said free speech was important, of course. But this incident happened on private property.

9 THE WTC COLLAPSE, JERRY HAUER, AND THE NYC ANTHRAX CONNECTION

Who could possibly have told Mayor Giuliani that the World Trade Center was about to collapse?

We are now entering territory where practically the entire diverse 9/11 Truth Movement is in agreement: The Twin Towers fell, in an unprecedented, sudden, freefall collapse. Something other than a "structural failure" caused that collapse. Over 1,500 architects and engineers formed AE911Truth.org to explain the scientific problems with the official story, and this professional association has petitioned Congress. The silence in response is deafening.

In 2006, even *The New York Times* published (online) over three hundred eyewitness accounts of strange anomalies down at Ground Zero that day. The World Trade Center Task Force report is one of the most underappreciated documents in the history of 9/11. It's a set of verbatim accounts from witnesses, many of them fire and building professionals. One hundred and eighteen first responders heard explosions or "secondary devices" before the collapses.

The *Times* suppressed its own report. Try searching for "World Trade Center Task Force" on NYTimes.com today, and you will get zero results. However, by doing a little digging, you can see some highlights in various blogs that have preserved the testimony.

Firefighter Timothy Burke recalls, "It seemed like I was going, 'Oh, my God, there is a secondary device' because the way the building popped, I thought it was an explosion."

Fire Marshal John Coyle, observed, " . . . The tower was—it looked to me—I thought it was exploding, actually. That's what I thought for hours afterwards, that it had exploded, or the plane, or there had been some device on the plane that exploded, because the debris from the tower had shot out far over our heads."[24]

EMT Richard Zarrillo's testimony stands out, from October 25, 2001.

> As I was walking towards the fire command post, I found Steve Mosiello. I said, "Steve, where's the boss? I have to give him a message." He said, "Well, what's the message?" I said, "The buildings are going to collapse; we need to evac everybody out." With a very confused look, he said, "Who told you that?" I said, "I was just with John at OEM. OEM says the buildings are going to collapse; we need to get out."
>
> He escorted me over to Chief Ganci. He said, "Hey, Pete, we got a message that the buildings are going to collapse." His reply was, "Who the fuck told you that?" Then Steve brought me in and with Chief Ganci, Commissioner Feehan . . . I said, "Listen, I was just at OEM. The message I was given was that the buildings are going to collapse; we need to get our people out." At that

moment, this thunderous, rolling roar came down, and that's
when the building came down, the first tower came down.[25]

So, if the Office of Emergency Management (OEM) was a source of forewarning that the WTC was about to blow, we should spend some time looking at who was connected to the OEM on 9/11.

The OEM was founded in 1996 by Rudolph Giuliani and Jerome Hauer. Hauer ran it until 2000. It was Hauer's decision to house the OEM in World Trade Center Building 7, where it would butt up against the local CIA headquarters and the Department of Defense. The decision was strange, because Hauer seemed to not be bothered by the 1993 WTC attack.

On September 11, 2001, Hauer was a managing director of the "CIA of Wall Street" a powerful, well-connected security company called Kroll Associates. Hauer was also a federal official that day, working for the Bush administration as a "national security advisor" with the Department of Health and Human Services. The morning of 9/11, Hauer was conveniently already downtown, at Ground Zero, as a part of a prescient bioterror drill, "Tripod II," a joint City of New York–Federal Department of Justice–FEMA drill that happened to be scheduled for that week, right near Ground Zero.

"Tripod II" stood for "trial point of dispensing." It sought to prepare "distribution of medication in the event of a biological attack." It seemed as if that day, Hauer and Company were already expecting the anthrax attacks. Mayor Giuliani's testimony to the 9/11 Commission was omitted from its website, perhaps due to the fact that he confirmed that FEMA et al. had set up a command center for Tripod II, near Ground Zero, *before* 9/11. His testimony contradicted later FEMA statements that claimed Tripod II was only set up *after* 9/11. FEMA was caught dispensing a desperate lie and claimed it was seeking to dampen "Internet conspiracy theories."

Let's go back and look at FDNY member Zarrillo's testimony to the World Trade Center Task Force. Why did Fire Chief Ganci and his right-hand man, Steve Mosiello, rebuke Zarrillo when he passed on word that the "buildings are going to collapse"? It's almost tragic how Zarrillo couldn't get anyone to believe him. They treated him like Chicken Little because his message was absurd. Steel-frame structures do not explode. It had never happened before. To believe otherwise would be to go up against years of professional fire safety training.

Later, around 2010, a fellow firefighter, Erik Lawyer, from Washington state, started up a new group, Firefighters for 9/11 Truth. Lawyer today delivers eloquent public presentations in which he points out that firefighters are professionally trained to recognize the signs when something is amiss in a fire situation. They know what can really make a steel-frame building collapse—jet fuel–based fires, or any carbon-based fire, just don't get hot enough.

To take a steel-frame structure down, you need a "secondary device." Lawyer also points out that the National Fire Protection Association's (NFPA's) fire safety manual teaches how to look for arson, but it was disregarded on 9/11. The existence of molten metal in the ruins, according to the manual, is a dead giveaway. If you go by the book, a real fire investigation concludes that "molten steel and concrete could indicate the use of exotic accelerants, specifically Thermite."[26]

Chief Ganci's primal "Who the fuck told you that?" is akin to its fairer cousin, the frank, raw disbelief of Dan Rather at CBS news. In his TV interview on the afternoon of 9/11, Rather asked OEM founder Jerome Hauer, "We have so few facts, at this point . . . Is it possible that just a plane crash could have collapsed these buildings, or would it have required the prior positioning of other explosives in the buildings?"

A tough question, Dan, but Jerry Hauer was ready. With almost scripted precision, Hauer retorted:

> *My sense is that just the velocity of the plane and the fact that you have a plane filled with fuel hitting that building, that burned, that the velocity of the plane certainly had an impact on the structure itself. And then the fact that it burned and you had that intense heat probably weakened the structure as well. And I think it was simply the planes hitting the buildings and causing the collapse.*

Rather pointed out that there were "few facts," but Hauer didn't have that problem. He had a high degree of certainty in this time of "few facts."

He was an oasis of cool in a broiling desert. In a short time, this crazy theory of Hauer's would morph into an official story of the collapse. What Hauer didn't tell Dan Rather was that he, Jerry Hauer, had links back to SAIC, the defense contractor with its fingerprints all over both the anthrax cover-up *and* the production of the nano-thermite-controlled demolition technology that a peer-reviewed scientific paper now widely believes was used at the WTC demolition.

Hauer's scripted speech to Rather contradicts the science and eyewitness testimony of the men and women on the ground. They heard forewarning from OEM, and then heard explosions, and then saw a volcanic collapse at the speed of gravity.

According to San Francisco–based *Bay Area News* and Wikipedia, Jerome Hauer later that day warned the Bush White House to go on Cipro, the anti-anthrax drug. I had the chance to interview Hauer in 2007, and he denied this allegation. But whether or not it was Hauer, on 9/11 the White House did go on Cipro. They knew an anthrax attack was coming.

Hauer's connections to U.S. anthrax are worth probing, if you get a kick out of stabbing a hornets' nest with a sharp stick. Six days after 9/11, the anthrax attacks started and sent the country back into paroxysms of terror. This time, we were all potential victims.

Watchdog group Judicial Watch sued to discover who warned the White House to go on Cipro. The Bush-Cheney administration stonewalled its Freedom of Information Act requests. Judicial Watch founder Larry Klayman stated, "The White House did know, and they went on the antibiotics . . . African American employees at Brentwood [U.S. Postal Service facility] were basically left out there to twist in the wind when the white guys up on Capitol Hill got immediate treatment."

Jerome Hauer is very well connected. He later testified alongside Giuliani to the White House–connected 9/11 Commission. I was there that day. It was a schmooze-fest, pats on the back and glad-handing. Shortly after 9/11, Hauer went on to lead a whitewash of his own, as part of the Department of Health and Human Services' immediate investigation of anthrax deaths. Hauer's report blamed Osama bin Laden and Al Qaeda.

"Suspects are Osama bin Laden and his Al-Qaeda network and sympathizers to U.S. right wing extremists." This report's theory is similar to that of the Bush White House, which also pressured the U.S. media and FBI Director Mueller to connect the anthrax attacks with either Al Qaeda or Iraq. According to a former aide, during the president's morning intelligence briefings, Mueller was "beaten up" for not producing proof that the killer spores were the handiwork of terrorist mastermind Osama bin Laden.

The Hauer-Bush assertion of a foreign source for the anthrax has been widely discredited. The five deaths in 2001 were from a fine, "weaponized" form of anthrax, the "Ames strain" that only the U.S. military and U.S. federal government possessed. Even the FBI's official investigation stated that this anthrax from 2001 was either from Fort Detrick, Maryland, or from Dugway Proving Ground in Utah, both U.S. military facilities.

Curiously enough, the Ames, Iowa, U.S. government database of all anthrax strains was destroyed in October 2001, with the permission of the FBI and the Centers for Disease Control.

Hauer's cover-up report on the anthrax attacks refused to do the obvious, which was to track the anthrax back to U.S. military facilities. Instead, he called for more deathly labs to be built. A contemporaneous National Institutes of Health report blamed a "serious shortage of high-containment laboratories in which to perform experiments using dangerous pathogens" in the United States. Next year, $1.5 billion more was added to the federal budget for biowarfare research.

So, let's compare. Hauer blamed Osama bin Laden. But in 2008, the FBI blamed a dead Fort Detrick scientist, Dr. Bruce Ivins. They can't both be right. But both can be wrong. Dead wrong.

Osama bin Laden was a popular topic for Hauer, even on the evening of 9/11 on TV with Dan Rather. In that same interview, Rather posited that the 9/11 attacks must have had state sponsorship. Hauer urged us to blame bin Laden only:

> **Dan Rather:** *Many intelligence people at very high levels say you can't have these kinds of attacks without having some state— Iraq, Iran, Libya, Syria, somebody—involved . . . Put that into perspective for us.*

Jerome Hauer: Yeah, well, I'm not sure I agree that this was nec-essarily state sponsored; it certainly has the fingerprints of some-body like bin Laden.

No investigation. No evidence. It was bin Laden. Scripted. Made for TV.

Hauer is a Democrat, and it was always odd that he was paired up with Republican Rudy Giuliani. He's a biological terrorism expert whose resume includes time working for the senator Evan Bayh (D-IN), IBM, and Science Applications International Corp (SAIC). SAIC is a military contractor doing work in nuclear issues, biowarfare, and PSYOP, and will soon reappear in this story. In a gross conflict of interest, in 2005, Hauer joined the board of directors of Emergent Biosolutions, parent company of Bioport, the sole manufacturer of the controversial anthrax vaccine. Despite its health risks, the vaccine became mandatory in some parts of the U.S. military.

Hauer's mother, Rose Muscatine Hauer, is a retired dean of the Beth Israel School of Nursing. She is also the honorary president of the New York chapter of Hadassah, the Daughters of Zion movement, one of the central Zionist organizations involved in the creation and maintenance of the State of Israel. In the volatile and oil-rich Middle East, Israel is a client state of the U.S. war machine. Its intelligence methods often ape those of CIA black ops.

BUILDING A "BIOBOMB": THE HATFILL CONNECTION

Jerry Hauer and anthrax go way back. In May 1998, Hauer spoke at the powerful and mysterious Council on Foreign Relations on the topic of "Building a 'Biobomb': Terrorist Challenge." That evening, Hauer co-presented on that topic with Steven Hatfill. Yes, *that* Steven Hatfill, who at one time (2002–2008) was *the* prime suspect in FBI's Amerithrax investigation.

A year after their CFR presentations, Hatfill and Hauer would be-come coworkers at SAIC's Center for Counterterrorism Technology and

Analysis. SAIC often works for the CIA—so often, in fact, that many in northern Virginia joke that if you spell "SAIC" backward, you can tell who it belongs to.

Steven Hatfill had also worked at Fort Detrick, the U.S. Army's bio-weapons lab in Maryland. Hatfill is the cartoon-size-beefcake bad guy. He had a thick black bandito mustache, but shaved it when the media were first onto him in 2002.

Hatfill was CIA, Special Forces, DIA, FBI, and SAIC, and through Hauer, he is two degrees away from Giuliani. Yet Hatfill was never convicted, or even prosecuted, for anything. Later we'll watch him exit this story with $5.8 million in cash.

In 2007, I tracked down Jerome Hauer in Alexandria, Virginia, and got him on the phone. (A quick $7.50 to Intelius, Inc., got me his unlisted number.) I waited to call him on Labor Day 2007, which I think was a good idea, because he sounded a little drunk. As you can hear from the MP3 on SanderHicks.com, Hauer's speech was slurred. He seemed sedated.

In our interview, Hauer was aware of the charges from the San Diego Citizens Grand Jury. He repeatedly referred to the grand jury as "a bunch of nutjobs," but he couldn't name something they had gotten wrong. On the phone, Hauer didn't deny his long relationship with his colleague Stephen Hatfill. How could he have, when the paper trail tying the two together is so voluminous? I argued with Hauer about whether one could describe his relationship with Hatfill as a "mentor-mentee relationship."

I was surprised Hauer stayed on the phone with me as long as he did. As with FBI agent Steve Hayes in Shreveport, it was as if part of Hauer wanted someone to empathize with him, or someone with whom he could come a step closer to confessing. I asked him three times over the course of twenty minutes, "Who did the anthrax attacks? Who killed those people?" The third time, it took him about five seconds to respond, "I don't know."

He claimed he didn't know, but at least this time he didn't blame bin Laden. Instead, he referred me to the FBI. At other times, on the recording, you can hear people laughing in the background, as Hauer puts me on speakerphone or has other people listen in on the call in some way.

We talked about Hatfill's long relationship with Hauer. I asked if Hatfill was innocent of involvement in the anthrax attacks.

> **Hicks:** *A lot of people are wondering, you know, where these anthrax attacks came from.*
>
> **Hauer was less than direct:** *I have, uh . . . no idea.*
>
> **Hicks:** *Do you think that Hatfill is innocent?*
>
> **Hauer:** *I . . . think that the FBI . . . should not have s-said anything about Hatfill until they knew more. I do not think Steve Hatfill is a murderer. I think Steve Hatfill is very passionate, but I don't think he's a murderer. I don't believe he did it.*

If Hatfill were innocent, the answer would have been a simple "Yes, he's innocent." So my follow-up question was:

> **Hicks:** *That seems to be not the most clear, specific response in the world. . . . Can you say conclusively that Hatfill was not involved in the anthrax attacks? Is that what you're saying?*
>
> **Hauer:** *I'm not going to get into those details.*
>
> **Hicks:** *So, you're leaving some room for ambiguity?*
>
> **Hauer:** *No, I'm not. I'm not going to get into those details.*
>
> **Hicks:** *Why not?*
>
> **Hauer:** *I just don't want to comment on it.*

(Ah, but Jerry, you already have.)

LET'S MEET STEVEN HATFILL

Steven Hatfill could be one of two things. First, he could be a red herring, part of a complex cover-up of the anthrax attacks, in which his role was that of the "official main suspect" for six crucial years, to distract the media's attention. (Kind of like the way Lois Ann Battuello worked to distract 9/11 Truth researchers away from the CIA.)

After all, it's easier for the media to focus on one bad guy. Meanwhile, all real international anthrax experts point out consistently that only a team of experts could have manufactured this military-grade, silicon-coated 2001 anthrax.

Or there is possibility number two: that Hatfill was one of those scientists involved, and not totally innocent (as Hauer implies). Hauer does create an air of ambiguity around Hatfill, as if Hauer himself were not sure of Hatfill's final fate. At the time of my Hauer interview, Hatfill had not yet been granted his $5 million payoff. Perhaps Hatfill made a deal early on and agreed to allow his public reputation to be destroyed in exchange for a big bag of cash.

Recall that early in the official investigation, in 2003, a significant *Washington Post Magazine* feature article presented some rather interesting evidence. Hatfill, we learn, started out in Rhodesia, where he trained as a medical doctor. The *Post* article touches on Hatfill's claims that he worked with the nationalist Rhodesian military group there: the Selous Scouts. (The claim is also on Hatfill's resume.) What the *Post* doesn't go into is that the Selous Scouts were a white supremacist militia that allegedly used anthrax in their war on black anticolonial movements in the late '70s.

(Of the five American anthrax deaths, three were persons of color. Both of the Brentwood postal workers who died were African American: Thomas Morris, Jr., and Joseph Curseen, Jr. The woman from the Bronx who died, Kathy Nguyen, was Cambodian American.)

The documentary *Anthrax War*, by Robert Nadler and Bob Coen, touches upon the Selous Scouts' use of anthrax but doesn't report Hatfill's claims that he was involved with them. But if you put the two facts together—Hatfill's documented claim that he worked with the Selous Scouts, and the Selous Scouts' video admission that they used anthrax in a racist war—it's clear that a real investigation into Hatfill's background is called for.

The five fatal victims of the anthrax attacks, from to right: Josep Curseen Jr., Thomas Morris, Ottilie Lundgren, Robert Stevens, and Kathy Nguyen. [Source: Reuters and Associated Press]

Steven Hatfill had worked with the U.S. military, at Fort Bragg, North Carolina, training with the Special Forces in how to defend against bioterror attacks. He had also done time doing biowarfare training at the United States Special Operations Command (USSOCOM). Recall, it was USSOCOM lawyers who cancelled Lt. Col. Shaffer's meetings with the FBI back in 2000.

Hatfill had a mentor, one Bill Patrick, a guy who kept a laboratory that could refine anthrax in his home. Patrick was like a dad to Hatfill. When Hatfill arrived at defense contractor SAIC, in 1999, he teamed up with SAIC vice president Joseph Soukup, and together they hired Bill Patrick to do a very interesting study: *a study to look at the potential dangers of anthrax sent through the U.S. mail.*

Hatfill was so connected, one of his former students at the FBI turned up as one of the agents who searched Hatfill's home when Hatfill became the "top suspect."

And then there is Hatfill's link to some of the information in the return address of the anthrax letters mailed in 2001. Whoever sent those letters used this fake return address: 4th Grade, Greendale School, Franklin Park, NJ 08852.

Back in Rhodesia (which was renamed Zimbabwe when the white colonial killers were kicked out), Hatfill (sort of) graduated from medical school in 1984. He claimed he had earned an MD, but that turned out to be false. One thing is true: His school in Harare, Zimbabwe, was next to a suburb called Greendale.

Another thing's for certain: The FBI was hot on Hatfill's trail. Then one day in 2008, the FBI turned around and blamed a guy who could not have done it: Bruce Ivins. Bruce Ivins did not have the technology to make "weapons-grade" microfine anthrax. He never had the sustained six-year investigations based on real suspicion. He lacked the complex web of military/intelligence connections that Hatfill had. Hatfill was declared a "person of interest" way back in 2002, but something, or someone, prevented a formal indictment and a trial. After the "limited hangout" or the dangling of what looks like imminent justice, the public was shocked to learn that Hatfill would not be indicted or tried at all. In a bizarre and sick surprise ending, Hatfill sued for defamation in court. He won a whopping $5.8 million from the Department of Justice, just as the focus of the Amerithrax investigation jerked around and focused its bureaucratic juggernaut force onto the weak and isolated Bruce Ivins.

DEAD SCAPEGOAT: BRUCE IVINS

FBI Amerithrax produced the dead body of "mad scientist" Bruce Ivins the way a proud cat makes the perfunctory drop of a still-warm mouse carcass. The timing was perfect: The sun was just beginning to set on the oily, engorged Bush-Cheney administration.

Almost the entire U.S. media accepted the verdict "Ivins acted alone," despite the lack of evidence. It seems like the only people who really protested were the members of Congress who had almost been murdered by military-grade anthrax.

Let's remember the psychological terrorization of the 2001 anthrax attacks. The targets were Democrats in Congress and the Senate, the media, and working people. A domestic population that hadn't ever been threatened with foreign invasion was suddenly thrown into political paralysis because of fear of being attacked in their houses. We in the United States were all plugged into a shared media experience, the spectacle of 9/11, the volcanic explosions and eight-second disintegration of the Twin Towers. These were terrible enough, rerun and rerun before our eyes until we were dizzy.

It was all so overwhelming. Nothing could top 9/11.

Unless something like anthrax attacks started the next week.

Which they did.

With the anthrax attacks, every single U.S. resident became the potential victim of sudden, chemical death. The media and the public went bonkers for duct tape and plastic sheathing, as America tried to wrap its bruised brain in an airtight cocoon. In this atmosphere, the United States PATRIOT Act was passed. Egged on by an atmosphere of terror, the United States took a long stride away from courage, freedom, and our Bill of Rights. Two illegal wars started in the next two years. The twentieth century had started out with some great strides for organized labor: people's revolutions in the '60s, and a victorious antiglobalization movement that had its moment in Seattle in 1999. But now someone was striking back.

Ivins's former boss, a veteran of the top brass at Fort Detrick, Richard Spertzel, said, in a 2008 *Wall Street Journal* op-ed, that Ivins could not have done it. "Ivins didn't have access to the equipment needed, because it didn't exist at Fort Detrick."[27]

In response to these widely held public doubts, the FBI commissioned an "independent report" from the National Academy of Sciences. In 2010, the FBI rejected the NAS's first draft. The bureau didn't like where the report was heading. Finally, in early 2011, the NAS report was made public. Despite having been being commissioned by the FBI, the report cast serious doubts on the science used to indict Ivins.

Ivins was married for thirty-three years and played the organ in his Catholic parish on Sundays. He liked to wear plaid pants. He was soft. He was quirky. The FBI claimed that Ivins drove seven hours, round-trip, to Trenton, New Jersey, to mail the letters, because he was obsessed with a Catholic sorority in nearby Princeton. The FBI offered Ivins's son $2.5 million and the "sports car of your choice" to say certain things to help create evidence of guilt about his dad. The son, bless him, wouldn't sell out his dad. If Ivins were guilty, why would the FBI try to fabricate evidence?

I imagine the FBI here was as desperate as special agent Steve Hayes sweating down in Shreveport. With Bruce Ivins, a desperate FBI found its vulnerable fall guy, alive, in Frederick. It would be easier, of course, if it could somehow be arranged for him to be dead. Patsies are more agreeable that way—just look at Atta, or Oswald.

With this mountain of evidence, we have a cause with no effect. There is something seriously broken in America, where we can all undergo a collective suffering, a collective experience of 9/11, plus anthrax terror. We suffer, but we lack the know-how to respond. And we lack some kind of moral compass; we lack the curiosity to really find out who did this to us. If we did it to ourselves, many of us don't want to know.

But don't despair—in later chapters we will meet American heroes, spiritual and political geniuses, men of courage, whose scientific analysis cuts through the fog of confusion. In the form of men like Kevin Ryan and Barry Kissin, Esq. (see Chapter 16), we will begin to be able to formulate a hypothesis about what anthrax was really all about.

THE HAUER MP3 REVISITED

I just listened to the Hauer MP3 again. I remember the night I made the interview.

After I hung up the phone, I used one-eighth-inch audio cables, some odds and ends, and a soldering iron to splice together and create the cable I needed. I had to convert the tape into an MP3. This ad hoc cable, held together with electrical tape, carried the audio signal from my phone recorder to my Mac. Thanks to the magic of free software, I downloaded an MP3 maker that converted the audio file into something we could all share.

It was exciting, because I felt I had just enough tools and knowledge to scrape together a low-tech/high-tech way to create an MP3. But it was exciting for a higher reason, too. I knew back in 2007, I began to feel in my bones, that the CIA and FBI would soon throw up a sloppy nonanswer for the anthrax attacks. They couldn't let Bush leave office with the investigation left open—someone might find out the truth. So, on that day, soldering together a cable to publish verbatim the Jerry Hauer interview online, I knew that someday this audio file would be especially relevant.

I called Hauer back a week later for a follow-up interview. I was honestly hoping we could continue to be just as friendly and honest with each other. The number was no longer in service.

Strange that in our interview, Jerry Hauer acknowledged that the FBI was mishandling the case, yet he still referred to them as the place to go for answers. That's called misprision of a felony, when you know that someone is committing a crime, like covering up the five anthrax murders, but you don't do anything about it.

10 THE NEW YORK 9/11 SPITZER-SILVERSTEIN INSURANCE SCAM

Figure 1: Art by Seth Tobocman

On March 13, 2006, at the West Side Institutional Synagogue, Eliot Spitzer clearly needed to be pressed to answer for his dereliction of duty. This guy was attorney general of New York City on 9/11. He enjoyed a well-groomed image in the media as a crusader, even as the "sheriff of Wall Street." And yet Spitzer never looked at any of the anomalies around 9/11. He could not claim ignorance; a published Zogby poll in 2004 showed that 66 percent of Manhattanites wanted Spitzer to investigate 9/11. He would not listen to the will of the people, and no one in the media asked him why.

The confrontation itself was actually quite easy. I wore a jacket and tie and waited patiently in the audience. The time was right when Spitzer was in the middle of rattling off a list of big cases he was proud of. I looked up at the ceiling of the synagogue and said, "In the name of the God of Truth, *there is one case you really missed*. Why did you not investigate 9/11 when the people of New York City asked you to?"

Spitzer laughed nervously and said something to the effect of, he had plenty he wanted to say to me, but in private. He acted as if he knew what I was going after. He asked me to call his office the next day. Like a fool, I even did call his office. The calls were not put through.

"Eliot Spitzer is like the good-looking bouncer in a bar who is secretly dealing drugs," forensic microbiologist Mike Copass later explained. It was July 2007, a year after my confrontation of Spitzer. I was back on the story, looking at Spitzer's social connections in the New York City power structure. Copass and I were in his local San Diego bar, down near the water in Ocean Beach. Copass had acted as a facilitator of San Diego's 9/11 Citizens Grand Jury, an extralegal group that had mounted a mock trial that April.

Copass is a progressive Democrat who has run for Congress inside his party. He's well aware of the corrupt leadership within his party, but he has yet to find a way out. He has degrees from Stanford and Harvard and an eager glint in his eye. Copass alleges that Eliot Spitzer acted as a firewall, preventing public disclosure of Spitzer's friends' roles in the anthrax attacks that occurred shortly after 9/11, in addition to facilitating his associates' windfall from the bloated insurance payouts at the World Trade Center. Copass seems to imply that Spitzer, despite his image as a crusader, played a role in the 9/11 cover-up.

In 2006, Eliot Spitzer was swept into the New York governor's mansion with 70 percent of the vote. The media went on and on about his shining image as a heroic fighter of white-collar crime. He bragged about being "very close" to Hillary Clinton. In Spitzer's lust for power, he made it clear he would accept an invitation to run for vice president if his pal Hillary got the nomination.

But in the summer of 2007, the Spitzer facade cracked. A year before the sex scandal that took him out of office, the allegedly "progressive"

Spitzer proved to be more than willing to use the state police to spy on his political rivals. His own attorney general (now New York state governor), Andrew Cuomo, investigated the governor's office's misuse of state troopers to monitor political rival Joe Bruno.

It became obvious, once the honeymoon was over, that Eliot Spitzer had a decidedly nasty side. To minority leader James Tedisco, he famously snapped, "I'm a fucking steamroller, and I'll roll over you."

The media increasingly reported that something was wrong with Spitzer. But no major media outlet would look at Spitzer on the 9/11 question. No media paid attention to the San Diego Citizens Grand Jury's indictments, which showed great interest in several of Spitzer's connections in New York City, including to ex-mayor Rudy Giuliani, his former "terror expert" Jerome Hauer, and Spitzer's former mentor from the New York district attorney's office, Michael Cherkasky.

And then there's the extra $1 billion Spitzer "facilitated" for his landlord at 120 Broadway: Larry Silverstein. Silverstein was the leaseholder of the World Trade Center, a deed he grabbed right before 9/11.

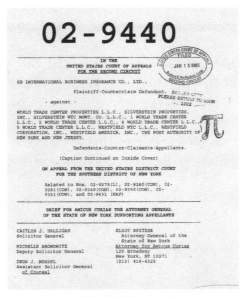

Page one: Spitzer's "friend of the court" brief intervening on behalf of WTC's Larry Silverstein

SPITZER AND SILVERSTEIN: THE AMICUS BRIEF

Prescient New York real estate baron Larry Silverstein became the primary leaseholder on the World Trade Center a mere six weeks before 9/11. What luck! The WTC's ownership had never changed hands before. For a down payment, Silverstein contributed a mere $14 million of his own money. His friends at the powerful investment bank Blackstone Group kicked in another $111 million.

After 9/11, Silverstein demanded a whopping $7 billion insurance payout, in the form of two $3.5 billion payments. He argued the two different plane crashes were two separate "occurrences" of two "separate attacks."

As attorney general, Spitzer got involved behind the scenes and in the courts, filing an amicus curiae ("friend of the court") brief on Silverstein's behalf on January 15, 2003. For years, this brief languished in the files of the public-records room on the seventeenth floor of the Second Circuit Court in Manhattan, until it was discovered and brought to this author by NYC attorney Carl Person (and his partner and wife, LuAnne Person). The court ended up agreeing with Spitzer and Silverstein, overturning the decision of a lower court. Spitzer helped midwife a fat compromise and an eventual $4.5 billion payout for Silverstein. The brief is available in full at www.sanderhicks.com/slingshot.html.

My multiple requests for comment from Governor Spitzer were ignored. Attorney Carl Person told me he "was surprised to see that Spitzer had used his position as attorney general to support one private litigant over another. Normally, this is not done." Person further suggested that "Silverstein could well have been someone who destroyed evidence concerning the 9/11 events by apparently ordering or consenting to the tearing ('pulling') down of 7 WTC and the removal of the debris from his multiple ground leased premises thereafter."

Silverstein's World Trade Center Building 7 collapsed at 5:20 PM on 9/11 without being hit by an airplane. Despite the many eyewitnesses warned in advance that the tower was coming down, the official claims a fire ignited a fuel tank in the building, prompting a sudden collapse.

WTC 7 housed the New York headquarters of the CIA, the Office of Emergency Management (OEM), and the SEC office investigating

Enron; 9/11 skeptics believe the building was taken down by controlled demolition.

Larry Silverstein himself talked too much about Building 7. He said in a 2002 episode of PBS's *Frontline* that he recalled having remarked on 9/11, "Maybe the smartest thing to do is pull it ... they made that decision to pull, and we watched the building collapse." Silverstein later claimed that by "pull," he meant removing firefighters, not pulling the building down. However, all firefighters had been yanked from the building three hours earlier. Dara McQuillan, a publicist for Silverstein, tried to spin his *Frontline* comments. In an odd coincidence, McQuillan later resurfaced as the publicist for the September 11th Victim Compensation Fund.

THE KROLL CONNECTION

In August 2007, another scandal radiated from the Spitzer circle. This time it was Nixon's arch strategist, Roger Stone, leaving a threatening voice mail for Spitzer's dad, Bernard. Stone allegedly claimed he would subpoena the elder Spitzer for the $5 million in illegal loans he alleged Spitzer Senior made to his son during Eliot's 1998 attorney general campaign. Stone denied he had made the call. To prove he had, the Spitzer family hired Kroll Associates to trace it. Why Kroll? Spitzer has a long relationship with this powerful, cryptic security company.

Kroll's CEO on 9/11 was one of Spitzer's old mentors from the Manhattan DA's office, Michael Cherkasky. Cherkasky investigated the Bank of Credit & Commerce (BCCI), which had links to both Islamic terror and the CIA, and the mysterious 1993 World Trade Center (WTC) bombing. Cherkasky's 2002 book, *Forewarned: Why the Government Is Failing to Protect Us, and What We Must Do to Protect Ourselves*, is a confused mix of fearmongering and insider's analysis. But there's one good reason to read Cherkasky's book: He sheepishly admits that the CIA *was* in part culpable for the 1993 WTC bombing, since it helped pull its own CIA asset, the known terrorist Omar "Blind Sheikh" Abdel-Rahman, into the country. This is widely known to be true but is rarely admitted by a former prosecutor. Cherkasky admits the FBI had a mole inside Abdel-Rahman's 1993 WTC bombing cell, and he lays blame for the bombing on the FBI. It's quizzical, therefore, that Cherkasky then hired a CIA-connected insider like *Jerry Hauer* to be his "managing director" at Kroll.

Cherkasky observed that the 1993 WTC bombing was an illusion. One could say it was a "dry run" for the 2001 attack on the same target. On the surface, Muslims were blamed, when really the story is more nefarious. With prosecutorial zeal, Cherkasky dug out the facts that showed the "Muslim" Jersey City Mosque "terrorist" operation in 1993 was penetrated by the CIA and controlled by the FBI.

The 1993 WTC bombing operation was a kind of experiment to see how much public opinion could be controlled by a collaboration between the FBI, the CIA, and major media. Cherkasky was an insider there, and he wrote a book with nuggets of gold sandwiched between layers of horseshit. He then decided, "If you can't beat them, join them" and became head of Kroll, the "CIA of Wall Street." Kroll took on the management of WTC after the 1993 bombing. Blackstone Group, the same financiers who backed Larry Silverstein, have also been involved with Kroll, owning big chunks of Kroll stock on occasion, according to SEC reports.

Cherkasky made significant donations of $14,500 to Eliot Spitzer's political campaigns.

THE DOOMED ZOGBY POLL

A 2004 petition gathered one hundred thousand signatures requesting then–attorney general Eliot Spitzer to investigate the 2001 attacks. A Zogby poll that year likewise found that 66 percent of voters wanted Eliot Spitzer to tackle these tough questions. What those poll respondents didn't know was that Spitzer couldn't investigate 9/11 or anthrax—he would have to indict his friends from Kroll, Jerry Hauer, and Michael Cherkasky. That's the *real* scandal.

So, despite Spitzer's public reputation as the former "sheriff of Wall Street," the truth is that he's an errand boy for some of the most powerful masters of cover-ups in New York City. No surprise that after his sex scandal, Spitzer would be allowed to come back into public life as a talking head, hosting his own TV news show on CNN, before it was canceled in the summer of 2011 because of poor ratings.

Back in 2006, after I asked my questions in my confrontation with Spitzer at the synagogue, the fundraiser was called to an abrupt halt. No money was collected. As Spitzer and his entourage slunk off the stage, I held an impromptu press conference at the back of the room. Nine days later, I held a protest in front of Spitzer's offices at 120 Broadway, near Ground Zero.

We presented a formal citizens' complaint to Spitzer. We never received a response. Spitzer still has a lot to answer for. He screwed a prostitute and destroyed his life. But his wife and CNN forgave him and brought his public stature back to life. What cannot be forgiven is Spitzer's allowing the crime of our time to remain uninvestigated. September 11 happened on the watch of an attorney general who, it turns out, has very flexible morals. Sex is not half of it. When it comes to the slaughter of almost three thousand New Yorkers, we cannot forgive if there is no regret.

11 A DIVE TO THE MAT: WHY DID THE TRIAL OF THE MAFIA'S MOLE IN THE NEW YORK FBI FALL APART?

I never bought into the hype about Eliot Spitzer. But I did get excited when the *Brooklyn* DA indicted former FBI agent Lindley DeVecchio on four counts of murder. The year was 2006, and DeVecchio was a Mob-connected FBI supervisory agent, a bigwig deeply connected to the cover-up of the 1993 World Trade Center bombing and to the Iran-Contra network. He had worked for the CIA to set up and take down the "rogue" CIA agent Edwin Wilson, who had been caught doing the CIA's dirty laundry in Libya.

DeVecchio's name had popped up regularly in the books of Peter Lance. Lance himself is something of an enigma: He's a Santa Barbara writer who has published three books on the 9/11 cover-up, yet he is not a Truther. In *Cover-Up*, *Thousand Years for Revenge*, and *Triple Cross*, Lance masterfully reported on the documented relationship between the U.S. government and terrorist assets like Ali Mohamed and Ramzi Yousef. But as a professional writer, he can be a tempestuous creative mind, as I have seen through personal experiences. But let's not focus on the negative.

I owe Mr. Lance a debt of gratitude for yelling into the phone at me that day, March 23, 2006. "Get your butt over to the Brooklyn Supreme Court," he said, so we could watch DeVecchio's "perp walk." DeVecchio had been indicted on four counts of murder while working for the Mob. He would be paraded through a column of media but protected by a horde of his violent and pissed-off FBI agent friends from the New York office. We might get a chance to ask questions. I got on my bike and rode a couple miles up from the Vox Pop coffeehouse.

Charles Hynes, the Brooklyn DA, called this one of the "worst law enforcement corruption cases in U.S. history." But no one in the New York media reported the full story on exactly how the boxers from the DA's office eventually took a dive in round two. The trial would quickly and quietly collapse, in the fall of 2007. DeVecchio's story shows that cozy networking with the Mafia means a lot when that network also includes the CIA, the Bush family, black-market financiers, and narcotics traffickers.

DeVecchio had been Mr. Organized Crime—the head of the Colombo crime squad, supposedly working against New York's Mafia family of Colombos, Gambinos, Luccheses, and Genoveses. DeVecchio was indicted for helping bloodthirsty Colombo don Greg Scarpa, Sr., kill informers and rivals. Even the final episode of *The Sopranos* includes a line based on something DeVecchio said while at the FBI. Tony Soprano's "we're going to win this thing" is what DeVecchio proclaimed victoriously to the FBI's Chris Favo when Mafia don Scarpa's rival was blown away. Favo grew alarmed at the time, and his concern prompted an internal probe. But within the insular FBI, the FBI's own Office of Professional Responsibility (OPR) probe went nowhere.[28]

In 2011, DeVecchio published a book and actually titled it *We're Going to Win This Thing!*. The book is not as bad as one would expect; with help from a cowriter, DeVecchio comes across as a real human being. But his personal knowledge of the murders he supposedly was "innocent" of participating in is rather eerie. He gives a detailed retelling of the killing of cocktail waitress Mary Bari, and at one point he refers to himself as a "bad cop."

The bad cop's trial halted abruptly in November 2007, when the *Village Voice*'s Tom Robbins produced eleven-year-old audiotapes of mobster Greg Scarpa's ex-girlfriend Linda Schiro. Schiro had been the prosecution's star witness. She had intimate knowledge of Scarpa's misdeeds and DeVecchio's role in them. *The New York Times* reported that these tapes "exonerated" DeVecchio. That claim is highly debatable. On the tapes, Linda Schiro details DeVecchio's role in the killing of young Patrick Porco. Schiro had in the past denied that DeVecchio played a role in *some* of the killings. Emphasis on "some."

Lead prosecutor Michael Vecchione told Peter Lance during a break in the 2007 trial, "Of course she made prior inconsistent statements back then . . . Lin DeVecchio was still checking in on her, still supported her and gave her a sense that he was protecting her . . . She may not have been telling the truth then, but she is now, under oath."

A day later, the prosecution reversed course and surrendered its case.

Free that night, DeVecchio flaunted his unrepentant love of Mafia culture by dining at Sparks, the Times Square restaurant famous for the 1985 mob slaying of Gambino godfather Paul Castellano.

How could the "biggest case of law enforcement corruption" be derailed by a couple of old cassette tapes, you ask? I called up Tom Robbins at the *Village Voice* office. In his combative interview with me, he also expressed some shock that the prosecution would quit so quickly. But he disagreed with the theory that the DA could have "taken a dive."

"What, did you go to law school? I'm trying to have a conversation with you here," laughed Robbins. He laughed, rather than answering my question about whether he believed DeVecchio was guilty or innocent.

The New York Times botched the facts about the tapes, reporting that they showed "Mr. DeVecchio had not been involved in the murders." Robbins himself said that that was not accurate.

"[Schiro] did in fact put DeVecchio into one murder," Robbins said—the killing of nineteen-year-old Patrick Porco. Porco had witnessed a Scarpa family hit on Halloween 1989. Lin DeVecchio told Scarpa, Sr., that Porco was likely to rat. "Come on, Dad, what are you, crazy?" the Mafia don's son Joey Scarpa pleaded with his father. "Patrick would never do that."

"He got killed for doing nothing else really except for hanging out with a bunch of numb-nuts." Robbins said in one of his better quips. "It grabs at your heart. He was a kid."

Robbins, however, became notably anxious when asked about his former writing partner, Jerry Capeci, who shared bylines with him at the *Daily News* back in the '90s. Capeci today writes about the Mafia for his column, "Gang Land News." I brought up the popular rumors that Capeci was being fed information by Lin DeVecchio himself at the time.

"You're backing something I know nothing about. But *look*, Sander, let me tell you something about *etiquette*. You don't ask other reporters who their sources are."

But, Tom, I wasn't asking you about your sources, I was asking you about your Mafia-centric writing partner. FBI special agent Chris Favo accused DeVecchio of feeding Capeci Mafia-related information. Favo said that he stopped talking to DeVecchio on Mondays so that FBI intelligence would stop appearing in Capeci's column, which ran on Tuesdays.

"I have no idea whether or not that's true," Robbins bellowed. "You're calling me and asking me a question, all right, and I can tell you this, all right, what I did and what I wrote had nothing to do with anything that Lin DeVecchio may have done for or against me, or anyone I know. Okay? I did it because I found some tapes, in a closet, that went directly to the chief witness in this case. And I didn't see how I could sit on that, since the guy was facing life in prison. So I went public with it."

As reporters, Robbins and Capeci shared bylines on important news stories regarding Greg Scarpa, Sr. They broke the bizarre, controversial pieces that revealed that Scarpa, Sr., had himself worked for the FBI in Mississippi, in 1964, to expose who murdered four civil-rights workers. Together, Capeci and Robbins wrote about the tainted blood transfusion that infected Scarpa with HIV and killed him.

Edwin Wilson at the time of
his arrest."

CIA CONNECTIONS

Edwin Wilson is a fifteen-year veteran of the CIA, released from prison in 2005 when a Houston judge redacted Wilson's conviction on smuggling charges. When I tracked him down on the phone, he was happy to comment on the DeVecchio case.

"I thought it was kind of interesting how the FBI guys all hung around [DeVecchio] real close to give him bail money and all this kind of stuff. Which really told me that there was a lot involved in this and they were sweating like hell."

Wilson is referring to the FBI friends who paid DeVecchio's bail. DeVecchio's support group, the Friends of DeVecchio Trust, included FBI heavyweights like James Kallstrom, the former head of the FBI in New York. For his "perp walk" out of court that day, DeVecchio enjoyed the escort of a phalanx of about forty-five angry FBI agents and retirees. They punched photographers and bragged on their website about "body-checking" reporters. (In high New York irony, Robert Stolarik, the *New York Times* photographer who was punched in the face that day, eventually sold one of his pictures to the publisher of DeVecchio's book. It graces the front cover.)

Edwin P. Wilson was a working-class kid from Idaho who showed bravery with the Marines in the Korean War. He worked for the CIA for fifteen years and then for the Office of Naval Intelligence (ONI). His specialty was setting up "front companies" to clandestinely ship materials for CIA operations, under the cover of legitimate businesses. Under the direction of Ted Shackley, Wilson worked with the CIA to monitor terrorist Carlos the Jackal.

But at some point, something went wrong. The CIA turned on Wilson and lured him out of Libya to be arrested on arms-smuggling charges in the Caribbean. The CIA claimed that he had not worked for them since his retirement.

The FBI's Lin DeVecchio was tapped to go into prison and record Wilson, who allegedly wanted to put out a hit on his prosecutors. Wilson had been sentenced to fifty-two years behind bars. Lin DeVecchio was a witness against Edwin Wilson at a 1983 trial, when the media, CIA, and law enforcement turned against the CIA "rogue." But after Wilson had served twenty-seven years in prison, attorney David Adler found eighty points of evidence showing that Wilson *had* been working for the CIA. Wilson was set free.

"Bad Cop" DeVecchio was on the side of the bad guys once again. The Friends of DeVecchio Trust points out that DeVecchio "saved" the life of a federal prosecutor. But it was never proven that the voice on the tapes had been Wilson's.

"It was just a railroad job, it really was. They wanted to put me away in a way that for sure I would never get out." Wilson, in his eighties, would still be in prison today if it weren't for a series of dogged Freedom of Information Act requests. Wilson proved at his original trial that for selling explosives to Libya, the CIA lied in federal court.

1993 WTC BOMBING

From the 1993 World Trade Center bombing to 9/11 to the present, the FBI's New York Office (NYO) has always had a bizarre relationship with terrorists. As mentioned in the previous chapter, in 1990, radical Islamist Omar "Blind Sheikh" Abdel-Rahman was pulled into the United States, despite being on the State Department's "terrorist watch list." Abdel-Rahman had been helpful to U.S.-CIA interests in the fight against the USSR in Afghanistan. He was also the spiritual leader of the Jersey City Mosque, whose members took the blame for the 1993 World Trade Center bombing.

The New York FBI, of course, had informants inside the Jersey City Mosque. One was named Ali Mohamed, the Special Forces– and Fort Bragg–connected Al Qaeda soldier who was bin Laden's head of security. Another was named Emad Salem. As the Jersey City terrorists planned the 1993 World Trade Center bombing, Salem made audio recordings of his conversations, including one with John Anticev, his FBI handler. After the attack, Salem told Anticev, on tape, that the terrorists had "built the bomb with the supervising supervision of the FBI."

It was the New York FBI that was in charge of "tracking" bin Laden. But just like Blind Sheikh Abdel-Rahman, bin Laden had been a key figure in the CIA's proxy war against the USSR in Afghanistan. His CIA code name had been Tim Osman.

The son of DeVecchio's Mafia informant, Greg Scarpa, Jr., became an FBI informant himself when he was incarcerated next to Ramzi Yousef, the supposed "mastermind" of the '93 World Trade Center bombing. Greg Scarpa, Jr., had been involved in murders with his father and had stories that involved DeVecchio.

Why, then, did Greg Scarpa, Jr., currently incarcerated in Colorado, not get called as a witness in the DeVecchio trial? Perhaps because the raw intelligence Scarpa, Jr., provided the FBI in 1996 showed that the FBI knew about terrorist "mastermind" Ramzi Yousef's planning new attacks on the World Trade Center five years before 9/11.

Or that Yousef was just a scapegoat, the patsy to blame for planning 9/11.

Richard Taus, FBI agent, in happier times.

THE TAUS RAILROADING

Was DeVecchio indeed working for the CIA when he was involved in the case against Wilson? It seems certain when you talk to someone who worked for DeVecchio at that time. Richard Taus is an ex–FBI special agent incarcerated inside Clinton Correctional Facility, in far-upstate New York. In our interview, Taus seemed healthy, unbeaten, and unbowed.

"How can you tell if someone is working for the CIA?" I asked.

"If it walks like a duck, talks like a duck, and looks like a duck, guess what it is?" he said with a tired smile.

Taus tells of observing Oliver North and New York–area CIA assets in Florida, moving narcotics as a part of a clandestine, illegal international operation in 1983. It was Iran-Contra, years before Iran-Contra became a household name.

At New York FBI, DeVecchio stepped in and tried to keep Taus quiet. When Taus refused, he was harassed and then arrested. Taus found himself sentenced to thirty-three to ninety years for pedophilia, in a lightning-fast Nassau County trial. The prosecution used no expert witnesses, and no parents of "victims" testified. Habeas corpus complaints Taus filed pointed out that his jury was tainted: The jurors were reading sensational newspaper accounts during the proceedings, and one was even a cousin of the DA.

"All of those guys, they start to believe their own bullshit. They put people away, they hide evidence, in order to get convictions," CIA vet Edwin Wilson told me on the phone from his basement apartment in a suburb of Seattle. "DeVecchio involved a lot of people."

The case had originally been recommended to the DA's office by a member of Congress, based on the work of New Jersey forensics expert Angela Clemente. Clemente broke her silence on the trial's collapse with this comment for this book:

> *Mr. DeVecchio and his supporters, representing our nation's top law enforcement officials, have demonstrated a public display of disgusting arrogance and utter disregard for the rules of law. The Federal Bureau of Investigation should be ashamed.*

The Brooklyn DA took a dive to the mat. Who pressured them to take that dive so early in the fight? The DA's office refused to answer my set of questions. But if it walks like a duck and talks like a duck, what is it?

PART FOUR

FROM BAD TO WORSE

"Sit back and watch.
It goes from bad to worse."
—Ian MacKaye

12 THE PROBLEM OF EVIL: FROM THE POPE TO THE DEVIL TO POSTMODERNISM

Let's go back and look through the thick plexiglass window of the Shreveport FBI office. I see special agent Steve Hayes again, clearly dying. He himself died a little as a part of the machine that killed David Graham.

Evil does exist. Not as Satan with horns, like in a cartoon, but as something more deadly. Not abstract, but physical. It's as real as the tremors, the hate, and the guilt pouring out of Steve Hayes's troubled soul. The more genuine part of his soul was begging for redemption, but the fear won out. He called security on two guys who could have helped him figure out just what the hell was going on, and why he was in a private hell.

Let's remember the insights of the legal minds at the Center for 9/11 Justice. William Veale, Esq., and his team wrote, "Evil does exist. Power is attracted to it."

Enlightenment polymath Gottfried Leibniz was a mathematician, philosopher, and Christian interested in reuniting all churches. He wanted Enlightenment science and reformed Christianity to come together and create a religion everyone could love. He explained the nature of evil in his *Essays on Theodicy*. ("Theodicy" means literally "God justice," or the philosophy of understanding God's omnipotent power in a universe where evil is also real. This is a world of both grace and suffering.)

Leibniz is most well known for his claim that "this is the best of all possible worlds." Of course, Voltaire had a field day with that, ruthlessly satirizing Leibniz (in *Candide*) through the character Pangloss, who witnesses a drowning without caring too much, always saying, "It's all for the best."

Call me old-fashioned, but I have outgrown Voltaire's punk sarcasm. I think Leibniz was onto something. When you take a look at what he really said, he made plenty of mistakes. But his theodicy is not one of them. The existence of evil in the world does not negate the existence of God; rather, it amplifies our need for truth, for God. Leibniz figured that God is real, even if evil is real. God is God, with all the goodness and omnipotence and creativity intact. God's world was designed with just enough evil in it to sharpen our wits, to enliven our spirits, to give us something to fight against.

Let's look at two Leibniz quotes to hear the man in his own words:

"When a truth is necessary, the reason for it can be found by analysis, that is, by resolving it into simpler ideas and truths until the primary ones are reached."

So, it seems that the process of truth is to recognize a universal desire for this truth, and then, when we "analyze" it (which literally means "to take apart"), we reduce the truth to simpler truths, until we come to a kind of logical "ground zero" of truth in its prime form. In the same way, in this book, I have started with 9/11, and the quest for justice amid all the Byzantine details because it is a compelling way to get into the complex subject of 9/11 Truth. But as I have written and rewritten the book, I see it going into simpler truths, and spiritual universals, toward the end. As Leibniz said at one point, "This is what we call God."

In my own thinking on the evil of 9/11, I have come to a conclusion that is startlingly Leibnizian. And I think many readers will get what I mean, regardless of their spiritual or philosophical background.

There is a perfection to things, to events, as they unfold. It is real, but we can see it only after the fact. God is marching through human history, but we can see this only after things happen. We need not view a tragedy such as 9/11 only as an act of destruction. The best of humanity is on display when catastrophe leads to great acts of compassion, when people overcome their feelings of vulnerability and help each other. It's an opportunity to grow. NYC itself saw this in the wake of 9/11: the selflessness of workers at Ground Zero, working on the toxic pile. Or the peace march and candlelight vigils in late September, asking for peace and nonretaliation.

Out of the death of 9/11 comes rebirth: a new way of seeing the world, a new way of going beyond hate, and a whole new way of doing politics.

The problem is that the candlelight vigils didn't work. At the heart of wisdom in all religions is the idea that "violence breeds violence" and "hurt people hurt people." But on 9/11, deeply hurt people (i.e., repressed, psychological strangers to themselves, like the Bush son and father) rolled out a plan based on hurt to create more hurt. The great tragedy led to more war and hate, as designed.

The twentieth century set new records for the proliferation of evil. New technologies developed so that we could kill each other with new speed and in greater numbers. Mass media developed so that we could watch it happen. Witnessing a great catastrophe creates another problem as well: Trauma can undermine our moral convictions and leave us vulnerable to manipulation. Fear encourages us to wallow in uncertainty and cling to the pithy slogans of the powerful, even if those reassurances are lies and reinforce fear of others. September 11 traumatized so many people that collectively we've accepted an obvious forgery. This would not have happened if people were more awake. This spiritually drifting world hasn't trained its eye to spot or even name evil.

Isn't it weird—as soon as I hear myself say "evil," I think I sound like some self-righteous cartoon character, like the old "Church Lady" skits on *Saturday Night Live*. The problem is that if you don't learn to say the word "evil" and mean it, evil sucks up power and kills people.

In the next few chapters, we'll look at how evil has perpetuated itself, how it has come to shape the actions of the most powerful interests today. How evil in its hidden American form is responsible for the events of 9/11. We'll explore the malicious influence of the outdated CIA, the clan of spies chartered to defend democracy. And we'll examine the ways truth is obscured in this country when fear becomes rampant.

But first, I will aim closer to home, by talking about a church struggling with internal evil. Catholicism is the faith of my birth. To understand the way power is attracted to evil and evil is attracted to power, the Catholicism and cover-up of Pope Benedict XVI offers us a prime example.

THE DEVIL IN THE VATICAN

The pedophilia crisis could have been an opportunity to reform the grand, battered, leaky ship called the Roman Catholic Church. Instead, with the election of Pope Benedict XVI, the Church chose more cover-up and denial. This resulted in a continued assault on the powerless, the very people it has promised to protect.

Leibniz would say that evil is an opportunity to face up to a crisis, to confront it, in order to become better. This was his rational Enlightenment Christianity. Of course, the current pope refers to the whole Enlightenment as a "thorn in the side" of the Mother Church.

I remember on Easter Sunday 2010, in downtown NYC, I was sitting at my piano in church. I had been the music minister for two years at the R.C. Church of the Nativity. I liked the place; it was boxy and modern, with a smart, progressive pastor, and there were free pancakes from the anarchists and pacifists around the corner at the *Catholic Worker* every Sunday.

But this Easter, at the climax of Pope Benedict's leadership through the storm of the pedophilia cover-up scandal, I cringed at the false claims I was hearing in the sermon. The Church is "under attack," and the pope needs our unqualified support, said Father Mike, a short, acne-scarred Filipino priest, and an assistant to the pastor. Jesus was a warrior, said Father Mike. Easter was a "battle victory."

Previously, Fr. Mike's most memorable sermons had involved his denouncing yoga, feng shui, and the idea that homosexuality could ever produce "meaningful relationships." Today, he was reading the company line. At the Vatican that same day, Cardinal Sardano turned the Easter Mass into a pep rally for Pope Benedict. Sardano claimed that pedophilia cover-up claims were nothing but "petty gossip."

What the Vatican was doing, and what Fr. Mike was parroting, were so different from the message of Jesus. The Pope is a man and a sinner, not a king.

While he was still cardinal in Germany, Joseph Ratzinger (Pope Benedict-to-be) signed off on an "untreatable" pedophile, Father Peter Hullerman, and let him return to work with kids from 1979 to 2010.[29] That's thirty-one years of child sexual abuse from one guy. How many more Hullermans were there?

From age fourteen to sixteen, Ratzinger was a Nazi in the Hitler Youth. Then he was a soldier in the Nazi army, shooting down Allied pilots. As a cardinal, he wrote Church policy that compelled priests to hide child-abuse evidence from the police. That's odd, because Jesus said that anyone who hurt or abused a child would be better off drowned in the sea with a millstone around his neck.

Betty Clermont's book *The Neo-Catholics* is a devastating history of the rise of the neocon Right. It turns out that rise paralleled a swing to the right inside the Vatican, as Reagan built up United States–Vatican ties. Has the Church gotten into bed with a certain kind of political evil? As a cardinal in 2004, Pope Benedict issued a fatwa against voting for John Kerry and tipped an extra 6 percent of the vote toward Bush in an especially close election.

In five short years, Pope Benedict reversed much of the interfaith work of Pope John Paul II. He brought back ornate, gilded ceremonial robes with twenty-foot trains, decorated with the coat of arms of the House of Medici. The Medici were the wealthy Italian banking family that got four of their own elected pope over the course of four centuries. They presided over the peak in the Church's power, from the Dark Ages to the Counter-Reformation to the Church's resistance to the Enlightenment.

According to Pope Benedict's previous statements, being pro-choice is akin to a reason for excommunication from the Church. Homosexuality is an "intrinsic moral evil," and violence against gays, though regrettable, is understandable. If some Nazis bash some fags, well, "When homosexual activity is consequently condoned . . . Neither the Church nor society at large should be surprised when other distorted notions and practices gain ground, and irrational and violent reactions increase."

Wow. This is the Church's new elected leader? This is Catholicism's response to accusations about its cover-ups?

You don't fight evil by giving in to it, by becoming more evil. Jesus was all about peace and love. He advised against divorce, wanted love to be sacred, and so got into some finer points about the law. But he never denounced homosexuality. In fact, he said some radical things about gender in a Gospel that this Church tried to erase from history.

Jesus would wince at this pope, at his Nazi past and his Nazi present. Pope Benedict seems to never have read the New Testament. He writes that within the Catholic Church, a diversity of opinion on issues like "the decision to wage war" is totally understandable. Meanwhile, abortion and euthanasia are not. Being pro-choice is a possible reason to be denied Communion at Catholic Mass, but being pro-war is not.

Pope Benedict was promoted by the worst forces in the Catholic Church to protect the Vatican's power and influence. He's zealously attacked those who stand up for victims of priest abuses (and the victims themselves). Perhaps this is the simplest expression of evil: power protecting itself at the expense of the vulnerable.

FRANKLIN SCANDAL

My friend the author Nick Bryant had a new book out around the same time as that Easter from hell, 2010, in which the Church, from the Vatican to my local, was preaching denial of the pedophilia scandal. Nick's book is the exact opposite; it's called *The Franklin Scandal*, and it shines a hard light on a specific abusive cult with links to the Catholic Church, the GOP, the CIA, and various D.C. politicians. The scandal reared its ugly, demonic head in 1989, when it was splashed across the pages of *The Washington Times*. The documentary *Conspiracy of Silence* alleges that a Catholic orphanage in Nebraska acted as a source of boys for a pedophiliac sex and power network.

Lawrence E. King, director of the Franklin Community Federal Credit Union and a rising black star in the GOP, was in business in the late '80s with Craig Spence, who was the "pimp" of the operation. Spence and his boy toys took midnight tours of the White House, thanks to military, intelligence, and Bush ties. Spence died a mysterious death in a hotel room just ten weeks after the first story broke in *The Washington Times*. *Conspiracy of Silence* was later pulled from the Discovery Channel, and *The Washington Post* went out of its way to attack *The Washington Times* for reporting the story. Two grand-jury investigations in Nebraska convicted no perpetrators and instead indicted two victims for "perjury," one of whom received an exorbitant sentence of nine to fifteen years.

Instead of going to Catholic services at Church of the Nativity that Good Friday, I spent time with Nick Bryant out in the sunshine. For taking on these powers, Bryant has been practically scourged: He has endured police searches, harassment, a death threat, and a media blackout. But in Washington Square Park, in the spring air, among cute NYU students and live bluegrass, it became easier to talk about the darkest evil. I asked Nick if he saw similarities between the Vatican's current cover-up and what happened with Franklin.

"It's exactly the same," he said. "Their MO is 'deny, deny, deny—if any victims come forward, slam them.' That formula has been used forever."

A practicing Quaker, Nick also pointed out that the original Protestant, Martin Luther (who was initially a Catholic monk), was personally revolted by the pedophilia and other sins of Pope Leo X (a Medici pope). Instead of reflecting on any of the "95 theses" Luther included in his critique, Pope Leo X attacked Luther as a "drunken German." What followed were centuries of bloody warfare between Catholics and Protestants throughout Europe.

Forsake the Kingdom of God, and you naturally create rebels, like Martin Luther and Jesus. If you claim the authority of God but don't do what God would do, then what do you turn into? You are like a dog asleep in a manger, not eating the food of life and blocking others as you sleep.

9/11 Truth has been both a political and a spiritual path. It's a form of citizen journalism, but it also requires a special kind of courage (or passionate stubbornness). Even as I've developed stronger convictions around 9/11 Truth, I've noticed that many people who earnestly want to do good in the world are hampered by their unwillingness to face evil in its most powerful form. This is why getting the message out about 9/11 is so important: It offers our best window into the problems we face as ordinary, well-meaning people.

I tried to give a copy of *The Franklin Scandal* to an editor at the *Catholic Worker*, but the topic was just too . . . *evil*. He just couldn't deal with a satanic network of pedophiles with ties to CIA, the GOP, and the Church. The book was clearly well researched, so the problem wasn't that it consisted of speculative theory.

Six months later, that same editor assigned me to review a big Howard Zinn book, an illustrated graphic novel called *A People's History of American Empire*. Zinn, a luminary of the Left, had just died. His graphic novel was an accessible way for more people to understand the United States's genocide of the American Indian, the violent suppression of labor struggles, the inhumane use of the atomic bomb, and the massacre of Filipinos in an imperialist debacle there, as well as the amorality of a country addicted to war and empire.

But my review was rejected. I had to take issue with the near gloating that Zinn and his coauthors indulged in. They open the book with the 9/11 attacks and make this weird, twisted point that in light of U.S. imperialism, the attacks could be seen as "understandable." In my review, I said this was knee-jerk, old-Left way of thinking:

The larger truth is that since 9/11, progressives, peace activists, and Truthers have been hotly debating just what exactly 9/11 *was*. This book ignores that question and lives in a single, simpler paradigm. Perhaps if Zinn were beginning his work today, he would find in this question, and in these peace movements, a new kind of "people's" history being actively written and lived. When asked in Montreal about 9/11 skepticism, Zinn retorted, "I don't know enough about it, and the truth is, I don't much care—that's past." He said that he did support a new investigation, yet called the Truthers "fanatics."

A different editor at the *Catholic Worker* rationalized the paper's decision to reject my review, saying, "Maybe we are not revolutionary enough to indict Howard Zinn for not being a 'Truther.'"

I was living in L.A. at the time, still practicing Catholicism but also beginning to add some Buddhism into the mix, too. In my reading, I was searching after the historical Jesus, and I wasn't sticking to Catholic reading lists. Doors were beginning to open. A copy of a remarkable document called *The Urantia Book* appeared in a box of books from the executor of the Richard Brautigan estate, who happened to be visiting the West Hollywood bungalow I was staying in. *The Urantia Book* was allegedly written by angels, so it's kind of appropriate to discover it in Los Angeles.

I went to Mass at the giant modern Cathedral of Our Lady of the Angels and had a chance to meet Cardinal Mahony. My Truther friends in L.A. later told me the Catholic Church had lost a huge amount of credibility because of the L.A. version of the pedophilia scandal and Cardinal Mahony's role in the huge cover-up. Out on the patio, I told the cardinal I was a peace activist and a 9/11 Truth activist. He didn't say anything at first—but then, quietly, "We have got a lot of work to do."

13 THE HOLOCAUST EFFECT

Looking under the rock of "U.S." politics inevitably leads to the taboo topic of Israeli influence in the United States. It's tough to navigate this territory because anti-Semitism and Nazi genocidal politics are still real in our day. But what is more real is that the tiny country of Israel is an international power broker. Its geographic size doesn't relate to its influence, both in the United States and worldwide.

We see that in the history of 9/11 and more recently in the Israeli attack on the humanitarian boat *Mavi Marmara*.

In Joseph Goebbels' seven-thousand-page diaries, on March 27, 1942, he wrote, "The procedure is a pretty barbaric one and not to be described here more definitely. Not much will remain of the Jews. On the whole it can be said that about 60 percent of them will have to be liquidated whereas only 40 percent can be used for forced labor."[30]

The Nazis confessed at Nuremberg. It looks like the Nazis did get about 60 percent of European Jewry, since about six million are reported to have died.

The Jewish Holocaust happened. There are volumes of evidence, and it's professional-grade material. See it admitted into a British court of law in the *Irving v. Lipstadt* case, for example. In 1993, Dr. Deborah Lipstadt of Emory University wrote *Denying the Holocaust: The Growing Assault on Truth and Memory* as a direct assault on the Holocaust deniers. In the book, she discussed a number of specific ahistorical scholars, including David Irving, whom she called a "dangerous spokesperson" for Holocaust denial. Irving sued her in an English court, where libel laws are very different from those in the United States and tend to favor the plaintiff. Yet Irving lost.

All Truthers should look at the evidence collected at her site, Holocaust Denial on Trial, or hdot.org. Why? Because you know people really hate 9/11 Truthers if they call us "9/11 deniers." That means they want so badly not to look at 9/11, they want to tar us with the neo-Nazi brush, aka the "Holocaust deniers."

Just as I am writing this chapter, I get a barrage of emails from a guy in Texas who wants me to believe the Holocaust never happened. I mentioned General Dwight Eisenhower, among the first U.S. soldiers to witness the camps. Eisenhower did write, in a letter to U.S. Army chief of staff George Marshall,

> *I have never felt able to describe my emotional reaction when I first came face to face with indisputable evidence of Nazi brutality and ruthless disregard of every shred of decency . . . I visited every nook and cranny of the camp because I felt it my duty to be in a position from then on to testify at first hand about these things in case there ever grew up at home the belief or assumption that the stories of Nazi brutality were just propaganda.*

The denier in Texas retorts that "Eisenhower didn't mention seeing gas chambers in his memoirs." He claims that the "truth about the Jews" can be seen in a document called the "Babylonian Talmud," clearly an anti-Semitic forgery whose sources were obscure neo-Nazi websites. Upon being probed, our friend in Texas turns out to have had some bad experiences in business with Jewish people. He was blinded by hate, and I couldn't reason with him. I found him to be a hothead, quick to spit out insults.

He claimed his entire political perspective is justified by his bad business dealings with the "Jews" and so thinks they are inherently a deceitful people. Based on my own experience, I could easily have rebutted by noting that my landlord at café Vox Pop was a careful, professional, generous, merciful Orthodox Jew.

I say this because I wish to make crystal clear that the places this chapter will go are not written out of hate for a people. But I do believe I have something to contribute here to advancing the truth on 9/11. I don't blame Israel for 9/11 as much as I point to the CIA, the Pentagon, and their handlers. But evidence is emerging here, as we are seeing that certain parts of the Israeli intelligence and corporate worlds did in fact play a significant role in the operation. Unfortunately for their own reputations internationally, Israel, alongside the United States, CIA, and Pentagon, is up to its neck in connections to 9/11.

ISRAEL AND 9/11

Let's begin at the beginning, by returning to the hero of our book, Dr. David Graham. The terrorists whom Graham was involved with tracking, Khalid al-Mihdhar and Nawaf al-Hazmi, were also on the radar of the Israeli Mossad, the CIA of Israel. Mossad had a complex operation of about sixty operatives posing as "art students" selling art to offices in southern Florida. But what they were really doing was tracking the Saudi intelligence– and U.S. intelligence–connected assets Khalid al-Mihdhar and Nawaf al-Hazmi.

Obviously, these Mossad agents were not clued in to the complete plan yet, and at times they found themselves at odds with CIA. When they got too close, someone on the U.S. side swiftly exposed them and deported them out of the United States on August 23, 2001. Eager to embarrass U.S. authorities, the Mossad published a list of terrorists planning a major attack on U.S. targets. They named names, including Mohamed Atta, Khalid al-Mihdhar, and Nawaf al-Hazmi. Only then, in embarrassment, did the CIA put these names on the Terrorism Watch List. The U.S. media never broke this story, but it did make the mainstream newspapers in Germany.[31]

URBAN MOVING SYSTEMS

Then there are the Israeli spies arrested in New Jersey on 9/11 for joyously high-fiving each other and videotaping the planes as they flew into the towers. Locals were so upset, they called the police. Taken into custody were a group of five Israelis, some of whom were Mossad agents, as reported by the BBC et al.

Fox News caved in to pressure from Jewish-interest groups to take this story off their website.[32] But in March 2002, a sanitized version of it made it into the *Jewish Forward*. The Israeli spies:

> . . . *were held for more than two months and were subjected to an unusual number of polygraph tests and interrogated by a series of government agencies including the FBI's counterintelligence division, which by some reports remains convinced that Israel was conducting an intelligence operation. The five Israelis worked for a moving company with few discernable assets that closed up shop immediately afterward and whose owner fled to Israel.*[33]

The article explains that two of the five were agents of the Mossad. All five worked for Mossad front company Urban Moving Systems. But the *Foreward* hastily explains that it's all okay, because the spies were all "working against a common enemy," i.e., radical Islam. Oh, okay.

Then, there's this line: "Sources emphasized that the release of all the Israelis under investigation indicates that they were cleared of any suspicion that they had prior knowledge of the September 11 attacks, as some anti-Israel media outlets have suggested."

Well, of course I don't want to sound "anti-Israel." But if these guys are "cleared" of suspicion, how to explain why they set up video cameras across the river from the WTC to watch the attacks?

The *Forward* is to be commended for reporting the story at all. The *New York Times* never touched it with a ten-foot barge pole, as *Salon* noted in May 2002. And *The Washington Post* remained content to publish U.S. State Department lies from spokeswoman Susan Dryden, who claimed, "This seems to be an urban myth that has been circulating for months. The department has no information at this time to substantiate these widespread reports about Israeli art students involved in espionage."[34] Even a voice as mainstream as that of *Jane*, the respected British intelligence and military industry publication, noted drily, "It is rather strange that the U.S.

media seems to be ignoring what may well be the most explosive story since the September 11 attacks—the alleged breakup of a major Israeli espionage operation in the United States."[35]

INTERNATIONAL CONSULTANTS ON TARGETED SECURITY (ICTS)

A particular security company always seems to be right there behind the scenes in all the major transportation "terrorism" cases. It happened in the Underwear Bomber case in 2009, the Shoe Bomber case in late 2001, the London bombings of 2005, and two of the hijacked flights of 9/11. It's the same company, and the "coincidence" warrants further investigation.

The company is International Consultants on Targeted Security (ICTS), a division of Huntleigh. ICTS is Israeli-owned, based in the Netherlands, and publicly traded on the U.S. NASDAQ. It was founded in 1982 by former members of Shin Bet, sort of the Homeland Security force of Israel.

ICTS is a case study in how anything Israeli connected to the mainstream "terror" narrative is treated with kid gloves in the U.S. media. While European media and even Israeli media will comment on ICTS's strange proximity to "terrorist" events, the U.S. Media stays silent. This should help clear it up for those still politically confused: It's not the Israeli power structure alone that ICTS are working for.

While there was no mention of it in *The New York Times* or *The Washington Post*, the Israeli newspaper *Haaretz* reported that the red lights should have been flashing like mad on the young Nigerian "Underwear Bomber," Umar Farouk Abdulmutallab, in late 2009.[36] He had no passport and no luggage. A "well dressed Indian man" helped Umar get on the plane. I have spoken to eyewitnesses who saw this "terrorist" get help boarding; they said the bombing was videotaped by other mysterious "passengers." But law enforcement was not interested in speaking to those eyewitnesses. It was a Christmas Day terror holiday, and the Obama White House milked it for all it was worth, promising more military violence in response.

On the other side, Rep. Pete Hoekstra (R-MI) found it politically expedient to let slip some of the deeper truth. "The U.S. government knew that Abdulmutallab was involved with Al Qaeda for at least a couple of months," according to his sources.

ICTS, which somehow let this obvious terror suspect through, was not censured or investigated. Just as they had on 9/11, when they had released "Islamic terrorists" onto the flights, they had done their job: to help stage an event that would be labeled a "terrorist attack," using an airline they were contracted to protect.

It's an opportunity to see how reality is a construction. The Underwear Bomber, like 9/11, was not an event as much as it was a staged production, a kind of 3-D movie, with actors, stage managers, and explosive special effects.

Why? To keep the Arab world on the ropes, to turn world opinion away from supporting a Palestinian state, to keep U.S. bases in the Middle East, and to keep the oil flowing, cheap.

COURAGE TO SPEAK THE TRUTH: NEOCON DUAL CITIZENS

Richard Gage runs the professional 9/11 Truth organization, Architects & Engineers for 9/11 Truth. Gage, with whom I have produced two events, gives well-polished presentations and has petitioned the U.S. Congress. Without making conclusions, he has made the case that the official story about the collapses of the three WTC towers is unscientific.

But we have a difference in strategy. Gage doesn't believe he can reasonably say whom a court of law should indict for 9/11, while I think we need a different tack, which the crimes of 9/11 warrant. I stand with David Ray Griffin and say that not only is there sufficient evidence to seriously doubt the official story, but there is also plenty of evidence to indict Bush, Cheney, and significant portions of their war machine. Even President Obama should remember that misprision, or perception of treason and subsequent inaction, is itself a serious crime, per the U.S. Constitution and case law. Remember, the U.S. Constitution wants treason to be treated with the utmost care. But if there is a case, then charges need to be brought.

People are inherently peace loving and truth loving, unless something deludes them. The Bush-Cheney administration was tasked with protecting, and was sworn to protect, the interests of the American people. Yet it served interests other than those of the people. "Citizenship," when you are serving in government, means that you are loyal to one country: your own. But a significant number of neoconservatives in the Bush-Cheney administration were dual citizens of the United States and Israel.

Total 9/11 Truth includes an analysis of the political ideology of neoconservatism and its close cousin, the quasi-religious/political ideology of Zionism. Both saturated the Bush-Cheney administration, ruining the members' ability to be objective. It roiled their own peaceful, divine-potential nature as human beings. From a legal standpoint, it created a gigantic conflict of interest, one that borders on treason, one that led to 9/11. It turned this administration into creatures obsessed with war, conquest, and demonizing the Muslim people. This is what theologian and Truther David Ray Griffin means when he talks about confronting demonic consciousness. The rise of neocon power is the manifestation of an amoral, Machiavellian demonic consciousness in which violence and power need no excuse.

The massive legal conflict of interest becomes apparent when one simply looks at a list of people in the administration who had dual citizenship in both the United States and Israel.

It was not just a few people. The list is rather long:

Attorney General—Michael Mukasey
Head of Homeland Security—Michael Chertoff
Chairman, Pentagon's Defense Policy Board—Richard Perle
Deputy Defense Secretary (Former)—Paul Wolfowitz
Under Secretary of Defense—Douglas Feith
National Security Council Advisor—Elliott Abrams
Vice President Dick Cheney's Chief of Staff (Former)—"Scooter" Libby
White House Deputy Chief of Staff—Joshua Bolten
Under Secretary of State for Political Affairs—Marc Grossman
Director of Policy Planning at the State Department—Richard Haass
U.S. Trade Representative (Cabinet-level Position)—Robert Zoellick
Pentagon's Defense Policy Board—James Schlesinger
UN Representative (Former)—John Bolton

Under Secretary for Arms Control—David Wurmser
Pentagon's Defense Policy Board—Eliot Cohen
Senior Advisor to the President—Steve Goldsmith
Principal Deputy Assistant Secretary—Christopher Gersten
Assistant Secretary of State—Lincoln Bloomfield
Deputy Assistant to the President—Jay Lefkowitz
White House Political Director—Ken Melman
National Security Study Group—Edward Luttwak
Pentagon's Defense Policy Board—Kenneth Adelman
Defense Intelligence Agency Analyst (Former)—Lawrence (Larry) Franklin
National Security Council Advisor—Robert Satloff
President Export-Import Bank U.S.—Mel Sembler
Deputy Assistant Secretary, Administration for Children and Families—
    Christopher Gersten
Assistant Secretary of Housing and Urban Development for Public
    Affairs—Mark Weinberger
White House Speechwriter—David Frum
White House Spokesman (Former)—Ari Fleischer
Pentagon's Defense Policy Board—Henry Kissinger
Deputy Secretary of Commerce—Samuel Bodman
Under Secretary of State for Management—Bonnie Cohen
Director of Foreign Service Institute—Ruth Davis

Again, this is not listed in the spirit of anti-Semitism or a kind of new McCarthyism, but in the love of the full truth.

I myself have investigated several of these people. In the case of Michael Chertoff, he was attorney and pulled strings for an alleged terrorist financier, Dr. Magdy Elamir, who had ties to ex–CIA asset Osama bin Laden. I knew this before Chertoff was appointed the first head of Homeland Security but was not able to get it published with my editor at *Long Island Press*. FBI whistle-blower Randy Glass also ran into a media blackout with a reporter, John Mintz, at *The Washington Post*. (I, too, phoned Mintz, and he was hostile on the phone, but the call made it clear to me that someone put the kibosh on exposing Chertoff's weird ties to terror.)

Or let's look at Douglas Feith, who was effectively running the Pentagon on 9/11. Colonel Karen Kwiatkowski, a Pentagon whistle-blower who worked for him, had this to say about the under secretary of defense:

> *"He served Likud interests. I don't think those are the same as Israel's interests, but instead those of a faction within Israel. He engineered Likud, outlined and desired actions by the U.S., and, in Feith's mind, I think he did it for Israel. I just don't have any countervailing information that would suggest he has ever done anything for America."*

Rich Wales is a California computer programmer who has lived in Canada. He maintains a website and a wiki on the topic of "dual citizenship." I find his work to be clean and sober, free of any kind of bias.

On the topic of U.S.-Israeli dual citizenship, he notes that:

> *Israel's "Law of Return' (under which any Jew may immigrate to and become a citizen of Israel) confers Israeli citizenship automatically, without the immigrant having to apply for it, attend any ceremony, or swear any oath of allegiance. The Israeli law may originally have been written this way to encourage American Jews to move to Israel; they could, in theory, argue that they had not explicitly requested Israeli citizenship and were thus still entitled to keep their U.S. citizenship.*

Thanks to that Supreme Court case, *Afroyim v. Rusk,* it is much easier to be a dual citizen of two countries—especially if one country is the United States and the other is the United States's main ally in Oil-land.

However, even if your dual citizenship is simply automatic because you are Jewish and you've traveled to Israel, it is certainly still a taboo topic, perhaps because of a sensitivity about Holocaust denial.

Using Google News, I went looking for any mention of the fact that so many Bush administration officials had dual citizenship. I found very little, in the United States or international media, but it's noteworthy to look at what's out there:

A liberal commentator in Cairo's *Al-Ahram Weekly* wrote in a 2002 op-ed that with the Iraq War, the United States's image worldwide has become that of another "God that failed," a historical heartbreak. The United States "has been hijacked by a small group of extreme right-wing ideologues. They are, on the whole, Zionist-leaning; some, too, have dual citizenship and divided loyalties. Their actions are turning the whole world against the United States." Israeli news service *Haaretz*, in April 2003, stated bluntly, "The war in Iraq was conceived by twenty-five neo-conservatives, most of them Jewish, who are pushing President Bush to change the course of history."

Israeli prime minister Benjamin Netanyahu frankly admitted, "We are benefiting from one thing, and that is the attack on the Twin Towers and Pentagon, and the American struggle in Iraq," because those events "swung American public opinion in our favor."

WIKILIKUD

When Julian Assange and WikiLeaks released two hundred thousand pages of documents but nothing critical of Israel, I got a sense that something wasn't right.

He told the *Belfast Telegraph*, "I'm constantly annoyed that people are distracted by false conspiracies such as 9/11, when all around we provide evidence of real conspiracies, for war or mass financial fraud."

Back when I was the anti-Bush indie publisher and was getting a lot of mainstream media attention, WikiLeaks was just starting out. Assange contacted me via email and said he would like to have me on WikiLeaks' board of advisors, or words to that effect. He would help me.

Then I became a Truther. I guess there are some taboo topics that even WikiLeaks won't touch. I wonder why.

That's not to say that WikiLeaks is not doing any good work. In the summer of 2010, WikiLeaks exposed U.S. assassin cabal Task Force 373 with "prima-facie evidence" of war crimes. Task Force 373 had killed seven children in Afghanistan.

Still, I wish Julian would take another look at 9/11. Unless . . .

RECOGNIZING THE HOLOCAUST EFFECT

Israel has its own equivalent of Task Force 373. In May 2010, Israeli commandos rappelled from their helicopters onto a flotilla of human-rights activists, the good ship *Mavi Marmara*. Nine aide workers, including one American, were killed in the violent melee.

Yet Israel was not censured by the United States.

The attack on the *Mavi Marmara* was so brutal, it has become historic. It may soon "turn the tide" against Zionism, according to Kevin Ovendon. Ovendon was a flotilla survivor. He overcame intense political pressure in the USA that attempted to stop him from speaking in New York. I was there that day, reporting for AlterNet.

After the killings on the *Mavi Marmara*, Israel was widely denounced by everyone from Amnesty International to *Foreign Policy* magazine to the *Daily News*. But President Obama's response was to "wait for details to emerge." Then he called Israel and offered help with its public-relations disaster.

Around that time in NYC, a battle was raging north of Ground Zero. Zionists and right-wingers tried to stop plans for an Islamic community center. Abe Foxman, of the Anti-Defamation League, said of the 9/11 victims' families, "Their anguish entitles them to positions that others would categorize as irrational or bigoted." It seems that the "Holocaust effect" refers to the idea that Holocaust-related suffering makes permissible everything Israel does, at least in the eyes of Israel and her allies.

I showed up at the Gaza Flotilla Survivors event at House of the Lord Church in Brooklyn on June 17. Flotilla survivors prepared to give rousing speeches. Before the event got under way, I had a moment to wander across Atlantic Avenue to hear from the twenty counterprotestors waving Israeli flags. Sometimes you learn a lot about an issue from the opposition.

I approached a tall, well-dressed man in a yarmulke, who introduced himself as Dov Hikind (without mentioning he was the New York State assemblyman who had organized the counterdemonstration).

Hikind told me, "What happened was a tragedy, without question. But the real story is the status of the 'IHH'"—the group who organized the flotilla.

Hikind claimed that the IHH was a "terrorist" organization, and he cited local New York politicians, like Jerry Nadler, who had recently made the claim. Israel itself had pushed this talking point and had blocked one of the survivors from being able to speak in the United States.

That visa was denied based on allegations that the IHH has "ties to Hamas and Al Qaeda." However, the sources for the assertion are sketchy, if not completely manufactured. The lead source is a paper on the IHH from the Danish Institute for International Studies. But that report was penned by a young, mysterious American named Evan F. Kohlman, a "terrorism expert" inseparable from the U.S. government he works for. Kohlman describes himself as a "private consultant in terrorism matters for the U.S. Department of Defense, the U.S. Department of Justice (DOJ), the Federal Bureau of Investigation (FBI) . . . and Scotland Yard's SO-15 Counter Terrorism Command." His "counterterrorism center" is located in his bedroom in New York. Kohlman claims his Nine Eleven Finding Answers Foundation is a group that works with 9/11 victims' families. In past military tribunals, Kohlman took $45,000 from the Pentagon to make an emotional movie, based in part on the Defense Department's own images, to show at a terrorism trial.

Assemblyman Dov Hikind complained that in Gaza, Hamas does not recognize the State of Israel. But even Hikind surprised me when he admitted that there *is* some truth to the theory that "Hamas is a creation of Mossad." He brusquely quipped, "Go on the Internet," if I wanted to learn more. Okay, Dov, let's go.

Since Hamas's founding, in 1987, Israel's strategy has been to use the religious Islamists at Hamas as a foil, rather than negotiate with the secular, left-wing Fatah movement. Are you finding peace talks with your Palestinian neighbors difficult? It's convenient, then, to keep on hand your own brand of radical Islamists to do something violent at key moments.

Hamas itself is a wing of the Muslim Brotherhood, a group with historical ties to the far right and the CIA. Hamas is a "terrorist" group on the State Department list, but its parent group is not. The Muslim Brotherhood is somehow "the preeminent movement in the Muslim world . . . something we can work with," according to a former CIA official.

WHERE IS GOD?

What we are seeing here is the power of victimhood elevated into the power of legend. Call it the Holocaust effect. The United States seeks to enshrine 9/11 within an impregnable cultural myth. Meanwhile, the Israeli Right seeks total freedom to kill.

Thankfully, due process still exists: 550 officers have been investigated for war crimes in Gaza. But the Holocaust effect is purported to be a kind of holy law now, or a cultural norm, as America and Israel attempt to justify their expanding territorial ambitions.

In my conversations with Zionists, Dov Hikind included, I have often wondered why they never talk about God. They tell me Zionism is not a religious movement; it's a nationalist movement. Well, that's a tragic development for the Jewish people.

It shows that the modern-day Israelis are still making the same mistakes they did millennia ago: turning away from God. Read the Bible, and you realize the ancient Jewish prophets were gifted with an insight into the true nature of the Supreme Being: change, mercy, peace. But today, instead of living the higher law of repentance, compassion, and understanding, the Likudniks worship a false god of revenge, power, and military might. "This is a stiff-necked people," God observed to Moses, in a bit of divine exasperation.

The host at House of the Lord Church, Reverend Dr. Herbert Daughtry, told me that his event was "faithful to the Biblical mandate, to prioritize the needs of the least in society, the excluded, the exploited, a call that is in both the Old and New Testament." Jesus would stand with the people of Gaza, not the soldiers delivering death from above.

Is it too heretical to ask if the reason that Holocaust denial is so popular in the Arab world is that the Holocaust of sixty-five years ago is now being used to justify brutal attacks on a similarly oppressed people?

Israel is the birthplace of two major world religions. Both preach the God of peace, mercy, and understanding. But Israel's huge heart, through Zionism, has turned to stone. Without a commitment to gutsy, God-based peace and nonviolence, Zionism has become an ugly practice of hate and murder. Politics alone can't address the problem—you have to know the Torah, the Bible. The prophet Ezekial says that God wants to say, "I will give you a new heart, and I will put a new spirit in you. I will take out your stony, stubborn heart and give you a tender, responsive heart."[37]

Violence perpetuates itself. Hate breeding hate is demonic consciousness in its simplest form. The Holocaust was bad enough. But the Holocaust effect perpetuates and echoes back the violence of the original Holocaust—on the Palestinians, and eventually, back on Israel itself.

The world owes Judaism a huge debt for advancing our consciousness. But the world owes Zionism nothing. The Zionists have tried to portray themselves as victims, when in truth, they have become a Goliath. But the truth of God is not complicated; it's simple and pure. Love alone can break the cycle of violence.

14 THE COMPANY OF DOGS: A PERSONAL LOOK AT THE CIA

Discussing the Catholic Church was personally difficult, but taking on the CIA also hits close to the bone. I grew up in the Washington, D.C., area. My father worked for the U.S. Agency for International Development (USAID), in Ghana, in the late '60s. When other moms and dads were dropping acid, going to Woodstock, practicing Zen, or joining Maoist book clubs, my folks were in Accra, working on economic development for the U.S. government. My dad was a PhD economist, and my mom was a teacher.

There's been much valid criticism of the Western attempt to use corporate capitalism and free markets to bring about real poverty reduction. But Ghana itself is quite a success story. The raging debate about international globalization has been a lifelong point of conflict around our family dinner table, but for now, let me just try to tell you the story from my parents' perspective.

The year before they came, Ghana had deposed its first president, Kwame Nkrumah. Nkrumah was an independent Marxist and Pan-Africanist whose vision of socialism absorbed some of Africa's precolonial tribal traditions. But Nkrumah's administration devolved into authoritarianism. He eventually outlawed strikes and imprisoned his political enemies without trial. He was deposed in a military coup but is today revered as the father of Ghana.

There's another perspective to all this, of course. Former CIA agent and author John Stockwell writes that The Company (the CIA's little nickname for itself) played a significant role when Nkrumah was deposed, in 1967.

I asked my father once about all the rumors and sources who say that the CIA regularly used the State Department's USAID as cover in various countries. Was CIA working in Accra through USAID? Dad said something like, "Oh, we hear that all the time—it's crazy . . . Well, there was *one* guy . . ."

Dad and Mom eventually moved back to the D.C. suburbs. He got a job at the World Bank, through contacts he met in Accra. He worked on economic development issues in the Philippines and Latin America, and he became a specialist in poverty reduction. He traveled often. One time in an airport, confronting some "crazy" protestors who were picketing against IMF funding of a certain agricultural program, he inquired about their cause. A protestor turned on him and said, "What are you, from the CIA?" I guess he looked the part.

When I was growing up in D.C., a close friend of the family actually *was* in the CIA. I was raised to call him Uncle Lee, although we aren't related. My folks first met Uncle Lee in Accra. When I was an antiglobalization activist, I caught hell at home for protesting the World Bank on the streets of D.C. The Battle of Seattle had just shut down the WTO meeting in Seattle in November 1999. It seemed like the movement in the streets had the upper hand, for a significant historical moment.

Looking back, I find it ironic, then, that it was Uncle Lee who gave me a copy of *Anarchist Portraits*, by Paul Avrich, when I asked for it as a high-school graduation present ten years earlier, in 1989. Uncle Lee had a strange interest in radical politics. He claimed he was an expert at economic modeling, but at one point someone in the family overheard him let slip that he was an expert at interrogation.

Christmas 2010 was especially hard. I was planning to begin writing this book, but there was intense pressure at home to give up the topic entirely.

When that didn't work, they called in Uncle Lee.

They sat me down with him at the kitchen table and demanded that he set me straight about 9/11. But Uncle Lee wasn't exactly forthcoming. When my folks asked him to please tell me that I was crazy, Uncle Lee stammered and said, "All I can tell you is . . . I can tell you this . . . I know who did 9/11."

But later, my dad would point out that Uncle Lee didn't actually say *who* this "who" was.

Pressed to be more specific, Lee became even more mysterious. He slowly raised one index finger to one of his eyes, staring straight at me, and then he said, in Spanish, "*Ten cuidado*" ("Show care" or "Be careful"). Weeks later, on the phone, Lee warned me, "Don't make yourself a target."

If I'm wrong about my 9/11 theories, why would CIA veterans imply that I'm becoming a "target"?

In order to more fully serve the interests of U.S. Big Business, the CIA has overthrown democratically elected governments at several key moments in its short history. If you have the courage to examine this taboo topic, the CIA's dirty work abroad, you will become more aware of what the agency is doing today at home.

Thanks to declassified documents, it's no longer a theory; it's a fact. The CIA now admits that it helped take out popular leaders like Mossedegh in Iran (1953), Árbenz in Guatemala (1954), Lumumba in the Congo (1961), Sukarno in Indonesia (1967, with help from Barack Obama's mom and stepdad), Allende in Chile (1972) . . . and the list goes on. The CIA helped set up dictatorships that were antidemocracy but friendlier to U.S. business interests. In Iran, it was the hated Shah Pahlavi; in Guatemala, it was the military dictator Armas; in the Congo, it was Mobuto; in Indonesia, it was Suharto; and in Chile, it was international war criminal Pinochet. The spy group originally chartered to protect "democracy" was destroying democratically elected governments and replacing them with thugs more willing to serve U.S. business interests.

On September 11, 2001, the top level of the corporate ruling class and CIA thugs overthrew another democracy. This time, the target was the United States itself. But some of us can't comprehend this, because we have no context. As with facts presented about 9/11, people's reaction is often *I just can't believe that could be true*. But denial doesn't negate truth.

Don't get me wrong. I'm not saying that the CIA did 9/11 because it was a capricious, diabolical whim. The agency was "just following orders," like the Nazi lieutenants confessed at Nuremberg. Those orders came from people with the power to enforce them.

OBAMA MARKETING VS. THE BURNING DESIRE FOR TRUTH

When it came time for Bush and Cheney to exit the White House, the CIA, the U.S. military, and all the top operators in the U.S. power structure had to make damn sure that the next president wouldn't look backward at the men behind the curtain. They had to put one of their own in the White House.

Obama's presidential campaign was an exercise in rank cynicism, because it exploited a universal human need people have. I call it the Burning Desire for Truth. This Burning Desire for Truth was manipulated by the Obama campaign's empathy rhetoric, when it's clear now that it never planned any real change, hope, or truth.

The problem of the CIA is not unique to the CIA. The "rule by secrecy" is an age-old pattern, as old as evil itself. The Vatican, the modern Zionist state, and the CIA all attempt to wield power by controlling information. When you see this, historically, you realize what a radical document the Bill of Rights is, for at least *attempting* to break any one party's grip on controlling information.

In the context of a world in which more and more people are cynical about the U.S. federal government, the war machine, the taxes for bombs, the Catholic Church's garish and ongoing pedophilia cover-up scandal, etc., the Obama campaign resonated on a deep, gut level with a simple message of "hope" and "change." The Obama campaign specifically promised a new level of government transparency, with C-SPAN cameras at health care hearings. On his first day in office, President Obama promised "the beginning of a new era of openness in our country." Two weeks later, he broke the promise. In the case of *Mohamed et al. v. Jeppesen Dataplan, Inc.*, the Obama Justice Department upheld the Bush-Cheney policy on rendition.

In the end, Obama's rhetoric was just a marketing campaign. What was delivered was not what we thought we had bought. We thought the vague language of "hope" meant that we could expect some substance. We thought that "change" meant a change away from evil, not a change of color. Obama, as president, is an even more staunch defender of the 9/11 official story: "I'm aware that there are some who question, or even justify, the events of 9/11. But let us be clear: Al Qaeda attacked us on that day . . . these are not opinions to be debated." Here, Obama shows himself to be a clever cover-up artist, equating those who question the events of 9/11 with those who say the United States deserved to be attacked. This sort of subtle rhetoric underlies a leader who has successfully continued the illegal wire taps, torture, war, and imprisonment at Guantánamo of the previous administration, all without receiving much criticism.

And yet the Burning Desire for Truth lives on. We know now that it's a universal, massively powerful desire. In the next chapter, we'll explore where Obama comes from. In the next *section*, we'll explore where our Burning Desire for Truth could really take us.

15 WILL THE REAL BARACK OBAMA PLEASE STAND UP?

Obama promised he would extricate us from Iraq in six months. Then it would be eighteen months. Finally, at this book's press time, the troops are being withdrawn, but not because of a change in U.S. foreign policy, but because the Iraqis voted to push them out. Obama's State Department wanted to stay indefinitely.

The people who promised a new standard in government transparency refused to even show us proof that they had really killed bin Laden. Obama promised to close the extralegal prisons and torture chambers at Guantánamo Bay, Cuba, but somehow couldn't make good on that vow, either. He promised universal, public health care, but what came out was a watered-down program, a failure on par with Hillary's nonsuccess early in the Clinton White House.

Obama is a rock star who lip-synchs. He's a pretty image, a darling of a celebrity-obsessed culture. He has never been seriously asked questions about his background. Despite his promises of transparency, on his first day in office as president, he sealed all of his records at the National Archives and Records Administration.[38] Why does he appear to have connections to the Chicago Far Left and yet rule from the Center Right? What can explain his meteoric rise to becoming the first African American president without his having had to create, produce, or stand for anything of substance beforehand? Obama is a lot like Hillary Clinton.

When you ask their fans what they have actually done, you get statements like "Well, he was the first black president" or "She was the first woman to go from being First Lady to being a U.S. senator." But those titles are just titles—what have these politicians actually *done?*

The answers to those questions are also crucial to the answers around 9/11. Part of the key to understanding Obama's meteoric rise is his backroom connections, which include the CIA. Beyond Obama's charismatic image lies a byzantine, homicidal reality. The American people have been fooled again. What they took for gravitas is an amoral listlessness. Obama's centrism, his "company man" cowardice, and his skill for cover-ups were bred in the bone.

CIA FAMILY: STANLEY, BARRY, AND LOLO

Previous media profiles, as in *Time* magazine, describe Obama's mother, Stanley Ann Dunham, as a free-spirited intellectual. But that doesn't tell us half the story.

A better source is my fellow writer Nick Bryant, author of *The Franklin Scandal*. Bryant penned an authoritative profile on Mama Stanley and her historic ties to the CIA. He writes:

Company Man: Young Stanley."

> *Obama's mother has a murky employment history, and the various organizations that employed her either provided CIA personnel with cover or are reportedly affiliated with the CIA; Obama's stepfather [Stanley's second husband] was an officer in the army of a CIA-backed genocidal dictator; Obama's first job out of college was with a company that had provided cover for CIA personnel . . . The person responsible for sending Barack Obama, Sr., to the U.S. was a CIA asset.*

Obama's biological father and Dunham divorced in 1964, when Barack was three. Dunham met her future husband, the Indonesian national

Lolo Soetoro, through the University of Hawaii's East-West Center, which had been set up with a $10 million federal grant.

The *Statesman* of India later exposed the East-West Center as a CIA propaganda vehicle, in 1998. "*Encounter* [magazine] and the East-West Center were funded by the CIA, to promote its own strategic pursuits, and that discovery horrified many people who had earlier been full of praise for them." Former CIA officer Frank Scotton says the East-West Center "was a cover for a training program in which Southeast Asians were brought to Hawaii and trained to go back to Vietnam, Cambodia, and Laos to create agent nets."[39]

Barack Obama's biological father went back to Kenya and was closely affiliated with the CIA-backed anticommunist president, Thomas Mboya. Obama's new dad, Lolo Soetoro, was also company connected, in his native Indonesia. When Indonesian president Sukarno attempted to forge a compromise between the powerful military junta and the Indonesian communist party (PKI), he was overthrown by the CIA-backed General Suharto. Suharto killed anyone who might be a leftist, including the members of a list of five thousand people provided by the U.S. embassy. His campaign of mass assassinations climaxed in the murder of two hundred thousand in East Timor, with tacit U.S. approval.

Lolo Soetoro was a killer. His violence against others had a deteriorating effect on himself. In *Dreams from My Father*, Obama himself reports that Lolo told him personally he had murdered people. Lolo would kill a man "because he was weak . . . Men take advantage of the weakness of other men. They're just like countries that way. The strong man takes the weak man's land. He makes the weak man work in his fields."

Is this the kind of man a free-spirited "flower child" woman would marry?

Obama describes how Lolo changed in Indonesia: "It was as if he had been pulled into some dark hidden place, out of reach, taking with him the brightest part of himself." Lolo wandered around the house with a bottle of whiskey and tucked a pistol under his bed before falling asleep. When their marriage disintegrated, Stanley Dunham sent her son, "Barry Soetoro," aka Barack, to live in Hawaii with his grandmother.

However, Stanley herself soon returned to Indonesia, to her job at the U.S. embassy. Her work there was not done.

Ex–NSA agent Wayne Madsen reports from inside D.C. at the Wayne Madsen Report,[40] where he goes into even more detail about Barack Obama's CIA connections. It turns out that Mama Stanley's *parents* also seemed to be working for CIA operations.

Grandma Madelyn Dunham was the first female vice president at the Bank of Hawaii in Honolulu. This bank was a favorite funding vehicle for various CIA black ops, including the bank that helped fund the Mujahideen in Afghanistan. And based on a photograph Madsen unearthed, it looks like Stanley's namesake, her father, Stanley Armour Dunham, was active in the CIA-sponsored airlift of Kenyan intellectual Barack Obama, Sr. That would make the story about the fetching young Ms. Stanley meeting the Kenyan Barack, Sr., in a "Russian language" class just a myth, set up to disguise some CIA-inspired matchmaking. Although her marriages to company men never lasted, the female Stanley *did* seem to have a more sustained relationship with an uncanny string of CIA fronts, and with the CIA itself.

In 1971, the *Boston Globe* printed a book review of a CIA exposé titled *Who's Who in the CIA*, which had been published in 1968 in Berlin. The reviewer, a former intelligence insider, noted that it shed some light on the cloaked workings of U.S. power—namely, how the U.S. Agency for International Development (USAID) often worked as a cover for the CIA. Leftist intellectuals, like William Blum, author of *Killing Hope*, have also long documented the interweavings of USAID and the CIA. In 1972, USAID administrator Dr. John Hannah even admitted to Metromedia News that USAID was being used as a cover for CIA covert operations in certain Asian countries.[41]

One example of such operations involves a USAID official in the Indonesian embassy, Dr. Gordon Donald, Jr. Donald ran the USAID program microfinancing loans to Indonesian farmers. Stanley Dunham started out at this embassy, teaching English classes, before graduating to work in "microfinance." Dr. Donald, it turned out, was outed as a CIA agent by *Who's Who in the CIA* when he was a USAID official in Lahore, Pakistan. Dunham's career also happened to follow his, in both Indonesia and Pakistan.

With USAID, the Ford Foundation, the World Bank, or the Asia Development Bank, Stanley Ann Dunham's career brought her to several hot spots where the CIA happened to be active. She was in Lahore for the birth of the CIA's proxy war against the USSR through the Mujahideen. She had young Barack visit her there, at the impressionable ages of nineteen and twenty.

Obama refused to discuss his mysterious New York years with *The New York Times*. But right after his "Columbia University years," he worked at a CIA front company, Business International Corporation.

How does all this relate to 9/11 and U.S. politics today?

The Obama White House is politically *to the right* of the Bush White House on anthrax and 9/11 investigation issues. It was the Obama White House's Cass Sunstein who recently declared that his office wanted to "infiltrate" and "disrupt" the 9/11 Truth Movement.

Likewise, as we'll see in the next chapter, this same White House has blocked an independent investigation of the anthrax attacks.

Once you know a few things about Obama and Bush, the CIA and 9/11, you realize that the president who followed Bush and Cheney *had* to be just as controllable. Otherwise, things like anthrax, or the nanothermite in the WTC dust, or the deaths of Dr. David Graham and Barry Jennings, or any of the many other tentacles of the 9/11 cover-up, would eventually be investigated.

But a dream deferred does not dry up like a raisin in the sun.

The justice that the CIA is denying us in our current world will only come back to haunt it sevenfold. There will be justice, and it will be in our lifetime. There are so many lies the system is holding back, it's like trying to hold back an entire ocean with a levee. Eventually, the levee breaks.

16 ANTHRAX AND NANO-THERMITE: CRACKS IN THE LEVEE

Even if 9/11 is too evil for some to comprehend, there are other ways to get a grip on the truth about that time.

If you just focus on something smaller—the anthrax attacks, for example—you get the same result. You come to the conclusion that parts of the U.S. government and their "quasi-governmental contractors" engaged in acts of terror against U.S. citizens. They created the fear that forced public approval for the War on Terror.

In March 2010, Obama fought off a few maverick voices in Congress asking for an independent anthrax investigation. The White House held up the budget for the nation's entire intelligence services for weeks over this sticking point, arguing that a probe into anthrax "would undermine public confidence" in the FBI's Amerithrax investigation of the attacks "and unfairly cast doubt on its conclusions."

The problem, of course, is that everyone already has "doubt on its conclusions." Who doesn't? A PBS *Frontline* special, *Wall Street Journal* editorials, and a National Academy of Sciences study commissioned by the FBI itself have all expressed serious doubts about the FBI's slapped-together scapegoating of a "lone gunman" scientist.

In response to the House and Senate Intelligence committees, Peter Orszag, director of the White House Office of Management and Budget, wrote the White House's refusal to investigate the anthrax attacks.

Perhaps Orszag couldn't live with himself afterward. Shortly thereafter, he quit to go work at Citigroup.

Back on November 11, 2004, Kevin Ryan, a chemist acting as "site manager" for Indiana's Environmental Health Laboratories (a division of Underwriters Laboratories), wrote a letter. It was addressed to the director of the U.S. Department of Commerce's National Institute of Standards and Technology's (NIST's) two-year investigation of the collapse of the World Trade Center. Ryan and Underwriters Laboratories had certified the safety of the steel and were concerned about their possible liability.[42]

UL's initial tests showed that "the buildings should have easily withstood the thermal stress caused by pools of burning jet fuel." The steel they had certified decades earlier was sound. In August 2003, UL had even published a preliminary report in which it was practically ready to "rule out weak steel as a contributing factor in the collapse." The temperatures of the burning jet fuel, and the short time the heat was exposed to the fireproofed steel, made it just impossible. After all, steel-frame structures never melt or weaken to the point of structural failure because of carbon-based fires.

But then something happened.

NIST started to embrace pseudoscience. It bent over backward, even ignored the laws of physics, to issue theories and statements that contradicted the science in its own original reports on the steel. Ryan's November 2004 letter soon led to his dismissal from UL.

Yet he kept going. Ryan's Christian faith fired him up, and his mastery of chemistry combined to give him insight into what was really going on. Government investigations and academic institutions had been co-opted to support what Ryan wryly termed the U.S. government's "genocide-for-oil program."

Ryan got fired for questioning the WTC's demolition, as a lone voice who rebelled from inside the cover-up. He was silenced at his day job, but he made his whole life about truth. He expanded his analysis. He found that in some cases, the same CIA-linked firms who make controlled demolition technology also make anthrax.

According to Ryan, the Battelle Memorial Institute should be at the top of a short list of possible suspects for the anthrax attacks.

Battelle has contracts to produce both anthrax and nano-thermite-based demolition explosives for the CIA and Pentagon, and is referenced several times in the FBI's Amerithrax investigation. But you have to know where to look. In the report's veiled language, Battelle is referred to four times, but never by name. The company is so powerful, it even had a mole inside the Amerithrax investigation.

Kevin Ryan was part of the international panel of chemists and physicists that in 2009 published a study of four samples of WTC dust. All four samples tested positive for evidence of the high-end professional demolition explosive nano-thermite. This peer-reviewed, academically rigorous study has never been scientifically disputed, nor reported by major U.S. media outlets.[43]

Ryan told me, "It is interesting that Battelle-managed facilities were related to nano-thermite and anthrax production. This leads me to suspect people like . . . the leaders of Battelle. The laboratories managed are capable of many types of high technology."

The "leaders of Battelle" are the masters of war. Some of them have ties to NIST and to the Pentagon. For example, Arden Bement, a former director at Battelle, was appointed director of NIST right after 9/11 by President Bush. Bement is a former deputy secretary of defense, a former director at DARPA (the research and development wing of the Pentagon), and a former executive at defense contractor TRW (developers of ICBMs).

In 2006, the U.S. agency NIST admitted that it had never even tested WTC steel for nano-thermite. The agency was asked, "Was the steel tested for explosives or thermite residues?" so many times that it published the answer in the FAQ section of its report: "NIST did not test for the residue of these compounds in the steel." Despite having experts in nano-thermite technology throughout its staff, NIST admitted that it chose not to look at the obvious. As Ryan points out in his "Top Ten Connections Between NIST and Nano-Thermites," NIST itself was testing nano-thermite technologies with Lawrence Livermore National Laboratories in 1999. Of course, NIST didn't test for nano-thermites in its WTC collapse investigation because it already knew what it would find.

Ryan also has plenty to say about Jerry Hauer and Stephen Hatfill's old employer, SAIC:

Science Applications International (SAIC) is the DOD and Homeland Security contractor that supplied the largest contingent of non-governmental investigators to the NIST WTC investigation. SAIC has extensive links to nano-thermites, developing and judging nano-thermite research proposals for the military and other military contractors, and developing and formulating nano-thermites directly (Army 2008, DOD 2007). SAIC's subsidiary Applied Ordnance Technology has done research on the ignition of nano-thermites with lasers (Howard et al., 2005).

Ryan goes on to point out that it was SAIC that "investigated" the 1993 World Trade Center bombing. SAIC publicly boasted in its own documents, "After the 1993 World Trade Center bombing, our blast analyses produced tangible results that helped identify those responsible."

It's telling, then, that despite the fact that Jerry Hauer worked for SAIC in 1999, where he would have had access to insider information on the 1993 WTC attack, somehow he knew that putting the Mayor's Office of Emergency Management in WTC 7 did not subject that office to grave risk of an outside terrorist attack.

KISSIN THE TRUTH

In my communication with Kevin Ryan, he recommended I talk to Frederick, Maryland–based attorney Barry Kissin, one of the country's lead advocates for exposing the truth about the anthrax cover-up. I told Ryan I was already there. Barry Kissin has spoken twice at conferences I have thrown in NYC and the Catskill Mountains. I have found him to be a passionate and sharp legal mind and writer, and a solid saxophone player, to boot. Kissin is on the ground in Frederick, home of Fort Detrick. He is in touch with the surviving family of Dr. Bruce Ivins. He writes a regular column for the *Frederick News-Post*. He is a bright light of hard curiosity amid a geographical area dominated by defense contractors and murky, amoral machinations.

Kissin recently wrote a detailed memo to New Jersey congressman Rush Holt, in which he noted that New York congressman Jerry Nadler asked the FBI's Robert Mueller some tough questions when Mueller appeared before Congress in an attempt to hawk the anthrax official story. The date was September 16, 2008. Nadler asked Mueller,

> *How, on what basis, and using what evidence, did the FBI conclude that none of the laboratories it investigated were in any way the sources of the powder used in the 2001 anthrax attacks, except the U.S. Army Laboratory at Fort Detrick, Maryland? Please include in your answer why laboratories that have been publicly identified as having the equipment and personnel to make anthrax powder, such as the U.S. Army's Dugway Proving Grounds in Dugway, Utah, and the Battelle Memorial Institute in Jefferson, Ohio, were excluded as possible sources.*

Seven months went by before the FBI responded to this question in writing. Its response read:

> *Initially, the spores contained in the envelopes could only be identified as Bacillus anthracis (anthrax). They were then sent to an expert, who "strain typed" the spores as Ames. Once the strain type was identified, the FBI began to look at what facilities had access to the Ames strain. At the same time, science experts began to develop the ability to identify morphological variances contained in the mailed anthrax. Over the next six years, new scientific developments allowed experts from the FBI Laboratory and other nationally recognized scientific experts to advance microbial science. This advancement allowed the FBI to positively link specific morphs found in the mailed anthrax to morphs in a single flask at USAMRIID.* Using records associated with the flask, the FBI was able to track the transfer of sub samples from the flask located at USAMRIID to two other facilities. *Using various methods, the FBI investigated the two facilities that received samples from the parent flask and eliminated individuals from those facilities as suspects because, even if a laboratory facility had the equipment and personnel to make anthrax powder,*

this powder would not match the spores in the mailed envelopes if that lab had never received a transfer of anthrax from the parent flask." [Emphases author's.]

According to Kissin, in his memo to Rep. Holt, "On its face, the FBI's response is absurd. The response literally says that after identifying 'two facilities' that received samples of anthrax from the USAMRIID (Bruce Ivins') flask, these facilities were excluded as possible sources of the attack anthrax because they 'never received' anthrax from said flask."

One of the purposes of this memorandum is to make clear why Nadler's question is the "most central" question to be asked about Amerithrax. This will serve to put in perspective Robert Mueller's professed inability to answer the question on September 16, 2008, the period of seven months it took for the FBI to fashion a response, and the disingenuousness of the response.

The FBI's response is not only absurd but, to the extent it states anything at all, it's demonstrably false. Bruce Ivins's "Reference Material Receipt Record," with respect to the anthrax flask designated RMR-1029, was posted on the Internet, now accessible at http://caseclosedbylewweinstein.wordpress.com/2009/07/25/usamriid-rmr-records-flask-1029/.

The original copy of said record is in the custody of the FBI. Said record documents that during the spring and summer of 2001, Bruce Ivins sent samples from RMR-1029 to both Battelle and Dugway. Practically all of the science underlying Amerithrax is about matching the genetic fingerprint of the attack anthrax to that of RMR-1029. Given that both Battelle and Dugway had RMR-1029, Battelle and Dugway are no less incriminated than Bruce Ivins by the science underlying Amerithrax.

Furthermore, as stated in a Los Angeles Times article dated August 4, 2008: "Dugway Proving Ground in Utah [is] a facility operated by the Battelle Memorial Institute in Ohio, a private contractor that performs top-secret work for the CIA and other agencies." According to Battelle's website, "Battelle is the world's largest private research and development organization . . . "

That the FBI has engaged in cover-up in its Amerithrax investigation is readily apparent. This memo addresses the crucial matter of what it is that is being covered up.

ANTHRAX IS ILLEGAL

In 1925, the United States signed on to the Geneva Protocol, which banned "the use of poisonous gases and bacteriological methods of warfare." Forty-four years later, upon realizing the United States was in gross violation of the protocol, President Nixon attempted to rein in the military-industrial complex and ordered all germ and biowarfare stocks to be destroyed.

In 1975, Congress's Church Committee discovered that the CIA had disobeyed the 1969 presidential order to destroy these nasty weapons. The CIA had instead retained pathogens and toxins, including anthrax, for its own use.[44]

According to *The New York Times*, in 2001, "Earlier this year, administration officials said, the Pentagon drew up plans to engineer genetically a potentially more potent variant of the bacterium that causes anthrax, a deadly disease ideal for germ warfare . . . "

The problem was, of course, that it was illegal, if you read the previous compacts. Yet, upon entering office, secretary of defense Donald Rumsfeld approved a plan to "weaponize anthrax" by producing a strain that was microfine, a billion parts per cubic inch, instead of a million.

Right before 9/11, on September 4, *The New York Times* published a useful, noteworthy article: "U.S. Germ Warfare Research Pushes Treaty Limits." The United States was considering allowing international inspectors to examine its biowarfare-making facilities in exchange for legal sanction to produce chemical and biological weapons.

Battelle makes an appearance in this article:

"Among the facilities likely to be open to inspection under the draft agreement would [have been] the West Jefferson, Ohio, laboratory of the Battelle Memorial Institute, a military contractor that has been selected to create the genetically altered anthrax . . . "

The next year, in 2002, an international effort came before the UN to reaffirm the Geneva Protocol, and the resolution passed unanimously except for two abstentions: the United States and Israel. Barry Kissin reports that the "U.S. abstention amounted to a veto, effectively preventing the resolution from being reported."

The year 2002 also saw the publication of a mainstream work, *Germs: Biological Weapons and America's Secret War* (Touchstone/Simon & Schuster), which includes this key information:

> *The CIA, [George Tenet] said, was looking for bold, imaginative solutions—something that would "break the back" of biological terrorism. . . . [T]he CIA and the Pentagon had been working separately for nearly three years on several highly classified projects to develop a better understanding of germ weapons and delivery systems . . . Officials privately acknowledged . . . the projects were bringing America much closer to the limits set by the 1972 treaty banning biological weapons . . . In the years that followed, scientists at Fort Detrick scrupulously confined their work. It was a different story at the CIA . . . A project took shape. CIA officials named it Clear Vision—an attempt to see into the future of biological warfare . . . The [CIA] went ahead without asking the White House for approval . . . White House officials say that President Clinton was never told of the program . . . In the ensuing months, Battelle, a military contractor in Columbus, Ohio, with sophisticated laboratories, conducted at least two sets of tests . . . The program had become controversial, one senior intelligence official acknowledged, because "it was pressing how far you go before you do something illegal or immoral."[45]*

Or illegal *and* immoral. Back to the story:

> *In the last days of the Clinton administration, the Pentagon gingerly moved toward doing its own recombinant work on pathogens . . . To make the genetically modified anthrax, the*

DIA turned to Battelle, *its contractor which had also worked on Clear Vision, the CIA project . . . [This] secret project was to be done as part of Project Jefferson.*[46] [Emphasis author's.]

When Rep. Jerry Nadler asked Mueller about why two U.S. labs had been arbitrarily ruled out as suspects, he was speaking of Battelle Memorial Labs and the Dugway Proving Ground in Utah. However, as we saw above, both are facilities managed by Battelle.

How could this story be so huge, so evil, and yet not reported by our mainstream media? The answer is that it *was* reported, by two "top reporters" who then found it convenient to look the other way. Scott Shane was at *The Baltimore Sun* before he moved on to *The New York Times*. While at the *Sun*, located less than an hour from Frederick and Fort Detrick, he did some good reporting.

On December 12, 2001, he published a piece titled "Anthrax Matches Army Spores: Organisms Made at a Military Laboratory In Utah Are Genetically Identical to Those Mailed to Members of Congress." It included language about the "weaponization" of the anthrax into microfine particles. It began to sketch a path to the obvious culprits:

> *For nearly a decade, U.S. Army scientists at Dugway Proving Ground in Utah have made small quantities of weapons-grade anthrax that is virtually identical to the powdery spores used in the mail attacks that have killed five people, government sources say . . . Anthrax is also grown at the U.S. Army Medical Research Institute of Infectious Diseases at Fort Detrick . . . [b]ut that medical program uses a wet aerosol fog of anthrax rather than the dry powder used in the attacks . . . Dugway's production of weapons grade anthrax, which has never before been publicly revealed, is apparently the first by the U.S. government since President Richard M. Nixon ordered the U.S. offensive biowarfare program closed in 1969 . . . [M]any bioterrorism experts argue that the quality of the mailed anthrax is such that it could have been produced only in a weapons program or using information from such a program.*

Around the same time, the *New York Times's* Judith Miller and William J. Broad were on a similar trail. On December 13, 2001, they published "The Investigation: U.S. Recently Produced Anthrax in a Highly Lethal Powder Form," which reported:

> *Intelligence officials say that Battelle Memorial Institute, a military contractor in Ohio, has experience making powdered germs. They say the contractor participated in a secret Central Intelligence Agency program, code-named Clear Vision and begun in 1997, that used benign substances similar to anthrax to mimic Soviet efforts to create small bombs that could emit clouds of lethal germs. Katy Delaney, a Battelle spokeswoman, would not comment on the laboratory's anthrax work except to say that the lab had always cooperated "with any and all legitimate inquiries from law enforcement."*

That's just wonderful. And may Battelle continue to do so. As more and more citizen groups explore ways to convene a citizen grand jury with subpoena power, there will be new forms of law enforcement, and Battelle should expect a presentment, soon, as we shall see.

THE NEW YORK TIMES: TRUTH REVERSAL

Despite these early reports in these and several other mainstream newspapers, the U.S. government and its allies in the media did an about-face, into a full-scale cover-up. They did so by attacking the idea that the anthrax from 2001 was in fact "weaponized" or "microfine." They did so using sloppy pseudoscience, in order to pin the blame on a "lone nut," Bruce Ivins, and not a corporation closely tied to the CIA. The scientists studying the case had been amazed that this new form of anthrax seemed to disperse itself weightlessly into the air, since it was coated in silicon at the microscopic level.

But the official story began to flex its muscle in November 2003. The reversal was observed in "Anthrax Powder: State of the Art?" by Gary Matsumoto, *Science* magazine.

> Early in the investigation, the consensus among biodefense specialists working for the government and the military [was that] . . . the powder mailed to the Senate . . . was a diabolical advance in biological weapons technology . . . In May 2002, sixteen of these scientists and physicianspublished a paper in the Journal of the American Medical Association, describing the Senate anthrax powder as "weapons-grade" and exceptional: "high spore concentration, uniform particle size, low electrostatic charge, treated to reduce clumping" (JAMA, 1 May 2002, p. 2237) . . . [But] by the fall of 2002, the awe inspiring anthrax of the previous spring had morphed into something decidedly less fearsome. According to sources on Capitol Hill, FBI scientists now reported that there was "no additive" in the Senate anthrax at all . . . The reversal was so extreme that the former chief biological weapons inspector for the United Nations Special Commission, Richard Spertzel, found it hard to accept. "No silica, big particles, manual milling . . . That's what they're saying now, and that radically contradicts everything we were told during the first year of this investigation."

Back in 2001, *The Washington Post* reported, "Law enforcement sources, however, said the FBI remains extremely interested in the CIA's work with anthrax, with one official calling it the best lead they have at this point."[47] But by August 2008, with Bruce Ivins three weeks in his grave, the FBI's "investigation" had clearly been captured and was now being controlled by the CIA, Battelle, and the masters of war. On August 18, the FBI gave a press conference at which its scientists and "consultants" agreed to speak with journalists from "well-respected scientific journals." What we see here is that not only was Battelle not considered, and not only was Battelle never named as a culprit, but it was a Battelle "scientist" who was helping to run the cover-up.

The full transcript of this little circus is available online at Sander Hicks.com. Key excerpts follow:

> **Background Official:** Leading today's discussion is Dr. Vahid Majidi and Dr. Chris Hassell of the FBI . . .

Dr. Majidi: . . . *After nearly seven years of investigation, we have developed a body of powerful evidence that allows us to conclude that we have identified the origin and the perpetrator of the 2001 Bacillus anthracis mailing . . . We have obviously done a number of other analyses [of the attack anthrax], elemental characterization, that drove us to conclude that there were no additives.*

Background Official: . . . *[The silica] was on the inside of the spore and not on the outside of the spore . . .*

Dr. Majidi: . . . *That's what the whole concept or methodology of weaponization comes from, is to weaponize. That's really—that's an ambiguous word, but what people mean by weaponize is that postproduction of the spores was silica added to it to make it more disbursable . . . So, one last time. No additive was added to the sample to make it more disbursable.*

Question: *Did you develop any theories on where the silicon and oxygen came from, and do you think it played any role in making the spores super buoyant?*

Dr. Majidi: *If I can actually pass that question to Dr. Burans, because he's our expert on processing.*

Dr. Burans: *In essence . . . the silicon associated with oxygen that was found within the spore, not on the surface of the spore, being present within the spore coat, which is covered by something called an exosporia, the silicon would not have contributed to the fluidlike qualities of the anthrax powders.*

[A comment from Barry Kissin: "Additives on the outside of the exosporium is pre-1969 technology. The current weaponizing technology, involving polyglass tightly binding hydrophilic silica, is located on the spore coat beneath the exosporium."]

Question: And as to where it came from?

Dr. Burans: *It's known that bacilli are capable of mineralizing different types of elements, including silicon, so as early as 1982 bacilli species have been shown to localize silica within their spore coat . . .*

Dr. Majidi: *Those locations [from where RMR-1029 was submitted]—it is not eight laboratories. I've got to be clear about that. They came from different locations. A good number of them came from USAMRIID itself. And we're not disclosing the [other] location.*

Question: How many were outside of the United States, and how many were non-governmental labs?

Dr. Majidi: *None outside the United States.*

Question: Were they all government labs?

Dr. Majidi: *There's a fine distinction there, and I don't know really what we call government and what we call quasi-governmental, so we're just going to leave that as is . . .*

Question: So, I've seen different estimates. How many people at Detrick or anyone else actually have access to RMR-1029?

Dr. Majidi: *The total body—the total universe of people [who] at some point were associated with RMR-1029—I'll qualify that. Roughly, about one hundred plus.*

Question: Hundred-plus. Were those all at Detrick, or other labs—

Dr. Majidi: *No, they were at Detrick and other labs.*

Question: Can you just tell us, of the eight samples that the letters matched to, how many places were they at? You were sort of vague earlier.

Dr. Majidi: Sure. Let's just say they're definitely not at eight places.

Question: But can you just give us the number? Why can't you give us the number?

Dr. Majidi: Because if I provide you with the exact number— well, there's a number of reasons; I'll just give you a generic one. We don't want you to bug those laboratories.

Question: Well, don't give us the names; just tell us how many.

[Laughter.]

Question: You've already told us a hundred people, right? So . . .

Dr. Majidi: Yeah.

Question: . . . How many labs?

Dr. Majidi: Hmm . . .

Question: Is it one?

Dr. Majidi: It's more than one.

[Laughter.]

Question: Can we keep guessing?

[Laughter.]

Question: Two?

Question: Is it ten?

Dr. Majidi: *Okay, it's total two laboratories.*

Question: *Total two. Including USAMRIID? Or—*

Background Official: *Two institutions.*

Dr. Majidi: *Two institutions . . . that means USAMRIID and one other institution.*

Of course, the other institution, the "quasi-governmental" lab, is Battelle. It bears pointing out that throughout the entire Amerithrax investigation, no one from either the FBI or the DOJ ever publicly mentioned the name Battelle.

During the formal introduction at the top of the press conference, Dr. James Burans was introduced as "associate laboratory director of the National Bioforensic Analysis Center," which is today called the National *Biodefense* Analysis *and Countermeasures* Center (NBACC). The NBACC is run by Battelle, but Buran's credentials hid the Battelle name from public view. The NBACC's own website shows: "On December 20, 2006, DHS selected Battelle National Biodefense Institute to conduct scientific programs and operate the NBACC facility."[48] As with Zelikow and the 9/11 Commission, Burans is Battelle. The "investigators" should have been the investigated.

THE SHAME OF SHANE

In 2008, the FBI and Battelle told the media that there was in fact no silicon artificially coating the anthrax. Burans was presented as the "expert" who made the outrageous claim that the silicon that was there occurred naturally, as a mineral by-product of the anthrax organism.

Where were those intrepid reporters from the big newspapers? The ones who in 2001 did the initial reporting that the anthrax was "weaponized," and that it therefore pointed back to the U.S. military, the CIA, and Battelle? In Judith Miller's case, we remember well that she destroyed her own credibility by actively selling the Iraq War to the American people, repeatedly writing stories with charlatan Ahmed Chalabi on the front cover of *The New York Times*. She effectively worked for the Bush State Department using *The New York Times*'s tattered credibility to sell Saddam Hussein's fictional weapons-of-mass-destruction programs. Her crimes against the truth recall the thesis of the book *The Record of the Paper*. From Vietnam to Iran-Contra, the *Times* has often acted as a mouthpiece for the State Department and the military-industrial complex. Indeed, the paper in recent years has even had William Kennard, an executive from the murky defense contractor Carlyle Group, on its board of directors.

So, when *Baltimore Sun* reporter Scott Shane moved up to *The New York Times*, his reporting on anthrax slipped significantly down the integrity scale. In 2001, Shane reported that "Dugway's [read: Battelle's] production of weapons-grade anthrax" pointed to U.S. military contractor involvement. But at the *Times* in 2009, Shane single-handedly reported something very different. The story was sold as the product of "the deepest look so far at the [Amerithrax] investigation." Here are some key excerpts:

"The *Times* review found that the FBI had disproved the assertion, widespread among scientists who believe Dr. Ivins was innocent, that the anthrax might have come from military and intelligence research programs in Utah or Ohio [read: Dugway or Battelle, respectively]. By 2004, secret scientific testing established that the mailed anthrax had been grown somewhere near Fort Detrick . . . By early 2004, FBI scientists had discovered that out of sixty domestic and foreign water samples, only water from Frederick, MD, had the same chemical signature as the water used to grow the mailed anthrax."

But water that is prepared for biological-weapons production has no "chemical signature." It must be 100 percent sterile, containing no minerals or anything that could track the water back to a specific place.

Even the *Times* partially retracted its nonsense, but phrased it in a half-assed way:

Postscript: February 28, 2009 (by Scott Shane)

A front-page article on Jan. 4 about Bruce E. Ivins, the late Army scientist who the Federal Bureau of Investigation says was responsible for the anthrax letter attacks of 2001, reported that FBI scientists had concluded in 2004 that out of sixty domestic and foreign water samples, only water from near Fort Detrick, MD, where Dr. Ivins worked, had the same chemical signature as the water that had been used to grow the mailed anthrax. That information, provided by a former senior law enforcement official who did not want to be named in the article, suggested that the anthrax could not have come from military and intelligence research programs in Utah and Ohio, as some defenders of Dr. Ivins's innocence had speculated . . .

On Tuesday at an American Society for Microbiology conference in Baltimore, an FBI scientist, Jason D. Bannan, said the water research ultimately was inconclusive about where the anthrax was grown. [Note: That's because Barry Kissin asked him a hard question.] An FBI spokeswoman, Ann Todd, said on Wednesday that the bureau "stands by the statements" of Dr. Bannan.

So, once again, the FBI effectively admitted it didn't have a case. Just as FBI Director Mueller couldn't rationally explain why Battelle and Battelle's Dugway lab were exonerated, the FBI and Scott Shane's nutty theory about a "chemical signature" in sterile water doesn't stand up to scientific scrutiny.

The entire anthrax official story resides, therefore, in a collusion between powers, the government and the media, *not to look at the truth.*

As a result, the people suffer. Every American who watched television or read newspapers in the fall of 2001 felt that a deadly chemical could come into their home via the mail slot. People felt powerless to protect their children, their spouses, their neighbors. They desperately bought the duct tape they were told to buy, until there was none left on the shelves. For what? Are we so frightened of the truth about anthrax that we will abide by the amoral intellectual mediocrities of *The New York Times* and the official pronouncements of FBI experts who actually work for CIA anthrax contractors?

In July 2011, PBS *Frontline*, in a collaboration with McClatchy News Service and ProPublica, released a hard-hitting documentary special on the anthrax cover-up. Meanwhile, Department of Justice lawyers waffled in Florida. The family of the first anthrax victim, American Media Inc. photo editor Bob Stevens, sued the U.S. government for negligence, asking for $50 million in damages. Obama's Department of Justice incompetently filed a response that said Ivins didn't have the adequate equipment to manufacture the anthrax. The DOJ then tried to retract that court filing, once it realized that it was effectively helping to expose its own big lie about the 9/11 anthrax attacks.

Every 9/11 anniversary in NYC, the city praises the "heroes" of 9/11, mostly the police and firefighters who gave their lives by charging into the inferno to save others. But there are some heroes we forget. It's the men like Kevin Ryan and Barry Kissin, who labor in obscurity to point out what many know but few are willing to state in public: that 9/11 is a rotten onion, and the softest part of the official story is the anthrax attacks—this Achilles' heel that will eventually topple the tottering 9/11 cover-up. At that moment, America will show its gratitude to its heroes not by giving speeches and throwing a ceremony, but by taking action to make a serious change, a turn toward peace and truth.

17 THE ANTIWAR LEFT'S CRISIS IN THE MOMENT OF TRUTH

September 11 is a funny political issue. Asking questions about it is taboo in the U.S. media. To the Right, it presents the possibility that the Bush–Cheney administration was in fact capable of an evil that is beyond our threshold. To some on the Left, 9/11 showed that U.S. imperialism got its "just desserts," and woe to those who question that logic. As a result, 9/11 skepticism is ignored more often than not. Still, the issue grows silently like a cancer, a growth that aims to kill the current form of crony-capitalist cover-up power politics. We express our deepest hopes for the world through our politics. But when those politics get hot and heavy, often our rationality goes out the window.

If you are against 9/11 skepticism, you tend to paint it with the brush of whatever you find politically most odious. If you are on the Right of the political spectrum, you claim 9/11 Truth is a crazy left-wing ideology. But if you are on the Left, you see 9/11 skeptics as nefarious neo-Nazis. Both positions are doomed to political obsolescence. In this chapter, I will confront the biases I have experienced in many different forms on the American Left, from everyone from radio-show hosts to socialists to a former friend who works at *The New York Times*.

All share a love of "correct" political ideology. But what if the truth were that they all in fact share a similar *bias*? What would happen if they were free to scientifically examine this issue, free from the kind of politics that create biases?

In my personal case, digging for the truth has expanded my mind and broadened my spirit. It has made me more open to others' views. I have become more interested in the world's diverse religious values, rather than one church's doctrine. I have become less hateful toward my so-called "enemies." After all, the notion of "enemy" is socially conditioned (another lesson that should be vividly clear in the post-9/11 world of scapegoating and paranoia).

With this chapter, I will make an important transition from 9/11 analysis to a broader worldview, both political and spiritual. I will focus in particular on several leftist/liberal voices I have encountered along the way. My own political background is on the Left, and yet, having been raised Catholic, I can also relate to the need to connect to a version of the "bedrock of traditional values." In my forty years, my "leftist" politics have been constantly leavened with a good dose of anarchist, traditionalist, and libertarian ideas.

What I am out to do here is form a place of unity. The "small government" politics of the Right could find common ground with the radical notion that we must disassemble the oppressive superstructure above us that wastes $700 billion a year waging U.S. wars of domination.

I have seen the shadowy side of the politics of liberation. The Left clings to this idea of purity and correctness; it forms political factions and Marxist "parties" that seek to weed out the incorrect ideologies within themselves. But it is so adamant about the ideology of correctness that it diminishes itself into smaller and smaller sects. The possibilities of creating a fun, vibrant, inclusive, compassionate mass movement are abandoned in the Left's anxiety to divide.

BILL WEINBERG AND RESISTANCE TO TRUTH

Former lefty radio host Bill Weinberg wrote an essay in 2011 that's a good example of losing sight of the ball in the thicket of political ideology. He is so married to the notion that 9/11 skepticism is a dangerous topic of discourse that he acted on his own essay by sabotaging the WBAI FM radio show he had hosted for twenty years. Ignoring warnings, he denounced the program director on-air and criticized other radio shows that he felt were too open to 9/11 skepticism. He was fired. He received sympathy only from a *New York Times* reporter, Colin Moynihan, whom I happen to know and who suffers from the same blinders. Colin and I have been friends since 1996, and I know that he cares a lot about principles and has a strong code of journalistic integrity. But he also hates 9/11 Truth with a passion, as evidenced by the article he wrote about Weinberg, in which Colin clearly tried to justify his own prejudices about 9/11.[49] It's a topic that we rarely discuss.

Weinberg's bias is evident even in the name of his anti-Truther essay, "9-11 at Nine: The Conspiracy Industry and the Lure of Fascism."[50] Weinberg promises to prove that, in the case of 9/11 at WBAI, "what began as an examination of seeming anomalies in the case of 9/11 has lured some of our best minds down a black hole of irrationality that ultimately leads—and this, as shall be demonstrated, is not just hyperbole—to fascism."

However, Weinberg never "demonstrates" any proof that 9/11 studies lead to fascism. He proves it's easy to use the word "fascism." Revolutionary methods of historical analysis are life-giving and fresh, but Weinberg is stubbornly wedded to a certain "leftist" viewpoint that is so disempowering, it's depressing.

In his essay's first paragraph, Weinberg sloppily conflates a variety of theories as he tries to appear rational about 9/11 skepticism: "It may begin with pre-planted explosives or missiles bringing down the Twin Towers . . . Once you abandon reason, anything goes."

There are no elements of the 9/11 Truth Movement that claim that "missiles" took down the WTC. Weinberg may be confusing this subject with the Pentagon, or perhaps he doesn't feel the topic as a whole is worthy of rigor.

If you "abandon reason," you forget to ask why there was molten metal in the ruins of Ground Zero for over three months after the attacks, or why seismic data show an explosion at Ground Zero *before* the buildings collapsed.

Weinberg, however, is clearly not writing for that audience; he's writing with a common leftist imperiousness that turns up its nose at new ideas outside the bounds of "leftist historicity." He assumes, or desperately hopes, that the reader shares his special disdain for anyone who asks these kinds of questions. So, without proving that such material is beyond "reason," Weinberg simply asserts that the idea of "pre-planted explosives" at the WTC is a theory that "abandons reason."

Weinberg also claims "historians are going to be arguing about [9/11] for generations to come, just like they are still arguing about the Reichstag Fire, the JFK assassination, the Gulf of Tonkin, and the sinking of the battleship *Maine*."

Actually, Mr. Weinberg, most "historians" heard the Nazis confess at Nuremberg that the Reichstag *was* a false flag attack blamed on a lefty scapegoat in order to foment support for militarism and the right. Just like 9/11.

Most rational minds agree that the "magic bullet" theory associated with the JFK assassination also abandoned reason. Recently, the U.S. military *itself* has admitted that the Gulf of Tonkin and the sinking of the USS *Maine* in Havana harbor were false provocations that the eager U.S. war machine used to expand its foreign military adventures.

It's only a glum form of subjectivism that alleges that there will never be any answers. The answers are out there for those who do the work.

Weinberg asserts that "the problem ultimately is not the power of hidden elites, but that we live under the capitalist system." He doesn't give details, but if he did, he might realize that this assertion is also contradictory. The capitalist system is *all about* hidden elites, by definition. Karl Marx said as much in *The Eighteenth Brumaire of Louis Napoleon*, his own study of how the elite used secrecy, conspiracy, and "bourgeois terror" to come to power.[51]

A radical critique of capitalism embraces the class analysis of history. Whether one is anarchist or Marxist, or beyond, radical ideologies understand capitalism as a rapacious system in which the working class is enslaved by economic conditions to work and to fight in wars based on lies in order to avoid starvation. This notion is illustrated vividly when one leaves the cities and goes to live in rural areas, where, it seems, the job opportunities for working-class young people these days are mostly at Walmart or in the U.S. Army.

Wars in this system are made attractive to potential soldiers with simple talk of adventure, training, and travel. But wars are sold to the larger public, the taxpayers, by the masters of a more nuanced form of propaganda. The events we observe are not clearly staged; it takes us years to see them for what they are: the products of a powerful network of hidden elites, aka the ruling class, who work under a cloak of secrecy, fueling the fires in this giant Platonic cave and keeping us chained to fear the shadows.

"Elites" is just another name for the ruling class. You learn fast in the 9/11 Truth Movement, with its sprawling diversity, that people coming from a more rural or "patriot" background may use the word "elite," while those coming from a more urban, "progressive" background denounce the "ruling class." Both are actually talking about overthrowing the same class, the "hidden elite" calling the shots atop this crystal pyramid of illusions we call capitalism. They teach us it's made of steel, but experience tells us it's built on sand and will fall at any time.

Even my own father, a lifelong defender of World Bank/IMF–style globalization, kept a copy of Karl Marx's *Das Kapital* on his bookshelf. I finally asked him at the beach in the summer of 2011 what he, an anti-Marxist, thought Marx got right, if anything. He said, "Not much. Well, there's one thing. Marx had a theory about why capitalism goes into crisis so much. No one else seems to."

Back to Weinberg: Let's take this out of the realm of theory. Instead of "hidden elite," let's look at one faction inside it: the Bush family. It's a historical fact that they make secrecy the currency of their power. George W. Bush's pathetic biography of cut corners and shady back-room deals was polished by GOP spin doctors just enough to make him quasi-"presidential." His father was a top manager of the narcotics/weapons/black-market power politics of the Iran-Contra network.[52] As CIA director in the late '70s, he spread disinformation about the assassination of Chilean ambassador Letelier on the streets of D.C.[53] Bush was involved in *and actually present at* the hit on JFK in Dallas in 1963.[54] During the 1981 assassination attempt on Reagan, Vice President Bush was put in charge of the "investigation." He failed to make public the strange and long relationship that the Bush family has with the Hinckley family in the Houston oil industry.[55]

But to those who have lost hope, like Bill Weinberg, the only acceptable response to ruling-class machinations like these is to shrug and terminate the debate by saying, "We'll never really know the truth."

Ah, but Mr. Weinberg, the light has not yet been smothered! For all the evil of the elite, there is an equal response: "We will never know the truth?"

We know what we demand to know. And we demand to know how to change this system.

Weinberg claims often in his essay that popular conspiracy author David Icke is a "neo-Nazi," but Weinberg never offers any proof for the assertion.

Icke is a lot of things, including a former Green Party UK spokesman (a fact Weinberg conveniently overlooks) and a sportscaster. He has quickly written numerous books on bizarre, fantastic forms of conspiracy theory. Icke's major thesis is that the ruling elite are so nefarious that they must be alien beings with an ability to "shape-shift" into human forms at will.

When you pick up Icke's books, you soon notice a startling lack of footnotes, or citations, or sources for anything. This is not for serious skeptics. Could it be that Icke is a red herring? A buffoon set in place to discredit the more careful researchers and critics of the global power structure? If so, Weinberg has taken the bait. By spending so much time on him, Weinberg is guilty of the "straw man" fallacy: The weakest and worst example of a class of people is held up as the example that proves the rule.

I prefer the analysis of Alex Constantine, a much more thorough analyst of the machinations of power. He calls Icke's work "an amateurish omelet of used conspiracy theories concocted by the John Birch Society and other far-right groups to discredit legitimate research on fascism, which is inherently conspiratorial. Most people, dumbed down by 'mainstream' media, can't tell the difference."[56] Bill Weinberg, despite his claims to radical analysis, can't seem to tell the difference, either.

Let's note what Constantine just said. Fascism is real. It is inherently conspiratorial. Therefore, the art of developing a radical theory of antifascism would be to work on exposing the fascist conspiracies. Our resistance to the crimes of fascism must be passionate and personal, disciplined and sustained.

Weinberg concludes his piece with "The conspiracy theory of history has right-wing roots, and remains inherently a phenomenon of the right."

To this, I would say, Bill, take a breath. Exposing the secret machinations of a militarist, right-wing, fascist system is actually quite liberating. It's wild, it's confrontational, and it's life-giving. And it's very "Left," if you choose to use that term. We are on the frontier of a new politics of liberation, and the old terms are just not relevant. In fact, I am reminded of America's genius poet Walt Whitman, who said:

> The learn'd, virtuous, benevolent, and the usual terms,
> A man like me and never the usual terms.

The never-the-usual "man" here is the movement. This Truth Movement is engaging in the making of history, free of the racist biases and the scapegoating of globalist, crony-capitalist disaster politics. History is not exclusively any single group's method, but the making of history is based on hard, materialist, political realities. Studying these realities is a part of liberating the global working class from the vampires.

Hegel teaches us that whenever people come together to think together, their ideas are always about freedom. Historian Howard Zinn said, "We all have an enormous responsibility to bring to the attention of others information they do not have, which has the potential of causing them to rethink long-held ideas."

But let's stick to the facts: A "conspiracy" is, after all, a crime that happens all the time. It's in our system of common law, prosecuted in the courts every day. Some on the Left reject 9/11 skepticism, but this lack of willingness to sit down, talk, and listen only creates more unnecessary drama and fanaticism. Tortured logic and twisted reasoning on the Left prevent social scientists from seeing that a new social movement is on the rise. It's dedicated to not letting Bush, Cheney, et al. get away with their crimes, and there are many: torture, rendition, reversal of civil liberties, fraud, election theft, and two illegal wars. But none of them could have happened without 9/11. While some wring their hands about the idea that "we may never know the answers," time is running out to bring Bush and Cheney to trial. We see the evidence and legal strategies as clear as day.

An obsession with the ideological side of politics has stripped some on the Left of their ability to even see the topic being addressed. This left-wing blindness is common in academic, intellectual circles, which prize precious postmodern theories over actual real-world evidence. A fear of working-class organization makes too many demonize anything not purely leftist as a "dangerous militia movement," or worse.

The 9/11 Truth Movement is an interesting social movement worthy of more serious study. The politics around 9/11 have led to real wars. The truth about 9/11 will lead to a real peace. And it's a truly radical theory of history that will get us there.

WEINBERG AND *THE NEW YORK TIMES*

I have been wrestling with whether to use Colin Moynihan's real name. I wasn't going to, but then he wrote that article on Bill Weinberg, and since I've been analyzing Weinberg's logic, it would be hard to keep Moynihan anonymous here.

His piece on Bill Weinberg's exit from WBAI is rather one-sided: He assumes that there's nothing credible on the 9/11 Truth side, and therefore he doesn't attempt to talk to anyone who will say anything good about the movement or about Weinberg's self-destructive crusade against it. Of course, the heads of WBAI, for some reason, chose not to respond to Moynihan's phone calls. Perhaps they assumed a bias on the part of *The New York Times*, which, after all, has a long track record of bias against fairly covering uncertainties surrounding 9/11.

On August 19, 2009, I took part in a nationwide campaign to ask the media to report the death of 9/11 witness Barry Jennings. We held banners outside media outlets in forty-two cities, planet-wide, with the simple message JENNINGSMYSTERY.COM. Jennings was a witness to explosions at the base of World Trade Center Building 7 before any tower collapsed. He voiced questions about how WTC 7 mysteriously imploded. He spoke to news outlets and appeared in the 9/11 Truth film *Loose Change*. He was a City of New York official, and yet the *New York Times* never covered his mysterious death. So, on the one-year anniversary of Jennings's death, I lead a squad of Truthers to the *New York Times* building, held the banner, and passed out flyers all day.

The confrontational Gandhian peace activist Dave Slesinger deserves credit for organizing this campaign, sending out banners and setting up squads from Washington, D.C., to Hollywood to Norway. I wanted this campaign to be comprehensive and impossible to ignore, so I also wrote a letter to *The New York Times* public editor Clark Hoyt regarding this issue. No response ever came.

Barry Jennings worked as the city's deputy director of the Emergency Services Department. He was in WTC Building 7 on 9/11, and he saw too much. He heard explosions at the base of WTC 7 and was led out of the building by a firefighter.

Later, Jennings said, "I'm just confused about one thing, and one thing only: why World Trade Center 7 went down in the first place. I'm very confused about that. I know what I heard—I heard explosions. The explanation I got was, it was the fuel-oil tank. I'm an old boiler guy—if it was a fuel-oil tank, it would have been one side of the building."

Jennings died days before NIST published its report on WTC 7. His death was not announced, and rumors about it swirled for a month, before an NYC Housing Authority spokesman offered this pithy comment: "Jennings did die from undisclosed causes, a month previous, he was a great man, well-loved, no further comment will be forthcoming."

For a quick overview of the other stories regarding 9/11 that *The New York Times* has been negligent about, just recall the contents of this book. The paper made no comment on the death of Dr. Graham, it missed the essence of Able Danger, and it misreported the anthrax attacks. September 11 was a crime of the CIA and the Pentagon against what was once one of the world's greatest cities, the namesake of what was once a respectable newspaper. The *Times* should be ashamed.

So, while writing this book in 2011, I had an argument with Colin Moynihan about his employer.

Osama bin Laden died, and I was disturbed at how problematic the event was. First of all, mainstream news in Pakistan had reported bin Laden's funeral back in December 2001. But if that was wrong, and this 2011 killing was in fact the real bin Laden, the body had swiftly disappeared at sea. The U.S. Navy reported that bin Laden had been armed, but then that story had to be retracted. Since bin Laden had never been wanted by the FBI for 9/11 specifically, I thought it was an opportunity to dialogue with Colin.

I said some of the above, and referenced Ed Haas's conversation with Mr. Rex Tomb of the FBI, in which this FBI spokesman said the bureau had "no hard evidence connecting bin Laden to 9/11."[57]

Colin responded by sending me the FBI's Most Wanted list, which did have bin Laden listed, but for the 1998 U.S. embassy bombings, and it insinuated that bin Laden might be wanted for "other incidents," without ever naming 9/11.

So, I pointed out that Colin had in fact just proven my point: bin Laden had never been wanted for 9/11, despite Colin's and others' claims that there were mountains of "evidence" that he was involved. But this point touched a nerve. Colin retorted:

> When I said I was interested in your personal feelings about the death of bin Laden I did not mean that I wanted to hear you repeat conspiracies coined by others . . . I feel as if you are taking this as an indoctrination opportunity. I have tried to make it clear that I want to stay away from what some call "9/11 truth," and which I consider to be an obsessive and unhealthy quicksand of innuendo, rumor, speculation, and fiction masquerading as fact. I'm not telling you not to immerse yourself in it; don't tell me that I should.

This section is hard to write. I don't want to write the epitaph for what has been one of the best friendships of my life. But it does seem that we have come to an impasse. The last time I saw Colin, it was on Avenue B and East Fourth Street. He was livid that I had suggested that perhaps his inability to look at some facts around 9/11 was linked to a fear of losing his job. He took that to mean that I was suggesting he was a coward, and he demanded an apology.

I'm not saying that Colin is a coward. But I *am* saying he needs to get out more. He has this automatic camaraderie with anyone else who works at the *Times*. So when the *Times*'s Corey Kilgannon laughed openly at me during the DeVecchio perp walk, because I had shouted out a question about the CIA, Colin's response later was "Corey's a good guy." So when the *Times*'s Ian Urbina arrived at Vox Pop, in our first year, to debate the merits of our book on the strange death of Senator Wellstone but chose not to do a story on Vox Pop or the book, Colin's response was "Ian's a good guy." Colin has a talent for cultivating stories that explore the FBI's use of informants—he's close enough to downtown radical people that he's trusted. So when the *Times* assigned him a story with older, more established reporter Scott Shane, I was worried for him. I showed him Shane's about-face on the anthrax cover-up. Colin never responded.

BARRIERS TO PERCEPTION

On my spring 2011 speaking tour of the country, I collected a few books that helped give me some insight into what we are up against. In New Hampshire, I learned about the libertarian Free State Project, an attempt to get ten thousand libertarians to move to a single state in order to live in true liberty.

Someone in the Free State Project gave me a copy of *The Sacred Non-aggression Principle*, by Brian Wright. He explores why people turn a blind eye to things that are clearly violations of their rights, like the TSA's body scans, for example.

"Many people—even those with high intelligence and, at least abstract, pride in critical thinking *who have a stake in* a political system and its corollary intellectual-authority system—are desperately bound to that system of belief despite overwhelming objective specific evidence that the system is deceitful, plundering, and murderous."

This helps explain why someone like Colin Moynihan, a man who has great ethics, sense of style, literary ability, and integrity, can turn into a tempestuous, angry, on-the-verge-of-violence guy when we talk about 9/11. He is bound to the system, through his class and family background.

His uncle, after all, was the famous Democratic Party senator Daniel Patrick Moynihan.

If you substitute the JFK assassination topic for the 9/11 Truth topic, this explanation from James Douglass's *JFK and the Unspeakable* speaks to this moment.

> *When we live in a system, we absorb a system and think in a system. We lack the independence to judge the system around us. Yet the evidence we have seen points toward our national security state, the systemic bubble in which we all live, as the source of Kennedy's murder and immediate cover-up . . . The extent to which our national security state was systematically marshaled for the assassination of President John Kennedy remains incomprehensible to us."*

Colin has been downtown a lot, covering Occupy Wall Street for *The New York Times*. He did a good job when he first reported the much-talked-about fact that when the NYPD arrested seven hundred marching Occupy protestors on the Brooklyn Bridge, the marchers had been guided there by the NYPD itself. It was a trap, and some on the street heard NYPD top brass boast, "They walked right into it."

Colin's article itself reported this information, including the line "After allowing them on the bridge, the police cut off and arrested dozens of Occupy Wall Street protestors." Twenty minutes later, *The New York Times* somehow decided to absolve the police of any wrongdoing, and Colin's exclusive byline was joined by that of an NYPD beat reporter.

18 TOWARD A MASS MOVEMENT

The word "anarchist" has both a vulgar and a sublime meaning. The vulgar is the stereotype of the crazy bomb-thrower, the "terrorist" who deserves nothing but annihilation. But once you actually talk to anarchists, you discover that the stereotype isn't real. Most anarchists are connected to a calling to forsake power. They seek to distance themselves from stale human institutions, which tend to do evil in the name of good.

After all, paying taxes today in the United States means that half of what you pay goes to a war machine. Is it ethical, therefore, to pay taxes? Is it Christian?

To some, radical politics have been crushed in the last ten years. A vibrant antiglobalization movement has been intimidated by the machinations of an uncontrolled national security state. This book is a resurrection. A call to compassionate insurrection. Our revolution is a moral one.

When we look at antiwar movements in this country, we see a landscape of fractured, mutually hostile, and ultimately ineffective factions. We are so concerned with the correct political ideology that we fail to stand united against the great evils of our time. This factionalism is one of the most challenging problems we face as an antiwar movement. But I have seen glimpses of a solution.

Occupy Wall Street is a new way to protest: It asks for more dedication and delivers more effect. Unlike the antiwar movement, which in the past has seemed to represent communists leading liberals around in circles, the Occupy movement is "the 99 percent," which means a lot more political diversity.

Seems like Occupy has learned something from the 9/11 Truth Movement. For ten years, the Truth Movement in the United States and globally shows Left and Right can come together around the idea that there is a massive superstructure above us all. The structure stitches together a cloak of "reality," but more and more people are beginning to see through it. The future of the revolution is a new politics of liberation, one that leftists, liberals, and libertarians can all relate to and act in. Even those words seem limiting, though. Let's just call it the 99 percent.

Skepticism about 9/11 is radical for its nonsectarianism, which encompasses elements of the patriot, the grassroots Right, the peace movement, spiritual people, and the radical Left. Plenty of regular, working-class, red-blooded Americans are wary of extremism. One interesting development is that there are also those who think that the whole Left/Right paradigm is a social construction, a part of the problem.

During the weekend of January 30 and 31, 2010, I attended the New England Antiwar Conference and the Northeast 9/11 Truth Conference and witnessed some historic and contentious events, as the left wing of the antiwar movement and the 9/11 Truth Movement inched closer to an understanding.

I hooked up with Boston 9/11 Truth as it participated in the New England Antiwar Conference, spearheaded by members of the Socialist Workers Party (SWP) and other peace and justice groups.

The good news is that through some careful diplomatic outreach, the Boston 9/11 Truth Movement got a "seat at the table." Boston 9/11 Truth ran an informational workshop and arranged for Peter Dale Scott to give a significant speech to the entire body. Scott spoke during the plenary session—titled "Debunking the War on Terror"—on the subject of history, deep politics, and the Truth Movement.

However, the Truth issue is still quite controversial, especially among the leadership of this conference. The socialists at times tripped over themselves to maintain a standard of political correctness. In doing so, they failed to perceive the great opportunities for mass anti-imperialist organizing presented by a Truth Movement/Peace Movement alliance. With more understanding and communication, we can create a bigger, stronger, mass movement against war and the terror of the state. We are all one antiwar movement.

WHAT PEOPLE SAID: THE NORTH-EAST 9/11 TRUTH CONFERENCE

On Sunday, January 31, the Northeast 9/11 Truth Conference started off with a group dialogue about what had worked at the conference the day before. Several insightful comments came from various members of New England 9/11 Truth groups about the fractured nature of antiwar politics. The following snapshots reveal the true diversity and creativity of the Truth Movement.

We were in a huge upstairs room in Boston's Chinatown—an office for some nonprofit, with big windows giving onto the gray January day outside. The space was littered with picket signs and posters from past antiwar, union, and activist campaigns. We were gathered in a big square made of long folding tables, so that everyone could see and hear each other. It occurred to me that what was being said was so good, someone should write it down. I started to take notes.

Liz Fenton pointed out that *Democracy Now!* and host Amy Goodman "freeze up" when asked about 9/11 Truth. "Why are they completely irrational? They act as if they are under tremendous threat." Liz also reported, "Tariq Ali got explosive when asked [about 9/11]. He said, 'It doesn't matter who did 9/11!' There's something really weird going on."

Frank Tolepko, paraphrasing something from *Monthly Review*, said, "Our ability to reform, our elections, are broken. The jobs of Amy Goodman and other progressive media outlets are over. [They advocate for a reform that is not possible.] 9/11 Truth shows just how broken the system is."

David Rolde pointed out why the Socialist Workers Party and other left-wing antiwar organizers fear/shun Ron Paul disciples. Ron Paul, it turns out, has called for a "separation wall" to be built in Mexico, to keep Mexicans out of the United States. (A quick online search later confirmed that this is true. Still, Paul's book *Revolution: A Manifesto* is worth a read.)

Susan, a Libertarian, said, "Antiwar activists . . . harken back to a by-gone day and tactics. Direct confrontation tactics are best. Really, there are two political parties: those who support freedom for people, and those who support the deprivation of freedom for people." To her right, Jonathan, also a Libertarian, added, "How can we blame the people when we don't have real elections in this country? We need *tax resistance!*" This is a great topic for the American Left to someday get around to: the idea that if you really are against wars of foreign imperialism, then it's a moral imperative to refuse to fund them via income taxes. Sound too radical? It's the view of Mahatma Gandhi.

Back in Boston, New Hampshire professor Bill Woodward spoke of his explorations into the psychological resistance to 9/11 Truth. He almost lost his job over this. Dan LaLiberté: "It's an issue of trust. They don't trust us. But who do you trust? Your friends and your family."

Richard expressed concern that perhaps he bent the truth a little in his representations of the 9/11 Truth Movement by deemphasizing the Ron Paul and Alex Jones elements and instead emphasizing the left/liberal side of 9/11 Truth. He said he felt guilt, but in my view, no guilt is necessary. The SWP and left-wing antiwar organizers are well aware of the Paul and Jones elements; they see these, plus some who are not there (witness their weekend-long fright of "LaRouchites" taking over the Saturday antiwar conference). What Richard *and* the antiwar Left do not recognize is that a lot of Alex Jones's fans are actually seeking a new politics that is beyond the Left/Right bifurcation. Jones talks often of the need to outgrow the Left/Right paradigm, because conflict among the people defangs a united opposition to the elite.

Rodney Lewis noted, "Peace activists are nice. They are afraid we will take over."

Barrie Zwicker recommended two books: *Pretensions to Empire*, by Lewis Lapham, and *Empire of Illusion*, by Chris Hedges. Zwicker has a funny quote about Canadians' view of the United States: "The 48th parallel is the longest one-way mirror." He also shared a good Chris Hedges quote: "Inverted totalitarianism . . . finds expression in the anonymity of the corporate state." The Hedges book includes this quote from Charlotte Twight: "Participatory fascism [is what we have now instead of democracy].

Washington has become our Versailles . . . politicians, pundits, media are our courtiers."

Alfons Olszewski said, "We need to work on our image. We need better PR. We are not just for 'truth,' we are for 'truth, justice, and peace.'"

Jack Shimek of New Hampshire said we have to understand that some people in the antiwar movement have a "need to belong" that is stronger than their need to question some stories. "It's not America did XYZ crimes and wars"; it's the U.S. government. Shimek argued that America is us, and we are separate from the criminal acts of our government.

Kelly Hawkins has been showing *Conspiracy Theory with Jesse Ventura: 9/11* episodes in the local library.

David commented on the Israel question. There is resistance on the Left to being too critical of Israel because of possible accusations of anti-Semitism. The Truthers there seemed to present the message that they reject anti-Semitism as racist. But they likewise reject Zionism as oppressive.

Mark Basile, also in New Hampshire, reported on his local efforts to get the 9/11 Truth cause recognized at his town meeting. As an independent Christian, he follows "two rules: Love God, love your neighbor. In the U.S., we have been wonderfully blessed. But we view the government (like Obama) as celebrities. Our government is unrestrained. This is a problem." Of the sixty to seventy people Basile approached in his town to sign his petition to get 9/11 Truth discussed at the town meeting, thirty of them signed—an impressive rate!

Edith asked, "Where are the blacks? It's time to go into those communities to expand the Truth Movement."

Doug from New Hampshire: "It's people closest to changing their paradigm who are most vocal about resisting." He also said, "How do people perceive us vs. how do we perceive ourselves?" Should we rebrand ourselves? Is the "Truther" label off-putting and didactic? (I would argue no, although it does pay not to be too strident, and to work on listening skills. On Friday, it was pointed out that one good thing about Dale Carnegie is his lesson that the way you win people over is by listening to their concerns and perspective first, then trying to connect what they are saying to your issue.)

Al said, "To those who say 9/11 was yesterday's crime and that we must protest today's wars: When you are bailing water from a leaky boat, it's also important to plug the leak. Any society that does not identify crimes cannot function."

Susan said she was "tremendously proud" of our professional participation in the conference on Saturday. "Patience is a virtue. Success does not come in an instant; it comes through persistence."

Tracy Blevins said, "We *need* a counternarrative."

Richard Krushnic said that he was "really quite pleased" that we were able to participate on Saturday. "We succeeded in securing a place at the table. We need to work with veterans' groups to build our movement."

Chris Gruneur suggested, "We are scared of two things: being called 'crazy' and being effective."

"Abdul" suggested outreach to the Nation of Islam. He pointed out that minister Louis Farrakhan wrote a 2003 letter that covered a number of false flag operations and the topic of controlled demolition. We all know how controversial Farrakhan is. Earlier, Abdul discussed his background as an American Muslim. Since he had no Christmas and lived outside the myths of American life, he saw 9/11 right away as a myth: "How does truth enlighten the spirit, and falsehood kill it?"

Susan discussed how, in New Hampshire, the Underwear Bomber scare led otherwise rational lawmakers to begin considering legislation that would have allowed full-body scans, and photos of all adults and children in the nude. This is a violation of child porn laws and was shot down, but it shows how much hysteria we are dealing with in an emerging police state.

(This conference took place before the TSA-body-scans controversy. At the time, when Susan said the above, I thought, *Oh, this is a pet issue for one person in the room.* Later, we as a country saw that a huge amount of mainstream America didn't want to be groped or scanned by the TSA.)

Mark Basile: "We are not going to drag people to 9/11 Truth. They have to walk with us." Mark recently held a public "Science Expo" showing the science of 9/11 Truth. It was well attended.

Richard Krushnic said, "People manage their worldview unconsciously according to their paradigm . . . People will go die for it, as soldiers. Their paradigm must protect them from things they can't handle. It's almost always subconscious . . . but people go to extraordinary lengths. It takes work to build a new paradigm."

Krushnic also pointed out that it pays to understand Noam Chomsky's objections to the Truth Movement, in order to bypass them. Chomsky and his followers argue that, in the United States, power resides with "institutions." Chomsky claims that conspiracy theorists don't understand this simple fact and instead argue that political injustices originate with "a few bad apples" who conspire against the majority.

Our response to this needs to be: *We agree with the institutional analysis.* Power *does* reside with institutions (e.g., the White House, CIA, Pentagon, media, lobbyists—all of whom represent the interests of capital). But our contribution to the resistance is to point out that *these very same institutions do, in fact, conspire to use shock and awe, media, spectacle, violence, and fear in order to quell a dissident and sometimes unruly peace- and freedom-loving people.* These institutions are smart; they have created a docile, frightened population willing to support and pay for an empire. (Chomsky admitted in late 2011 that al Qaeda was never proven to have done 9/11.)

CONFRONTING RESISTANCE TO TRUTH

I was impressed by the diversity of ideas and incisive commentary at the gathering. Synthesizing some of the concerns others had, I've come to see a number of reasons why the Truth Movement has had trouble gaining steam, which I shared at the gathering.

First, COINTELPRO. Students of U.S. state repression first have to realize that nothing is what it seems at first glance. Every potent social movement in U.S. history has been infiltrated and disrupted by agents of the complex state apparatus. It happened in the Black Panthers, the American Indian Movement, Martin Luther King, Jr.'s, circles, Earth First!, the IWW, and other groups. Jules Boykoff's *Beyond Bullets* is a great manual for opening your ability to identify and root out destructive police tactics. There is evidence that this is some COINTELPRO-style disruption in the Truth Movement.

At the gathering, someone pointed out that Cass Sunstein, the Obama White House official, allegedly said in regard to 9/11 Truth, "This movement must be crushed . . . Disinformation agents should be sent out to infiltrate the 9/11 Truth Movement." My personal reaction at first was, "Surely Sunstein didn't say this!" Sunstein, after all, was a renowned constitutional scholar, supposedly an advocate for the freedoms enshrined in the Constitution.

Ah, how naive I was. In a white paper called "Conspiracy Theories" prepared in 2008 but only discovered in 2010, Sunstein proposes a plan to execute "cognitive infiltration of extremist groups." In it, he writes: "Government agents (and their allies) might enter chat rooms, online social networks, or even real-space groups and attempt to undermine percolating conspiracy theories by raising doubts about their factual premises, causal logic or implications for political action." He goes on to argue that the practice of enlisting nongovernment officials "might ensure that credible independent experts offer the rebuttal, rather than government officials themselves. There is a tradeoff between credibility and control, however. The price of credibility is that government cannot be seen to control the independent experts."

Of course, this sort of intervention would violate prohibitions on government propaganda aimed at domestic citizens. Like Obama, Sunstein is a "constitutional scholar" whose words and actions are contemptuous of the Bill of Rights.

Another factor in the Left's unwillingness to embrace the Truth Movement is fear. On Friday, at the pre–antiwar conference meeting at Krushnic's house, an email from Marc Stahl, one of the antiwar organizers, rejected our proposal to have Canadian journalist Barrie Zwicker replace Peter Dale Scott, who could not attend in person. Stahl claimed that the Canadian liberal's politics were "far right," and that his "long association" with Webster Tarpley suggested that he was a "LaRouchite." It was an absurd fear, one that did not bear out: No LaRouchites attended the conference. It seems that some antiwar organizers are letting their fears inform their perceptions. I noted that Webster Tarpley is not a LaRouchite; he made a very public break with LaRouche years ago. Tarpley's book *9/11 Synthetic Terror: Made in USA* is quite good. (Though we noted with regret the damage Tarpley did to his reputation with "the Kennebunkport memo," and the unfortunate spat with Cindy Sheehan.)

In addition to fear, institutional political correctness holds back the Truth Movement. The partisan Left suffers from a set of assumptions that a certain brand of labor and working-class organizing, along economic lines, is the only valid form of organizing. The 9/11 Truth cause is more "populist." It is a working-class movement, but it doesn't use those terms. So, at first glance, the Truth Movement looks like a politically confused movement with no class struggle understanding. Antiwar organizers and partisan lefties dismiss the Truth Movement for not having the "correct" position on class and imperialism. But the objection over "class" is actually a superficial distinction, and the objection over "imperialism" is just plain wrong. It is instructive to consider that *everyone* at the Truth meeting—including progressives, Marxists, lefties, "political atheists," Christians, and Libertarians—was against empire, and all felt that the 9/11 Truth Movement was the best way for them to live out that creed.

For some leftists, an immature understanding of media and power relations becomes an obstacle. Probably one of the funniest moments at the Saturday antiwar conference was when I was having a heated conversation with three young lefties in the lobby. They were adamant that there was nothing worth knowing in 9/11 Truth. Their primary argument was that if there was a story here, *The New York Times* would have covered it. I pointed out that the *Times* is the prime media vehicle that sold the Iraq War to the American people. They remembered that, and then countered that well, then, the 9/11 Truth story should be on *Democracy Now!*.

The truth is that no one mainstream media vehicle is comprehensive, or objective, or free from outside foundation or U.S. intelligence influence. That conclusion comes from my own twenty years as an antiwar activist studying U.S. media. Or you could go online and see the recently republished piece by Carl Bernstein (originally published in *Rolling Stone* in 1976) regarding CIA influence over the U.S. media. Holding up either the *Times* or *Democracy Now!* as a trusted filter against disturbing realities is unsophisticated and politically immature.

After recent events in NYC and Cambridge, I have begun to realize that a significant difference between 9/11 Truth activists and non-Truth activists is passion. In Sun Tzu's *Art of War*, the author notes that a small army can defeat a much larger army if that smaller army has the "oneness" of purpose. After a recent 9/11 Truth event at the *Catholic Worker* in NYC, some older antiwar activists accused Truthers of being "fundamentalist" in their dedication to the cause. They were critical of Truthers' lack of willingness to listen to opposing opinions. Some of that is understandable. But in the same way that there have been factual distortions about Truthers' politics, there seems to be some deliberate denigration of our passion and dedication for what we do.

For example, I approached Ashley Smith, of the International Socialist Organization, during the lunch break on Saturday. He had just denigrated the 9/11 Truth cause, saying that it was distractive, when "most people" were already on the antiwar side. I pointed out that choosing to be dismissive of an issue that many people care about creates an unnecessary barrier between different sections of the antiwar movement and was a tragic lost opportunity for the ISO. I also noted that of all the admirable passion I have seen on the Left, I have never seen the level of dedication and passion that I have seen in the Truth Movement.

Ashley, unfortunately, took this as a personal attack and, in a high-pitched voice, responded, "I have *plenty* of passion!" Shortly thereafter, he left the room in a huff.

Many people at this Boston antiwar conference denounced imperialism. The Truth Movement does so as well, but we also act. We are a movement that directly confronts political criminals. We freely distribute information on the Internet and on cheap DVDs. We move. We are growing. Every year, something new happens in the world that makes the Truth Movement more relevant, whether it's the Underwear Bomber and his tenuous "ties to Al Qaeda in Yemen," or the impending (and constantly delayed) military show trial of Khalid Sheikh Mohammed.

But perhaps the greatest attribute that Truthers seem to possess is a kind of conviction. I remember having a flash of insight when I read a manifesto called *The Coming Insurrection* by French radicals known as the Invisible Committee. They write, "You can see the dogmatism of constant questioning give its complicit wink of the eye everywhere . . . No critique is too radical among postmodernist thinkers, as long as it maintains this total absence of certitude."

At last, someone has hammered the final nail into the always-dying zombie of postmodernism. The entire *Insurrection* book indicts our age—in which a once strong resistance has had its tendons cut by a zeitgeist of uncertainty. Everyone is "radical," but no one is certain.

Postmodernism is a system of problems: Truth is dead, language is broken, capitalism is schizophrenic. But with truth dead and language broken, how can we create a counterforce against corporate control?

Perhaps, then, the best form of resistance to the permanent war state, the national security terror state, will be to declare certainties. Here is what I am certain of:

September 11 is a rotten onion. We have seen in previous chapters that the Bush-Cheney official story is a complex ruse; the onion has many rotten layers. It could not have happened *without* the postmodern zeitgeist. Put another way, the uncertainty and lack of truth in daily life right now created a fertile ground for new lows in human political corruption.

September 11 shows a new nadir in evil, surpassing anything seen previously. Never before has a state spent $700 billion a year on weapons and military and *created* an enemy to justify the cash flow.

September 11 shows us that we are ill equipped to go into battle against evil armed with a philosophy that is based on relativism, subjectivism, lack of certainty, lack of faith. Foucault and his followers would say, how can we approach "truth" with a language so broken? My response is "Check yourself before you wreck yourself." Is the language really all that broken? Or is that the bias of the time?

Let us simply present the world. The post-9/11 world, as presented thus far in this book, shows that beyond the Bush-controlled 9/11 story, a clearer picture is beginning to emerge. September 11 was the crime of our time, and underneath the Muslim garb are the colors red, white, and blue. September 11 happened when it did because our age offers the right mix of media manipulation, emotional spectacle, and cultural bias. You find truth by examining its suppression.

I am certain that the philosophy of the future will be a hybrid of two very different strains in modern thought. The Left has a great mission to change the world, to bring justice. But the Left forgets what the Right has. It's something also essential: a sense of the "eternal things." There is a solid sense of authority (without desperate authoritarianism) and trust when you can cite time-trusted notions like "the good": freedom, truth, democracy. This is what the Western tradition and the Judeo-Christian ethos are built on: creating community around a common dedication to the light. (That, and invading smaller, browner countries for their pelts, gold, or oil.)

You look at the Truth Movement today, and you get a sense of the future of American politics. The political struggles of the post-9/11 world will not be about Left versus Right. They will be about truth versus lies.

September 11 shows us that the enemy is within, sleeping in a cocoon of self-justification woven in the wool of postmodern morals. The democratic centrists and the neocons are all in truth postmodernists who have no moral core. Everything is pragmatic, usually to advance the interests of the U.S. big-business ruling class: the big banks, the megacorporations.

Parts of both the Right and the Left get this. Both have risen up against the 9/11 official story. A new political leadership will hold high the banner of truth. It can be simple and pure. It can be beautiful. It can be empowering. It can touch the star inside us all, the third eye, the love of God's wisdom that we all have in our heads and hearts, just waiting to open.

Remember: The current Occupy Wall Street movement is about making the revolution a universal experience. The media can try to peg us as the same old left-wing organizers, but when you actually go and experience an Occupy, you realize that something very special is happening. It's very new and very old. People are reaching in and turning on the better part of themselves, and then they're reaching out to each other, by getting involved, by dreaming big, by acting together. Some people call that God.

PART FIVE

SYNTHESIS - REVOLUTION

19 REVOLUTION MEANS A SPIRITUAL SOLUTION TO A SPIRITUAL PROBLEM

Spiritual starvation is rampant in this country. Our problem is not just political; it goes deeper than that. Our problem is one of a spiritual nature. We do not know what to believe anymore. We don't believe in ourselves; we turn away from God and from reality. We are dominated by our own egos, and we don't reach out beyond ourselves. We don't have the guts to admit we are vulnerable and that we need a bigger, loving higher power, whose existence we run away from. We are scared of something simple and pure, like the truth.

Instead, we get addicted. To marijuana, beer, and Internet porn. To anxiety, stress, and worrying about what other people think. To cable TV news, sports, and celebrity shows. We get used to watching and reading "news," knowing that it's not even half-true, but consuming it anyway. Sugar goes down easy.

We get addicted to our jobs, to our own identities. We cling to what other people say we are instead of finding out ourselves. We eat up what the media tells us to believe instead of doing a little extra work and finding the truth ourselves.

The problem is that the powers that be do know that there's a spiritual malady at the core of our society. They use it for their own ends. It's one of the things they were banking on when they pulled the strings at the CIA and the Pentagon to make 9/11 happen when it did. They were banking on our political and spiritual lethargy.

Ironically enough, though, it was the 9/11 event, its cover-up, and the Truth Movement that arose in response that resulted in a spiritual rebirth. It's crazy, but for all the death, bombing, lies, and torture, 9/11 also led me to realize that the peace movement needs to strike out on a fresh new path to the truth, using the pulsing heart of the world's religions to guide it.

September 11 also showed how the current revolutionary Left is bankrupt in many ways. The Left lacked the courage to really penetrate to the truth of this historical event. Instead, many of its adherents simply clucked that the United States had it coming—just look at what this country has done—and this, of course, was such a vindictive thing to say. Devoid of mercy, it served only to further alienate the Left from mainstream American society.

The reason the Left has no mercy is that it abstains from all things spiritual. Most leftists think Marx said, "Religion is the opiate of the masses." But there was no period at the end of that phrase, for it continues, " . . . the heart of a heartless world." An insistence on dry rationalism has created a Left in the United States that is exclusionary. In my own experience, trying to be a member of the International Socialist Organization (ISO) in 1997, I was kicked out for being a vocal individual, for being a nonconformist, for having a vibrant personality in a culture of drones. I came to realize that these leftists were so doctrinaire, so humorless, that they were scared of human creativity (especially in the form of a quirky punk-rock guy with his own publishing company). Eventually, I also came to realize that they lacked a process with which to foster and nurture their own compassion for each other. These "revolutionaries" were fast becoming inhuman authoritarians.

Right after 9/11, I was an atheist, ex-Catholic punk publisher, licking my wounds and mourning the mysterious suicide of the Bush biographer I had published. I was carrying a lot of pain and guilt for the things I had done and the things I had failed to do. I needed badly to make sense of the sacrifice that I had witnessed. In my Long Island days, I decided to give God and the Church another shot. It was a good risk that paid off immensely. I started going back to Mass again and praying for the soul of that departed, troubled, working-class writer and felon Jim Hatfield. I thought of him every time we sang the new Catholic song "We Remember."

We remember how you loved us
to your death
and still we celebrate, for you are with us here.

I started giving up alcohol and herb every spring, for the forty days of Lent. It was tough, but it got me out of my habits. It helped me get ready to someday go sober for the long haul. I went to confession and found a priest there who wasn't into making me feel any worse for the things I had done. Instead, with no judgments, he took my burden off my shoulders. I wept like a baby. I realized confession is not just a Sacrament; it's a no-cost form of therapy for the poor. I was forgiven, and I was freed from my own mental slavery. Eventually, I moved to New Mexico for a while, where the truth of God in her many forms just continued to pour out to me: A celibate, gay Catholic priest who had been kicked out of the Jesuits introduced me to Gandhi and the Catholic peace radical Father John Dear S.J. (who somehow is still in the Jesuits).

I read a lot. I studied the tarot. I got so high just by walking in the desert and saying the rosary.

I have found that a religion is like a language. You don't have to know only one language; it can be helpful to know a couple. Then you see the overlaps. These days, I go to Catholic Mass, even though I am highly critical of the cover-ups and the lies coming from the Church hierarchy. I practice Zen meditation every morning and visit a Buddhist Zendo in the Catskill Mountains.

I have found that understanding religion and false religion helps me to understand exactly what 9/11 was: a collaboration between fake Christians who used fake Muslims. It was militarists, GOP Far Right "fundamentalists," atheists, Zionists, and Leo Strauss–ian neoconservatives, and their partners, the postmodern-centrist Democrats.

The peace and liberation of truth is the last thing on their minds. Subversives and liberators, like Jesus or Buddha or Allah Himself, are strangers to them. But they know their Machiavelli cold. They teach that the appearance of religious passion is essential to accumulating power. They pretend to be spiritual, but what they are really doing is exploiting our vulnerable need for a spiritual truth. So if you have ever wondered how the GOP has been able to turn "Christianity" into a political program that is full of intolerance, violence, and hate, understand that this is a part of a calculated power-grab. It has nothing to do with the God who knows all truth and is known as all-merciful, all-compassionate, and all-loving.

The false religionists attempt to smother the light, but the light has not been smothered. Despite what they have done, there's a way to understand people's inherent need for spirituality and to work toward the community and fellowship that support it. A true understanding of what Jesus actually said, and what Buddha was actually all about, will create a whole new rebirth of positive, peaceful values in America and in the world.

It's time to connect to the ancient wisdom, the mercy of God in the Bible, the true, unedited teachings of Jesus and Buddha and modern practitioners like Martin Luther King, Jr., Gandhi, and Father John Dear. It's time to set peace and nonviolence as the new national standards for the good old U.S. of A. It's time to give the United States a new job to do. Instead of competing to win the award for "most violent," we must make better use of our gifts. We can become a country that says, *In the name of the freedom we were given, we are here to become emancipators of all people from all violence, for all time*. And there's no better way to lead than by example. There's no better way to save our wheezing U.S. economy than to stop wasting $700 billion a year on weapons and military expenses we simply do not need.

I'm not proposing this as a pie-in-the-sky goal. Rather, if you simply read the Bible, read some Gandhi, or read the U.S. Constitution, you see that it's about time. Nonviolence is not some impossible dream; it's the minimum expectation that the higher power has for us. It's the simple, rough-hewn door made for us to walk through as a people.

The first step is to admit that we are addicted to death. We have to admit we are vulnerable, far from perfect. That we need the higher power of all truth, all mercy. We all have to park our egos outside and admit that we all have a damaged worldview and that we all need to come together, from various backgrounds, and listen to and learn from each other. We can bring out the truth that we were born for, the light that we are made of.

This is the beginning of a path to spiritual sobriety.

I want to start something called the Truth Party. But instead of an old-fashioned, top-down, hierarchical "spider"-like organization, I want this to be a "starfish."

(As we go, I will mention a book called *The Starfish and the Spider*. It talks about the unstoppable power of leaderless organizations that don't use a hierarchy. Instead, a culture of shared values is written on their own hearts. You don't need authoritarian power when everyone is guided by the organization's norms.) So, in this section, I will talk about something I have started to convene: It's called the Truth Gathering.

"Truth Gathering" is a funny phrase, because it can mean two things: a gathering of the truth into one place, or a gathering (like a get-together) done in the name of "truth." I am not out to start a new religion, but the lessons from history about how we people have sought out the divine, the truth, through community are too important to ignore. A shared sense of purpose makes a group become so alive, it becomes animated by a spirit, it grows, it becomes unstoppable.

In "Bad to Worse," "New York Stories," and "Among the Living and the Dead," we saw some pretty gruesome, isolating situations. Some people get into 9/11 Truth, and the darkness they look into starts to really look into them. What I have found is that 9/11 Truth is just a portal, a special kind of black hole that has transported me to a whole other world. It's a world where the revolutionaries know how to talk to the religious, and vice versa. Where spiritual struggles and political debates are lovers. Where justice and peace kiss, and kiss hard, with passion.

Our days of wallowing in "Bad to Worse" are over; we are in a whole new world now, and it's right here, right now. Welcome to the Truth Gathering.

GATHERING TRUTH

American politics is like a schizophrenic coquette, teasing the American people with promises of love and great sex and serious commitment. But she systematically and consistently delivers none of these.

We are seduced by the slick marketing machine that created President Obama, then disappointed by his militarist centrism. Liberals feel betrayed by his expansion of war and torture, and then wonder why his opposition surges at the midterms.

American politics seems locked in a pattern in which two parties stand mostly just to negate each other, passionate about nothing so much as the other's annihilation. Yet when you step outside their drama, you see that their economic and foreign policies are almost identical. The loud rivalry is all sound and fury, signifying about as much as a feud between two egomaniacal celebrities.

Who will break the pattern?

What ideas and practices are compelling enough to break us all out of this seductive trance?

The answer is a new politics that addresses the whole body politic. A comprehensive politics that is spiritual, one that understands history. A spirit that understands the unique nature of the United States, that has empathy for both Right and Left, without being limited by either.

In August 2010, I had had enough. I picked up on patterns I had observed in the Truth Movement and invited the world to take it to the next level. I started something called the Truth Gathering, an informal conference to found the Truth Party. I wanted us to do something practical around peace and truth.

There are elements within the U.S. Constitution that directly support what the Truth Movement has been trying to do: the First Amendment's support for the free flow of information, the handling of the question of treason. It turns out the most radical thing to do is also the most traditional thing to do. The revolution that we need is actually very similar to the path of enlightenment and freedom that the founders of the United States originally chartered us with.

The Truth Gathering was a lot of fun. We had lefties and constitutional conservatives. We had Christians and postmodernists. We lived and ate together in a house in the Catskill Mountains. A bunch of people were spooked about Cass Sunstein's scheme to "infiltrate" and "disrupt" the 9/11 Truth Movement. And, ironically enough, we had a guy who had known and admired Sunstein through his work on "crowdsourcing," and on how the Internet can make knowledge more democratic (as long as that knowledge is not 9/11 Truth).

We were only around sixty people. And yet we all came away inspired, fired up. We saw something. We saw a future.

The New York Times blogger Dr. Stanley Fish noted how happy and united everyone seemed. He wrote a blog entry about the event that started out cynically, like most mainstream reporting on the Truth Movement. But eventually, this writer had to recognize that in his own life he was surrounded by "Truthers."

I got up to the Catskills early and did four days of constant, mantralike promotion of the Truth Gathering. The experience of marketing the event in small towns like Roscoe and Livingston Manor provided new insights.

In a bar in Liberty, New York, I was able to connect with a soldier who had just done three tours in Afghanistan. The right-wing bouncer set us up, thinking I would get my ass kicked. Instead, I thanked the vet for risking his butt over there. Then I told him I was doing the same thing here at home. I told him I, too, love the Bill of Rights, and that I needed his help now, in this police state that rules through shock and awe. We had a nice talk.

I wish I had had more time with him—I would have asked him if the promises of the U.S. military have measured up to the reality. I would have asked him to volunteer his time to help with the counter-recruitment movement. (I thought of that guy when I read the kick-ass book by a veteran and lefty activist called *Army of None: Strategies to Counter Military Recruitment, End War, and Build a Better World* (Seven Stories, 2007).)

To soldiers and strangers alike, I consistently got good responses when I told people the gathering was all about "peace activism through 9/11 Truth." On the streets, with my arms full of postcards for the Truth Gathering, I had this moment of insight: There's something *there* in the slogan "peace through truth." What is the deeper reality that it points to?

It's this: If the U.S. government system can go to war only through an artificial event, then this leads to a startling conclusion. *The days of war itself are numbered.*

If only a highly charged emotional stimulus will get us to permit war, then that means war is naturally fake. The masters of war show us this themselves. They make their own business obsolete. They dig their own graves.

What is the future of the United States as a political influence on the world? Are we here on this planet to brutally display the same old enforcement of bloody empire? Look at American history a certain way, and you'll see that we were not meant to become a new empire in the wake of the British empire; we were rebels *against* that empire. We were not meant to become a new Roman empire; we were founded by deists and Protestants, who were into the Enlightenment rebellion against the control of information, just like Jesus was a rebel against the mental control of the Pharisees. The United States is not meant to be an *empire*. We are an original creation. We have not yet become a fraction of what we are chartered to be. Do you hear that? It's the Spirit of Truth, telling us to go higher.

In L.A., talking to fellow activist-author Daniel Pinchbeck, I asked him what he thought about 9/11 Truth activism: "9/11 is a black hole," he said.

Now, this can be true.

9/11 Truth is only good as a path to go *through* the black hole. It's important to have the courage to confront the truth about the darkest evil of our day. The weakness of American culture is that we are raised on a diet of very little substance. We are not raised to respect truth.

But if we go to the opposite extreme, into the facts of 9/11 Truth, only to stew here as an obsession, we risk stagnating in the "black hole." (And in ten years, I have noticed that people who *obsess* about 9/11 Truth exclusively don't last.) How can we come back out into a place of light, of peacemaking, of understanding?

The idea behind the First Amendment is that it is better to let a free flow of information exist, so that the reason and light within us all are the supreme authority. There is something very Zen about detaching from the authoritarian tendency to control truth. (Which itself reminds me of something I hear around AA meetings: *Live life on life's terms.*) The spirit of the First Amendment runs contrary to zealots who won't listen. You can't allow yourself to be obsessed, to cling to your paradigm of reality. Let the truth about things exist, despite what you want to think is true. The spirit of the First Amendment is like Zen: It asks you to slow down, breathe, listen, become more aware of what is real.

Communism is dead, thank God. That dry, authoritarian system couldn't last against the truth and freedom that are at the core of human need. Unfortunately, there isn't too much truth or freedom at the core of our modern crony-capitalist system, either.

So, in order to build up more Truth Gatherings, in this final section of *Slingshot*, we will discuss how to build the Truth Party and Truth Gatherings. But first, we will discuss why. We will meet the real Mahatma Gandhi, the real Jesus, and a few Zen masters. We will mix, chill, and serve. We will discover that the radical things I am proposing can happen only in the radical truth machine that the United States was built to be.

We're not there yet. But we're headed there. When you read this stuff, you eventually realize that there's no other place for us to go.

20 TRUTH FORCE IS THE FUTURE: MEET MAHATMA GANDHI

I remember one night in the '80s, at a crowded punk show in the huge basement of a church in Washington, D.C., before Fugazi played, the band's pal Tomas Squip took the stage. He wore a floppy straw hat and seemed to be floating on a wave of bliss. His short speech ended with an exhortation: "I want everyone here to promise to go out and read a book of Gandhi." The command was a bit vague, so I ignored it for fifteen years. But then one day in New Mexico, I read the Jesuit peace activist John Dear's new collection of the essential Gandhi wisdom. I understand why Father Dear thinks Gandhi is a saint, and why Tomas Squip believed Gandhi had something to teach a gang of anarchists, progressives, and punks.

Gandhi was in the streets in a wildly open way, like an antiglobalization activist. Among his tactics was the graphic, public destruction of private property. Dear's book shows Gandhi was an antiracist, anticapitalist, anti-imperialist die-hard who gave his life to the cause. For us today, Gandhi left behind a set of new tactics that could revolutionize the international Left. Not enough of today's anarchists, progressives, and punks have read him. Ironically enough, a book by a Jesuit priest who has done six months' hard time for banging on an F-16 with a hammer could change all that.

John Dear read all ninety-eight volumes of Gandhi's *Collected Works* and condensed the best into a little paperback with the power to change the world. While reading it, I woke up earlier every morning, with Gandhi on the mind. I burned to get back into this man's "greatest hits." Reading Gandhi feels like a distinct step closer to enlightenment.

Before *Essential Writings*, I thought of nonviolence as a negative concept. As for most of the Left, nonviolence meant a cold blanket on my romantic vision of direct action and revolutionary swagger. But after *Essential Writings*, my worldview has shifted completely. Nonviolence is a rich, dynamic, supple living idea, and might be the most potent threat to the system. Before *Essential Writings*, I assumed anyone in the antifascist or antiwar struggle who espoused nonviolence just wasn't comfortable fist-fighting Nazi skinheads or cops. I assumed the non-violent harbored a sense of prissy, ultra-leftist superiority over the blows and slaps of daily life. But Gandhi spoke out against cowards and condemned the fear that compels some to flee confrontation. To expand our revolutionary arsenal, Gandhi instructs us, we must use the human emotions of our opposition, suffering in the face of our oppressors so that we "melt their hearts."

To Gandhi, prayer and spirituality are peace tools, essential forms of discipline for revolutionaries, "soul" in a world where simple mental focus is itself elusive. Gandhi redefined God not as a harsh father figure who tells us to bomb the Arabs, but as truth itself.

In an age in which the Left finds itself on the defensive in a U.S.-dominated globe, without heroes, goals, or popular leadership, Gandhi points to a way forward. The old Left sought the militant seizure of the state in order to develop a new state in the interests of the people. The fine print was that the workers' paradise would by its nature have to be fiercely defended against counter-revolution from the deposed fat cats.

Gandhi points out a superior alternative: Rather than spending energy fighting, killing, and imprisoning your opponents, wouldn't it be more efficient to appeal to their emotions, melt their hearts, have them join you? If your cause is good enough, don't you trust the truth of it?

This is not idle theory; these are practices that have born fruit in real-world applications. As John Dear points out, Gandhi and his movement used these living, life-giving ideas to change the world. They won the liberation of India without the autocratic tyranny of Stalin or Pol Pot. And if the conversion of opponents seems impossible today, look at an example from Dear's book. When Gandhi was fighting racism in South Africa, in his first twenty years as an activist, the aptly named viceroy General Smuts was Gandhi's harshest critic in the media and courts. But after several years of persistent practice, consistent sacrifice, and intense prayer, Gandhi won General Smuts over to the anticolonial cause. Smuts influenced others in the ruling-class establishment when he became Gandhi's biggest supporter.

TRUTH-FORCE

Whenever English didn't serve Gandhi's ideas, he turned to his original Sanskrit. His philosophy on nonviolence in practice, *satyagraha*, translates literally as "truth-force" or "soul-force." John Dear calls it "a holy strategy for social and political revolution and widespread social change." The English word "nonviolence" carries a weakness by sounding inherently negative, but *satyagraha*, or truth-force, is a positive term.

Dear's definition is worth meditating on: "a holy strategy for social *and* political revolution." Political revolution is only half the solution; what about the social? As Marx himself said, if the mandatory social ethic of greed isn't purged, the revolution has won nothing. (He pointed out that human nature was defined as capitalistic, of course, by the capitalists.) Only in combining political *and* social transformation is there real hope for change.

Gandhi goes even further. If internal change in people is necessary, then a new spiritual practice must be part of the revolutionary program. Prayer, to Gandhi, wasn't blind supplication to an unknown entity; it was the only thing that kept him from becoming a lunatic after what he had been through. Gandhi's life mission was to "see God face-to-face." Gandhi's desire is an extreme, radical, high-risk spirituality for a world that has grown beyond some of Moses's ancient tribal prejudices and instead glows in terror from economic meltdown, out-of-control wars, environmental catastrophes, and a lack of moral leadership.

"Seeing God face-to-face" was possible for Gandhi through persistent visualization and silencing the mind and all its chatty, worldly desires. With a nod to Buddhism, Gandhi discovered that the glib monkey-mind caused suffering through its attraction to idols and illusion. Among the idols are violence and revenge. If God is truth and violence just breeds more violence, then "seeing God face-to-face" demands renouncing that which is repetitive, noncreative, sadistic, unthinking, and brutal. Gandhi once told a young labor activist that even if the professed "ends" are social justice, the means must also be just. Why? "It's questionable whether there is an end."

Maybe it's time for the Left to stop blaming the fall of the Soviet Union/Iron Curtain on flaws in ideology and admit that political violence promises an end that never comes. Political violence means you need violence to stay in power. Political violence makes you as tyrannical and ugly as the lies of the Bush and Obama administrations.

Out of *satyagraha* flowed Gandhi's other commitments. Among the fourteen vows at his first commune, or ashram, were the vows of "fearlessness" and *swadeshi*. The first vow speaks volumes about our modern paranoia—without fear, many people in the modern world would have to start using their other emotions. The vow of *swadeshi* was a promise to never use any clothing or consume any product that had been made by exploited labor. This sets the bar high for North American consumers living on the products of globalized sweatshops. No wonder Gandhi never won the Nobel Peace Prize.

Another vow of *satyagraha* was a commitment to not be married to outcomes. The Heart of Wisdom sutra at the heart of Zen teaches us to let go of our clinging to "The Goal." We can't control the future. Gandhi said that our universal task is to just engage in experiments in peace and truth. He led by example.

Our role is to engage in a loving confrontation of racism and war through truth-force. Trust your higher power to take care of the results. The truth will take care of the future. The events of Gandhi's life proved that. A man who never sought political office became one of our most lasting international political influences.

LIVING THE LIFE

After being thrown out of a whites-only section of a train in 1893, Gandhi spent twenty-three years in South Africa, starting newspapers and communes, developing truth-force theory and refining it in practice. At the time, South Africa was intent on degrading its Indian population through mandatory fingerprinting, ID cards, and threat of deportation (eerily similar to the recent detention of Muslims post-9/11).[58] After he helped win the Indian Relief Act from the South African government in 1915, Gandhi returned home to India.

At first, Gandhi's homeland saw him as a potential revolutionary messiah from the bootheel of foreign occupation. Gandhi was well known as an antiracist activist who blended the religious and political consciousness of his native people. "Anyone who thinks religion is apolitical doesn't understand religion," he said. His first major blow against British imperialism was both economic and spiritual. In protest of the Rowalt Acts, which had suspended civil liberties during wartime and kept them suspended after the war, Gandhi called a *hartal*, or general strike in 1919. He called on the entire country not to go into work for one day, and asked people instead to spend the strike fasting, praying, and purifying themselves. The British responded the only way they knew: Troops opened fire on peaceful protestors boxed in at the stadium at Amritsar, mowing down men, women, and children. In total, 379 were killed and another 1,200 were wounded.

After Amritsar, it was not all peace and love. In retaliation, revolutionary Indian nationalists stormed a British police station, killing twenty-one officers. In response, Gandhi suspended the entire anti-occupation movement, a move his fellow activists found extreme. Gandhi wouldn't let the cause degenerate into a gun battle. According to their own investigation, the British at Amritsar would have used a powerful machine gun on the protestors if it had fit through the stadium gate. Nonviolence made sense to the Indian cause on multiple levels, especially because the British outmatched the Indians militarily. Gandhi needed something bigger than machine guns.

The struggle in India expanded with Gandhi's 1922 arrest for "sedition." In his famous courtroom speech, he challenged the judge to either fully exonerate him and admit that the colonial laws were unjust or to pass full sentence on him. This act later inadvertently brought world attention to the criminality of the laws themselves, when the judge gave Gandhi six years.

Before he was led away, Gandhi made a speech. It electrified the nation. "Noncooperation with evil is as much a duty as cooperation with good." There was no longer any middle ground. Gandhi condemned the mild toleration of colonial oppression. The nation of India heard the call.

Gandhi submitted "cheerfully" when the judge sentenced him to six years of breaking rocks in the hot sun. He taught his community to go to prison and remain there with joy—the state can jail the body, but never the soul. Truth-force and nonviolence were spreading across India and shaking the foundations of British colonialism. The masses were beginning to realize that nonviolence isn't *less* radical, less virtuous, or less effective than violence—it's actually *more* potent. It makes the revolutionary more powerful, more of a full human being. Gandhian spirituality is about a new path to the Absolute; it grants self-knowledge, knowledge of "God," knowledge of the full emotional human being. To Gandhi, truth-force wasn't about "meek submission to the will of the evil-doer, but [about] . . . pitting one's whole soul against the will of the tyrant."

Gandhi continued to thrive on blending spiritual revolution with economic resistance. In 1930, when the British imposed laws protecting their own salt companies and taxing local Indian salt, Gandhi led a march across 240 miles to the salt mines at Dandhi. The British met the marchers and beat them with steel rods. Although they crushed skulls and killed activists, the people did not fight back. When the clash was reported in the media, the truth went viral. The British looked like thugs.

Worldwide opinion shifted.

British imperialism in India saw its days were numbered. The salt tax was repealed in 1931, and all political prisoners were freed. Gandhi was invited to London for a round-table negotiation but was promptly arrested upon his return home. In 1947, when the UK finally did yank up stakes and leave, it was not an unmitigated victory for India. At that moment, Gandhi and the country were swept up in the ethnic strife between Hindus and Muslims as the continent was gradually partitioned. East and West Pakistan twenty years later became Pakistan and Bangladesh.

World War II was the last nail in the coffin of UK imperialism. Gandhi devotee Thomas Merton once said, "If we fight Hitler, we will become Hitler." The UK proved this true, since it joined partially in Hitler's defeat: The war crippled London financially and contributed to the end of the British empire. In the United States, dropping atomic bombs on Japanese civilians paved the way for the "American century," an era of U.S. militarism and empire building that Hitler could have only dreamed of. The "big lie" that Goebbels talked about at Hitler's propaganda office became the "big lie" of 9/11, as fomented by the CIA and U.S. corporate media. Gandhi once said that the difference between fascism and militarism is only a matter of degree.

Back in India, one million died in the ethnic/religious strife as the land and social fabric were ripped apart. At age seventy-eight, Gandhi walked barefoot to forty-nine Muslim villages in Noakhali, the poorest and most remote backwater. At the height of potential civil war, in 1947, Gandhi steered the country away from further violence by undertaking a seventy-three-hour fast. Hindu and Muslim leaders rushed to the negotiating table to avoid causing the death of India's most beloved spiritual leader.

When Gandhi was assassinated, he left this world with God's name on his lips. God to him meant big ideas like truth, love, and truth-force. God meant immediate engagement in social struggles. If we find God elusive today, maybe it's because we lack the faith to even conceive of the big ideas that Gandhi loved. They led him, like they call us, into the most important questions of our time.

GANDHI: RADICAL AMONG THE ANARCHISTS

I'm struck by the similarities between Mohandas Gandhi and today's direct-action, consensus-based, radical democratic politics. At the height of his influence, masses of two hundred thousand would gather to watch Gandhi burn huge piles of British clothing. A stadium-size, Dada-esque performance event, Gandhi's act was an artful expression of his vow of *swadeshi*.

To awaken consciousness about exploited sweatshop labor, Gandhi smashed the mystique that surrounds private property in a capitalist culture. It's comparable to the anticorporate globalization protestors who take a swipe at corporate greed by smashing the window of a Starbucks, McDonald's, or bank. The mainstream media will tut-tut and falsely describe this kind of thing as "violence." But Gandhi never used violence. Of course, he did destroy private property on occasion. But then, Jesus did the same thing at the clearing of the temple.

A reporter once asked Gandhi to summarize his message in three words or fewer. Gandhi cheerfully obliged: "Renounce and enjoy." Gandhi had the radical view of capitalism that not only does it keep most people in low-paying, spiritually dead jobs, but socially it also creates layers of false needs: bright, clean fears; colorful addictions; empty, unsatisfying desires. It's an unhappiness that stems from an inherent lack of meaning. It's a hunger that stems from not getting paid enough to live on. Once you renounce all of it, you are on the road to being able to enjoy true happiness. But "happiness" seems too light a word to describe the fulfillment and satisfaction that Gandhi lived. "Enlightenment" is more like it. But was Gandhi special? He always claimed to be of just average intelligence. "Truth and nonviolence are as old as the hills," he was fond of saying. He claimed his life was only a series of "experiments" in truth-force and social organization.

When I mention "anarchism," it should go without saying that there is bad anarchism and good anarchism, as with any system of praxis. One good thing I learned in the ISO is the Left's critique of anarchism: There is ultra-leftist posturing, the product of a naive lust for radical chic. But what the ISO never really got is that there are also anarchists and red anarchists who lead by example, who live lives so committed to abandoning the capitalist matrix that they inspire masses of others. Gandhi was in this tradition, that of Thoreau, Emma Goldman, even a little bit like Eugene Debs (all of whom did hard time under repressive U.S. regimes).

With Gandhi, the "anarchist" label isn't totally accurate. There are times when Gandhi's life is more of a challenge to anarchists than a comparison. First, there is the hurdle of spirituality. All too many modern radicals fall into the postmodern trap of relativism: Truth is just a story, a "master narrative," and history itself is "subjective." Gandhi would argue that this is just an academic conceit. Truth and peace are relevant and real when you are being bombed by the U.S. military.

What's most radical about Gandhi is that he offered people the option of renouncing false needs through a new form of pan-religious spiritual discipline. The swift effect of the *hartal* showed that it was a gift gladly received. Then Gandhi went further. The vows he developed with his friends at their communal farms are what amount to a philosophical system.

Gandhi presents a way of seeing every human as intelligent, sensitive, capable of change.

Gandhi's legacy impacted the United States fifteen years after his death by gunshot. The reverend Dr. Martin Luther King read about truth-force and experienced an epiphany. Up until that point, King had seen Christianity through the lens of capitalist individualism; he thought that the New Testament was a lesson in individual behavior. But, after reading Gandhi, King wrote, "It was in this Gandhian emphasis on love and nonviolence that I discovered the method for social reform that I had been seeking. I came to feel that this was the only morally and practically sound method open to oppressed people in their struggle for freedom."[59]

In his introduction, Fr. John Dear points out that Gandhi could have been the first president of India, but he shied away from the corrupting influence of high office. "Have nothing to do with power" was the newest vow he told a reporter, right before his assassination. He was more effective in the streets, anyway. His critique of power is linked to his critique of capitalism. "The economic war is no better than armed conflict . . . economic war is like prolonged torture," he wrote in 1926. So, then, how to reconcile the need to move society beyond the economic war that is capitalism, without seizing power?

SPIRITUAL WISDOM FOR POLITICAL TIMES

Gandhi's definition of spirituality involves an accessible, clear, open system that even atheists can use. He makes no demands in terms of dogma, because his system isn't Christian, Hindu, or even "Gandhian." To the

Mahatma, all established religions are valid because at the heart of them lives the truth-force *satyagraha*.

We see this bottom-up, egalitarian legacy in vibrant grassroots organizations today, like the compassionate communication movement, or even Alcoholics Anonymous, which uses spiritual truths, without dogma, to address a spiritual need.

In these times, when the U.S. nation-state fishtails in a state of confusion, roiled by a culture of militarism and unbridled corporate avarice, our opinions and perceptions are managed by a complicit, corporate media. It's becoming obvious that Gandhi was onto something. The truth is something we should all respect. It's the bitterest enemy of political corruption and the number one tool for revolutionaries. It's the reason so many radicals get involved in alternative media. It's where anarchists agree with Maoists, it's where liberals agree with conservatives—public opinion is something created.

To Gandhi, *satyagraha* involved "fighting untruth with truthful means." War can't exist without the managed spectacles and opinions of the big-business media. The question becomes, how do we make our lives into a kind of truth that is naturally stronger than these institutions' "untruth"?

Gandhi's answer is to live and work communally in a place that combines economic justice and spiritual truth. He calls on new revolutionaries to subject themselves to constant self-purification. Gandhi's religion was experiential; his spirituality today is confrontational and transformative. John Dear called Gandhi's system a "foolproof method" because faith in the humanity of a political opponent naturally leads you inside his or her heart, to melt it. Spirituality to Gandhi is the process of becoming "fully human."

Before I read Gandhi, in August 2003, I went to Washington, D.C., for a direct, violent confrontation with the National Alliance and neo-Nazi skinheads. When a few of us had the opportunity to fight them face-to-face, we took it gladly. I won't pretend I didn't enjoy the hell out of it. But what was the long-term effect? In the end, I think it just made things worse. I hit them, I wrote about it, and neo-Nazi websites urged people to beat people up at my band's next show.

Did fighting the National Alliance change any of them? And by fighting them were we assuming, falsely, that they were beyond redemption? Isn't that a cop-out? A bicycle activist I know wished that we could have "showered them with love" instead. I'm beginning to realize that trying something like that would have been the bigger challenge. That would have been artful. It would have been much more "punk rock." In the long run, it would have been more successful.

Most people don't know that Gandhi loved Jesus and loved what he said. The root of all religions is peace, and the best expression of that to Gandhi was Jesus Christ's Sermon on the Mount. Christ here called on the world to forsake revenge and abandon hypocrisy and public displays of piety (and public displays of antifascist bravado, for that matter).

These simple, classic teachings have been abandoned by the superficial fundamentalism that plagues our time, as it plagued the time of Christ. "The meek will inherit the land . . . love your enemies . . . You have heard that it was said, 'An eye for an eye and a tooth for a tooth.' But I say to you . . . When someone strikes you on your right cheek, turn the other one to him as well."[60] Gandhi said this was the ultimate expression of truth-force and nonviolence, even better than the *Bhagavad-Gita* of his native Hinduism.

During his administration, President Bush claimed that God told him to attack Saddam Hussein. I'm reminded of the time Gandhi said, "The only people who don't understand the nonviolence of Jesus Christ are Christians." Rather than starting a new religion (which would have been a sectarian, fractious process in this analytical and skeptical age), Gandhi simply asked us to start living out the creeds of the religions we already have.

But as I will show in the next chapter, Christianity has grown talented at ignoring the historical truths about who Jesus was and what he said. And when Christianity divorces itself from Jesus's nonviolence, it's not worthy of even being called Christianity.

Gandhi's spiritual system can almost be described as a spiritual form of grassroots anarchy. If "God's will" revealed throughout the world's religions is peace, then the way to keep this in mind is constant prayer and meditation. If it's true that "God is in everyone," as Gandhi said, then by this logic, to learn "God's will," we simply have to quietly search for it and find it among the best parts of our individual and collective will.

"The purpose is within yourself," as Fugazi's Ian MacKaye once sang (in an earlier, great band, Embrace). "God's will" doesn't mean docile supplication; it doesn't ask us to become passive drones to an authoritarian system. God's will is a revolution of peace. "*Satyagraha* is both easy and difficult," said Gandhi. Easy to know, but hard to do. "The world has no other really effective remedy to offer."

Gandhi is a doorway to a new arsenal of revolutionary tools, more powerful than nuclear bombs. Truth-force makes us undefeatable. With truth-force, we the people can go straight through solid steel.

21 JESUS TRUTH

*"Lies make people weak. To live a life based on
the truth makes people strong."*
—Daisaku Ikeda, president, SGI

GOD FOR ALL: GOD-LOVE FOR ATHEISTS AND THE RELIGIOUS ALIKE

When you seek the truth about the historical Jesus, you realize that the full story is something the world hoards selfishly. Power is based on secrets. We saw this with the 9/11 cover-up, and it's the same with the Jesus cover-up.

But the truth about Jesus is a rich, life-giving place. Jesus is the ultimate subversive, a rebel of great intelligence and wisdom. Jesus's philosophy of action transforms people from selfish creatures into generous, sensitive ones. At their best, his practices are viral, spreading from person to person, turning us from selfishness and violence to empathy, peace, and happiness.

To really understand Jesus, you have to dig. You have to embrace the full historical spectrum: Jesus's lost years, his nature as a traveling prophet on the road in India, in Asia, in Egypt. We see in his words that this guy not only had the Old Testament down cold but also was influenced by something else. Several somethings, in fact: His teachings bear the mark of Buddhism, Gnosticism, Zoroastrianism, the Essenes, etc. According to Muslim historians, Jesus was called "the traveling prophet." He got around. He was the original multicultural mixer. His message of compassion is simple, and yet it's easily disfigured by the world.

Jesus was a revolutionary who transformed the definition of God. In the Old Testament, God was a warrior, a jealous father figure who was capable of such rage as to wipe out all life on the planet with a flood. When the prophet Elisha was teased by young boys for being bald, God sent wild bears that popped up and ate the kids on the spot. No one questions this violent God of revenge in the Old Testament. God is like a wild bear.

Jesus came to show us another side of God. He came to elevate God out of human violence. He wasn't here to put himself up on a pedestal as "the son of God." He came to say that we are *all* the daughters and sons of God.

Jesus is the jewel of history, a fulcrum between ancient and Western history. As with a prism, when the subject of Jesus is held up to the light, one sees many different angles, and light itself is broken into a prism of rich primary colors.

JESUS AS ANARCHIST

Jesus was not a "king" or a worldly leader. In fact, he was the opposite; instead of an object of worship, instead of a man of power, he was a man of empowerment, giving power, empowering. His magic was free magic.

Let's look at another teaching of Jesus's from the Synoptic Gospel of Mark:

> *You know that the rulers in this world lord it over their people, and officials flaunt their authority over those under them. But among you it will be different. Whoever wants to be a leader among you must be your servant, and whoever wants to be first among you must be the slave of everyone else. For even the Son of Man came not to be served but to serve others and to give his life as a ransom for many.*
> *(Mark 10:42–45)*

Politically, the closest Jesus gets to a modern description is that of a nonviolent, spiritual anarchist. I say this because there have been some terrible misunderstandings about Jesus in the past two thousand years. He has been called Christ the King, and the Catholic Church even created a special feast day to celebrate this moniker.

It's a name the working-class peasant carpenter Jesus would wince at. Jesus never declared himself a king. In Mark, we see he teaches that hoarding power, politically or spiritually, is a distinct step away from God.

Remember that Gandhi, under the influence of Jesus's Sermon on the Mount, said, "Have nothing to do with power."

Jesus suffered under the brittle sneering power of the Pharisees, the Judaic religious authorities. This is how he described them:

> *Everything they do is done for men to see: They make their phylacteries wide and the tassels on their garments long; They love the place of honor at banquets and the most important seats in the synagogues; They love to be greeted in the marketplaces and to have men call them "Rabbi." But you are not to be called "Rabbi," for you have only one Master and you are all brothers.*

Call no one "Rabbi." No one had supreme authority over another. Jesus said the only supreme authority was God. And God is alive in each of our hearts, a divine spark. We are talking about the ironic fact that what makes us most human is also what makes us divine. We're talking about the inner light inside us all, the star between our eyes.

Jesus was consistently a rebel against church corruption. Then, as today, for every good rabbi, priest, or minister in the Church, there are nine fakes, nine hypocrites, nine closeted Catholic pedophiles smothering the light of the one.

The Catholic Church bases its authority on some flimsy assertions. But at no point in the Bible does Jesus clearly start a church. He rather seems constantly restless, always traveling. At no point does he feel like he's done enough. The Church cites as its moment of conception a single conversation Jesus had with with Peter: "Peter, do you love me . . . if you love me, feed my sheep." But "feed my sheep" can be interpreted any number of ways. Jesus never made it clear whether he was out to reform Judaism or start a whole new religion. Some Buddhists point out that the answer is likely neither. Jesus (like Buddha) in essence said, *Here are some practices, they work for me, try them for yourself.*

Peter's interpretation of "feed my sheep" was to appoint himself the first pope. The giant, private-property-owning, political powerhouse that is the Catholic Church is often the kind of thing Jesus opposed by resisting the Pharisees. At its worst, sometimes it seems the Catholic Church shows that hierarchy and authoritarianism drive the spirit out of an institution.

Look at the fact that in the pedophilia scandals of the past twenty years, the Church's first concern has been to hide the truth, rather than "confess" and ask the world's forgiveness. Where is their faith? Why don't they do what Jesus would do? What Jesus would call for is a rigorous honesty, a community of forgiveness and understanding. It's like the Catholic Church doesn't believe in that anymore.

What really *was* this Holy Spirit that Jesus seems to have called into existence? In the fifth chapter of Luke, Jesus does this radical thing in the temple, by reading from the Book of the Prophet Isaiah, "The Spirit of God is upon me . . . to announce a time acceptable to God, a time of Jubilee, when all slaves are freed and all debts are forgiven." Then he says that the prophecy there is fulfilled right now in him. Such a controversial move, the crowd rioted and was about to stone this rude carpenter for blasphemy. But Jesus slipped away through the crowd, like a wily anarchist hiding his face and dissolving back into the group.

Jesus was a life lived by example, a life of direct action. He was "religion" in its true sense: *re*setting the *lig*ament of the divine, reinforcing that bond through constant spiritual seeking, a life of intimate prayer and self-examination, a cycle of retreat, meditation, and direct engagement against the injustices of the day. Expanding your compassion for others means developing a deeper political commitment to justice.

When Jesus meets the Samaritan woman at the well, he says, "There's a time coming, and it's here now, when we will worship not at this well, or in the Temple at Jerusalem, but in Spirit and *in truth*." So, the Holy Spirit was a practice—not so much a person as a procedure.

JESUS WAS A TRUTHER

Jesus loved the truth. He came to get us closer to the truth. He taught us to hold the truth close to our hearts, with tender care.

The Pharisees and the scribes had turned religion into a set of secrets, similar to the way the swamis of the economy today mystify a simply unjust system, or the way U.S. foreign policy is based on a complex rotten onion of 9/11 lies. But to combat all of these complex webs of anxious lies, Jesus promises a cleansing rainfall of simple truth:

> *Therefore do not fear them, for there is nothing concealed that will not be revealed, or hidden that will not be known.*[61]

In Jesus's time, religion was a cover-up. The Pharisees were so superficial, they made religion seem like a big sham.

Jesus is at the heart of 9/11 Truth. The first writer of a 9/11 Truth book was theologian David Ray Griffin, who published *The New Pearl Harbor* in 2004. Since then, Griffin has produced a miraculous number of other 9/11 Truth books, nine as of this book's publication. My favorite is *Christian Faith and the Truth About 9/11.*

In chapter seven, he exposes the lie that the United States is a "Christian nation." We are actually an empire shockingly similar to the Roman empire of two thousand years ago. We have this aloof sense of divine mandate and overwhelming military power, and we use terror and war to intimidate. Jesus's message was what Griffin calls the "anti-imperial gospel." That message didn't "resist" the oppression and idolatry of the Roman empire militarily. Instead, it subverted hate itself, universally and across history, by melting it with love. Jesus was the ultimate warrior, but one who didn't fight with weapons. He was the ultimate emancipator.

Jesus was widely read. He spoke Aramaic and Hebrew and was probably reading Greek. He was a devout Jew with ties to the Jewish radicals of his time: the Gnostics, the Zealots, and the Essenes. We learn in the New Testament that one of his Apostles was Simon the Galilean, which is shorthand for "Simon the Zealot." That means Jesus didn't shun violent revolutionaries who wanted a militant revolution against Rome;

he sympathized with this national need. He just felt, and he knew, that he had a better revolutionary tactic to subvert the terror.

His tactic was truth-force, Gandhian *satyagraha* two thousand years before Gandhi. And here we see the influence of a Jewish cult called the Essenes.

The Essenes are very interesting and aren't studied enough by modern Christians. They lived outside the urban sophistication of Jerusalem in a desert community called Qumran. They all took a vow of nonviolence. They wore white. They grew their hair long. Sound familiar?

Anyone could join, with the lone exception of a manufacturer of weapons. War was no longer holy. War was never from God.

While we aren't sure Jesus was a full "member" of the Essenes, their influence on his philosophy (and his fashion sense) is unmistakable. Jesus's cousin, John the Baptist, was almost certainly an Essene. This is John who acted as a herald of the coming of the Messiah, and who was a lot like Jesus. He was Jesus's cousin on Jesus's mother's side. John also stood up to the corruption of the Pharisees. The missions of Jesus and John were very similar: Both battled the stasis, the sham religion, of the institutionalized Jewish establishment.

Jesus's mother, Mary, seemed to be influenced by a radical class-leveling ideology, as we see in the prayer she utters early in the Gospel of Luke:

> *He has pulled down princes from their thrones*
> *and raised high the lowly.*
> *He has filled the starving with good things*
> *sent the rich away empty*

Jesus's mom raised him right, reading him the right things. Thanks to his mom's spiritual and political insight, Jesus was on the path to do something huge with his life.

According to the New Testament, we don't really know where Jesus was from about age thirteen to age thirty. But if you look at the religions surrounding the Middle East at the time, you'll see that Jesus was likely way out there somewhere. If you study the basics of Buddhism, you'll begin to see some similarities between the teachings of Jesus and the older teachings of the Buddha. It's likely that Jesus spent his "lost years" gaining wisdom in India. Or it could be that Buddhist missionaries came to his home turf.[62]

Buddhism teaches us to not identify our selves with our minds. Our minds are full of anxiety, and they chatter like monkeys. The average Westerner can't seem to allow a thought to happen without letting an anxious emotion follow.

Jesus's Buddhist influence comes out several times, even in the mainstream Gospels: "Do not worry about your life . . . can any of you by worrying add a single hour to your span of life?"[63]

And here:

> *Therefore I tell you, do not worry about your life, what you will eat or what you will drink, or about your body, what you will wear. Is not life more than food, and the body more than clothing?*[64]

Buddhism teaches that our minds create drama. But it's just noise most of the time. We all have this Buddha nature inside us; we all have the capacity to reach enlightenment in this lifetime. Jesus may have been riffing on his and your Buddha nature when he announced that we are all sons and daughters of God.

"The Realm of God is within you."[65]

There's always been something missing in Christianity. It took Jesus's empowering nature and sucked out the righteousness and turned empowerment into just power. Western civilization turned Christianity into a power tool. The human ego ruined Christianity. But there is a practice that makes space for compassion, truth, love, and forgiveness and that also has a method of keeping in check the wild horses of the ego and mind. Calm the mind, pray, chant, call on the truth. I have found new paths to Jesus and truth through Zen and Buddhism. We'll dive in and explore this "pure land" in the next chapter.

How could this radical, empowering, anti-power-hoarding Jesus have been changed into the namesake of a church that excuses war, inequality, and oppression? The simple answer is that there has been a Jesus cover-up. Jesus's history has been distorted in the name of power.

Jesus's "empowering" nature is the opposite of Christianity's "power-hoarding" nature. This becomes most clear as we begin to study Jesus of the Gnostic Gospels. These rediscovered texts were almost obliterated from history by the nascent Catholic Church in the second and third centuries AD. In 323–325 AD, at the Council of Nicaea, much of the early Gospel was cut out, but the Spirit of History laughed at this puny attempt at human censorship. Three months after the United States's use of atomic bombs against Japan, the Spirit of History opened up the Gnostic Gospels to us in December 1945 in a cave in Egypt. It was time. Perhaps it was some wise, subversive angel who broke the seal.

Shortly after Jesus's death, there were about two hundred Gospels floating around. But at the Council of Nicaea, the Roman warrior-emperor Constantine forced Christianity to clean up its message, sanitize Jesus's biography, and turn the two hundred–plus Gospels into four. Jesus of Gnosis ("immediate knowledge") became the "Christianity" of the Roman empire. Jesus's views on gender and sexuality had to be sanitized and distorted. The Jesus of liberation became the Jesus of control.

The legend of Jesus's birth has the event first announced to shepherds as a sign that Jesus came to save regular, working people. The Nag Hammadi Library—ironically, in Egypt—was discovered by shepherd boys, who found manuscripts that had been buried almost 1,700 years ago.

My favorite text from Nag Hammadi is the Gospel of Thomas. It's a collection of revolutionary sayings attributed to Jesus. Despite what the Church tells you, it can't be dismissed as the scribblings of a heretic. This is Jesus, raw, uncut, and with scholarly documentation. About half of the scholars on the Gospel of Thomas say its authorship *predates* the Gospels of Matthew, Mark, and Luke. That means this Gospel of Thomas may have been the first Gospel.

Reading it will be eerily familiar to anyone who has read the Bible, as half of the quotations come from the "Q document," which the other Gospels also use as a source. The other half of the quotations show an anarchist, surrealist Jesus who is no friend of empire, social control, "soft clothes," or the rich.

Ever heard of "doubting Thomas"? That story is in the Bible, but in only one place: the Gospel of John, which paints the Apostle Thomas with the taint of uncertainty. Only in John's Gospel does Thomas speak at all, brashly urging the Apostles to go die with Jesus in Jerusalem, at one point. At the Last Supper, John depicts a thick Thomas ignorant of Christ's mission. John wrote his Gospel last, probably around 100 AD, and he had an axe to grind. The author of John was likely surrounded by rival "Thomasite" Christians with their incendiary, uncontrollable, sexy Gospel. John decided that Thomas had to be taken down.

It's a historical fact that the Apostle Thomas was sent to India, perhaps by Jesus himself. Thomas died there, in the Holy Land that was itself a source of some of Jesus's own spiritual education.

THE RADICAL JESUS IN THOMAS

The Gospel of Thomas itself can be read in a single sitting, the language poetic, fiery, and at times cryptic. Good books have been written on Thomas, such as Elaine Pagels's *Beyond Belief: The Secret Gospel of Thomas* and Neil Douglas-Klotz's *Hidden Gospel: Decoding the Spiritual Message of the Aramaic Jesus*. But the "interpretation" of Thomas has only begun.

In the midst of the Catholic Church's crisis of legitimacy surrounding pedophilia and its cover-up, and amid its larger crises around questions of female ordination, gender equality, power, sexuality, and misogyny, a deeper interpretation of Thomas is called for. Remember that one of the last things Jesus said, according to the Gospel of John, is that he would send us his spirit, and it would be the Spirit of Truth. It seems like the Catholic Church sure could use some of that right about now.

Reading Thomas brings out two major themes. Jesus is opposed to power, and Jesus is opposed to gender oppression. Both notions are just human constructs, and Jesus's liberation is a world beyond them. This is the Jesus of the wild, an uncontrollable Jesus, pure spirit, against power. Read Thomas, and you can see why the Church decided to suppress this Gospel for 1,700 years and counting.

Jesus warned against the intoxication of power, especially political power, and advised his followers to renounce it, like Gandhi did. That means not engaging in the domination that traditional gender roles help enforce. To make this point, Jesus engages in a "meta-parable" in which clothing is a metaphor for social control and gender. A running theme of nudity and freedom pops up in this anarchic Gospel.

Here's a great quotation from stanza twenty-one:

> *Mary said to Jesus, "What are your disciples like?"*
>
> *He said, "They are like little children living in a field that is not theirs. When the owners of the field come, they will say, 'Give us back our field.' They take off their clothes in front of them in order to give it back to them, and they return their field to them."*

Notice no great respect for the religion of private property? Emperor Constantine and the early bishops and popes must have loved that.

From stanza twenty-two:

> *Jesus saw some babies nursing. He said to his disciples, "These nursing babies are like those who enter the (Father's) kingdom."*
>
> *They said to him, "Then shall we enter the (Father's) kingdom as babies?"*
>
> *Jesus said to them, "When you make the two into one, and when you make the inner like the outer and the outer like the inner, and the upper like the lower, and when you make male and female into a single one, so that the male will not be male nor the female be female . . . then you will enter [the kingdom]."*

Wow. The exact opposite of Paul's "wives, be subject to your husbands." Jesus instead advises a step away from the part of gender that is built by society. Why? A step away from the power dynamics of the world means having a deeper curiosity about who we really are.

What are masculinity and femininity? What part is just a social construct? What part is natural? Jesus says to mix it up and make those two one. Get away from maleness or femaleness as you were taught it. Come up to something higher. Maleness does not mean violence. Femaleness does not mean submission.

"Make the two into one" is also eerily familiar to students of Zen. Zen attempts to collapse dualistic thinking. It proposes that the me/you construct is just a mental illusion.

In stanza seventy-eight, Jesus demands, "Why have you come out to the countryside? To see a reed shaken by the wind? And to see a person dressed in soft clothes, [like your] rulers and your powerful ones? They are dressed in soft clothes, and they cannot understand truth."

Later, he says, "When you strip without being ashamed, and you take your clothes and put them under your feet like little children and trample them, then [you] will see the son of the living one and you will not be afraid."

The final stanza, stanza 114, completes the theme of radical rethinking about gender. In it, Simon Peter (the first pope, according to the Catholic Church) makes one of the Church's first statements to subjugate women: "Simon Peter said to them, 'Make Mary leave us, for females don't deserve life.' Jesus said, 'Look, I will guide her to make her male, so that she too may become a living spirit resembling you males.'"

I think what he meant there was that Jesus wanted to "make her male" in the sense of making her equal. But there's something more going on here: Jesus's message is to bring "life" and make us all into the "living spirits" we were made to be. It empowers us to become more alive, blowing past the strictures and conformity of social mores, be they Jewish, Roman, or American rules.

To the Jesus of the Gospel of Thomas, gender is a lot more fluid than any of us is willing to believe, especially now, in our tough-guy, militaristic society, based on bluffing and secrets. Gender is just a part of man's rules. God has no rules. Well, not the way humans set up petty regulations and codes and classifications. God is truth. Once you work hard to remove the separations between yourself and God, then you don't need rules, because you are already living a good life.

What happens if we don't listen to this Jesus? Well, look around you. You end up with a Catholic Church that subjugates women to a second-class status. It does not allow them to enter the priesthood, has a Dark Ages attitude about gender studies, and relies on the darkest scriptural passages, about "stoning homosexuals," for advice about how to address the wide range of our God-given human sexuality.

To all the leaders of the Catholic Church, and to Christians and people everywhere, I urge you to go read the Gospel of Thomas. Go read the historical Jesus in his own words. Quit faking it. Practice the raw honesty you taught me. A Church of cover-ups will not stand.

How do I know?

I follow the real Jesus, the raw one, the radical of the First Gospel, the Gospel of Thomas.

FACE REALITY AND ANNIHILATE FANTASY: ZEN, TRUTH, AND PUNK ROCK

The Urantia Book says this about the modern Church: It often confuses the riverbed for the river. The river is the full truth about Jesus, God, and reality. The Church itself is the riverbed, and it's the riverbed that the Church seems most concerned about.

In the previous chapter, the summary lesson from all those prismatic facts is that there is so much more historical information about Jesus than the Church "authorities" are willing to deal with.

It's a classically Western problem to want to "control" truth. The lesson here is that you can't. You can't "pick and choose" what information you want about Jesus if you want to be a "religion" about truth.

The Church has not found a way to control its own tendency to give in to delusions. But there is a practice that preaches against "picking and choosing" your reality. It's called Buddhism. Like the Trappist monk Thomas Merton, I have found that Buddhism makes me a better Christian.

Christianity needs a revolution in consciousness, one path to which would be to learn about the rigor of Buddhist practice. While the Western mind adds layer and layer of detail, the Buddhist ethos is to simplify.

I am not alone in my generation in seeing the wisdom here. Part of the process of deciding to do this book was deciding that I had to break out of my spiritual shell. I had to become like a wet chickadee, to break through the membrane of the eggshell of "Christianity as I knew it" to become something more active, more new.

Today, Buddhism is enjoying a rebirth, with a new rigor coming particularly from people in punk rock. It's kind of similar to the '60s, when Zen Buddhism became popular in the West, largely through the work of its chief emissary, D. T. Suzuki. He made connections to the more spiritual parts of the counterculture.

Today in L.A., Nicherin Shoshu Buddhist (and former Hole guitarist) Eric Erlandson leads these great open-chanting sessions in his loft downtown (sometimes followed by delicious potluck vegetarian meals). Here, the Nicherin Buddhist chant "Nam Myoho Renge Kyo" is the essence of the Lotus Sutra, in which the constant musical repetition of a single phrase launches your mind into a heightened state. You meditate on the law of karma, the law of "cause and effect." You put aside anxious thoughts and tap into your internal Buddha nature.

It occurs to me that Jesus wanted to create more Jesuses. This is clearer in Buddhism: We all have a Buddha nature, we all have a Christ nature. It's just a question of calling it forth.

Buddha is not a "god" externalized outside your self. Do the work of polishing the lens of your perception to bring forth the Christ/Buddha/Light within you. Too radical? Well, isn't this what Jesus said to do? "Don't do what you hate . . . bring forth that which is within you," he says, according to the Gospel of Thomas.

Punk rocker Noah Levine has created a whole new Buddhist subculture, the Dharma Punx. His newest book is a radical take on politics: *Heart of the Revolution: The Buddha's Radical Teachings on Peace and Nonviolence.* I like this guy a lot. He is clear. What he says about the original Buddha in India could have been written about Jesus:

> *The Buddha was a revolutionary, a radical advocate for personal and social transformation. He rejected the religious forms of his time and renounced all forms of greed, hatred, and delusion. He dedicated his life to going "against the stream," to the subversive path of an outlaw transient. He wasn't afraid to speak out*

against the ignorance in this world's political, social, and religious
structures, but he did so from a place of love and kindness, from
an enlightened compassion that extended to all living beings. The
Buddha's teachings are not a philosophy or a religion; they are a
call to action, an invitation to revolution.

On the Zen side, Brad Warner's book *Hardcore Zen*, which details the author's personal journey from hardcore punk rock in Akron, Ohio, to becoming a Zen priest living in Japan, shows the rigor and process of Zen: "Zen replaces all objects of belief with one thing: reality itself."

Zen takes it to a whole new level. Zen literally is the hardcore of Buddhism. It traces its lineage back to the first Buddha, the man with many names, Shakyamuni, or Siddhartha Gautama, who lived in India around 800 BC.

Punk, as a subculture, has lasted thirty-five years. Not bad, when you compare that to the subculture of the late '60s, which fast dissolved into disco and drugs in the late '70s. Somehow, punk rock has improved the staying power of alternative cultural forces. Did punk do that by making a more hardcore commitment to certain values? By making culture more political? More practical? More spiritual? More self-critical?

Let's consider that the answer to all the above is yes.

There is something inherently Zen about punk rock. It is anarchic, but it keeps going because it's empowering. There is a Buddhist quality to the way punk rock is about ripping the blinders off your mind and embracing reality in all its sweaty detail.

In this chapter, I will attempt to continue a "Jesus" tradition—East meets West—in order to go beyond. Way beyond. I am breaking my Christianity out of its little corral. I want to jump into something lesser known, but a thing that will be historically catalyzing for social change. Gandhi showed us the massive potential of spiritual revolutionary movements. A Christian-Buddhist dialogue leads to a lively, multicultural, interfaith consciousness, where the radical-roots Jesus gets back in touch with his Easter-Buddhist influences!

Writing about Zen is itself breaking all the "rules." I am not an expert in Zen. I can't pretend I am qualified to write about it. Zen is not supposed to be about scriptures, or words, or "intellectualization." Zen is not a religion, but a practice. There are many books about Zen, and they all say it's not about books with Zen.

So I will make this personal. I will also rely on some classics.

The Zen master Yuanwu, from the Song Dynasty of China (1000 AD), wrote a collection of *Zen Letters*.[66] I have found his wisdom to be a good guide. Yuanwu promises, "Those who realize transcendence pass through words and phrases and can make them come to life."

Zen is about collapsing the dualities: subject/object, self/others, means/ends, theory/practice. Zen is a practice that puts you into direct contact with reality. It strips us of our Western tendency to deal with reality through "concepts" and is a path to the truth in itself. Martin Heidegger was once discovered in his office with a book on Zen by Suzuki. The father of modern existentialism startled his student by remarking, "If I understand this man correctly, *this is what I have been trying to say in all my writings!*" Zen says what the best minds of the Western tradition have only struggled to say.

Zen is like 9/11 Truth. It demands we vigorously forsake illusion and fantasy to practice a "turn to reality." This turn ends up ridding our minds of terror and illusion. The effect is that we become less self-centered and more compassionate.

Although I am new at it, I approach Zen with devotion. Having been raised Catholic helps, and there are many similarities between the reverence and the rituals of both faiths. Bowing to the Buddha upon entering the meditation room of the Zendo is a lot like genuflecting to the tabernacle in a Catholic church.

I feel like Zen is the modern incarnation of the Holy Spirit, the Spirit of Truth. Many of my discoveries have taken place at the Dai Bosatsu Zendo, a Zen temple on top of a mountain in the verdant Catskills. But many more discoveries have taken place in my daily Zen meditation. I sit in *zazen*, keep my eyes open, get centered on my breath. I become more awake than "awake." It has led to a change in my bones.

Christianity and Western civilization have ruined their credibility. Simply look at the current ability of the Church to ignore certain political questions, at how it views the 9/11 event, and at the wars waged in the name of 9/11. Step back and face reality here, and you'll see that the Church's position is dominated by illusion.

Let's treat this as a lesson in how reality is constructed in the Western mind. The Western reality is a collective domination of the Western ego. As we saw in the "Left Resistance" chapter, the ego clings to reality, and it only clings harder when confronted with evidence that demands a reconsideration of what is real. Evidence is not enough; a revolutionary spiritual approach is needed.

Simply sitting in silence for a half hour each morning has begun to work for me. I exhaust all my words and empty my mind. A Catholic way of looking at it would be to say that the Spirit comes to us in the silence. Instead of my life being about "I," I have steered it toward being about "eye." On the advice of a Zen teacher, I have worked on opening up a new way of seeing things, opening a third "eye" that penetrates reality more deeply.

But it's not an intellectual process. Rather, it involves slowing down. Breathing. Smiling. Being perfectly still. I imagine shaking the dust from my mind like shaking out a backpack. Reality opens up like the lotus flower. In *Zen Letters* a thousand-plus years ago, Yuanwu had an eloquent way to describe the Zen mission. He said that the practice of Zen was to "face reality and annihilate fantasy."

Yuanwu would have loved the 9/11 Truth Movement: "All those who are truly great must strive to overcome the obstacles of delusion and ignorance. They must strive to jolt the multitudes out of their complacency and to fulfill their own fundamental intent and vows. Only if you do this are you a true person of the Path, without contrived activity and without concerns, a genuine Wayfarer of great mind and great vision and great liberation."

When I reflect on "delusion and ignorance," I don't think immediately of any one tragically uneducated person. I think the greater tragedy is the unspoken consensus of "liberal" media outlets, like *Democracy Now!*, NPR, and the *Huffington Post*, all of which have clung to the idea that 9/11 is not a topic worthy of serious investigation. The taboo against looking at certain realities deprives us of the liberty and peace that are in our hearts, in our peace-loving nature.

There's the law of cause and effect again. It's instant karma, like the title of the John Lennon song. A bad cause creates a bad effect. Just as soon as someone decides to not report the truth, the world becomes instantly more inclined to support war.

OBJECTIONS TO KILLING THE INTELLECTUAL HORSE

One of my favorite Yuanwu quotes is about Zen practice:

"You should train your mind and value actual practice whole-heartedly ... Go to the spot where you meditate and kill your mental monkey and slay your intellectual horse. Make yourself like a dead tree, like a withered stump."

Weird, huh?

A dead tree? And what monkey is he talking about?

The mind is a chatterer. It just never stops yammering on, with its thoughts leading to thoughts and worries building into stress taking a physical toll on our bodies. It won't stop unless you decide that you have control over your mind, not the other way around.

Likewise, the "intellectual horse" here describes this mythical quality we give to our intellect. We think of intellect as this strong beast that will serve us, so much so that we identify our "selves" with our intellect. But there's a deeper, truer way to think of the "self."

My friend Priscilla looked at my collection of favorite Yuanwu quotes as this chapter was coming together, and she protested the line about graphically "slaying" the intellectual horse. With a punk rocker's ferocity, she said it sounded vaguely "fascist." She went on to explain, "It is the intellect that informs us and guides us toward meaningful connections to our communities, friends, and families, many of which are defined by intellectual connection. It is also our intellect that allows for analysis of social circles and interactions so that we can choose to engage with healthy practices/work/goals or not."

As I tried to argue to Priscilla, Zen is not "anti-intellectual," per se, but it also doesn't find the path to peace through intellectualism. There is a big, beautiful library up at the mountaintop Zendo—but the Zendo doesn't rely on it. The *roshi* (head) of the Zendo said to me in a letter, "Yes, Zen is not an intellectual path, yet reading is really important, and then experiencing for yourself, tasting the transformative moment for yourself, is essential."

Zen is about finding enlightenment, which is really just a new way to see the world. To find this new way to see, we go beyond Western rationality, beyond normal intellectualism.

I remember pulling out a copy of my 2005 book on 9/11 for Ten rai, a monk at the Zendo. I was yammering on about "my philosophy," and he said something to the effect of, "We don't rely on philosophy here." I wouldn't stop blathering about some point that I wanted to make about "my philosophy," so Ten rai simply walked away. At the time, I thought, *Oh, my, how rude, what a jerk, I am so insulted.* But now I realize that he did me a great service. I was centered on my own ego, my own thing at that moment, *I, Me, Myself, My Book.* And Ten rai had been trying to point out the Zen difference. He sort of tweaked my nose, but it was a pain that got me one step closer to enlightenment.

If killing the intellectual horse seems too graphic, just look at our world today. We cling to this "rationality," and it fails. We cling to solutions that also fail. Our capitalism, our socialism, our "Christianity," our "authority," have resulted in this insane world. This is all expressed perfectly in all the anxiety, the multiple wars, the 9/11 official story. Our entire society is a fortress of denial.

Zen is part of the way to find the new path. Although it's not a religion, it is an attempt to describe the essence at the core of all religions.

Yuanwu talks directly about people like Ten rai, dedicated monks of the Rinzai Zen school. Rinzai Zen believes that we can all achieve enlightenment, which Yuanwu says is just a "new viewpoint on life."

Yuanwu praised the Rinzai monks of his day. What he wrote around 1000 AD sounds almost like he's describing a great rock band playing live: "Even having the mettle to storm heaven, and upholding the truth outside conventions, even defeating people's weapons without fighting—even this does not quite resemble what the Rinzai school is getting at."

Stand for truth outside conventions. There is a truth, but it's not what we have been programmed to expect. There is a reality, and it's much bigger than our anxious clinging to our image of "reality."

Let's go back to *Hardcore Zen*'s Brad Warner. His book features this Zen take on truth:

> *Truth screams at you from billboard cigarette ads. God sings to you in Muzak versions of Barry Manilow songs. Truth announces itself when you kick away a discarded bottle of Colt 45 Malt Liquor. Truth rains on you from the sky above, and God forms in puddles at your feet. You eat God and excrete truth four hours later. Take a whiff—what a lovely fragrance truth has! Truth is reality itself. God is reality itself. Enlightenment, by the way, is reality itself.*

Later, Warner makes an important distinction between truth and the human mind:

"Truth can never be found in mere belief. Belief is restricted. Truth is boundless . . . Truth doesn't screw around and truth doesn't care about your opinions. It doesn't care if you believe in it, deny it, or ignore it."

CHANGING THE BONES: ZEN'S SOBERING EFFECTS

I felt something resonant in my marrow when I read this part of Yuanwu: "You should realize that on the crowns of the heads of the Buddhas and enlightened adepts there is a wondrous way of 'changing the bones' and transforming your existence." I was sitting on a rock across the lake from the Zendo in the Catskill Mountains. I felt something well up inside me. I wanted to shave my head and become a Zen monk immediately.

The night before, I had made one of the great discoveries for myself in my time at the Zendo. I went to an Alcoholics Anonymous (AA) meeting that happened to be taking place there. I was up during a *samu*, or volunteer work, weekend. I was repairing the sheetrock in the ceiling in the guesthouse but also doing the Zendo ritual of getting up at 4:30 AM to sit *zazen*, before a formal breakfast in silence.

I stumbled into the AA meeting that night with a vague intuition that there was something there for me to learn about. In the context of

Zen, I needed to further my mastery over my mind. I needed to learn how to get sober. I had decided that it was not very Zen of me to smoke pot and drink beer every night. It was fun sometimes, but I did not want to do it anymore. I needed a formal way out, and wasn't sure I could keep myself dry without help.

Zen had already taught me to scrape the top layers of ego off the skin of my self. Things were getting clearer to me, but there was still a problem. I was an addict. Not to a drug as much as to my own ego, my sense of importance, my grandiosity. (When I later heard that all addicts have to confront an addiction to grandiosity, I said to myself, *They can have my Purple Haze and craft IPA, but they will* never *take away my addiction to grandiosity! And show business!*)

I walked into the room, where a group of New Yorkers had gathered around a roaring fireplace. I was blown away by just how careful and loving people were with each other. They really listened to each other and supported what each person was going through.

The parallels between Zen wisdom and AA are uncanny. AA says that you can't make your process of recovery all about "me, myself, I." It can't be "self-willed." You don't have all the control you think you do. That's an illusion, and it's a dangerous one.

It pays off when you realize that addiction is a spiritual sickness, an unmet need for truth, for love, for connection to a higher power, to the love of other people. So, the essential third step in AA's twelve-step process is to recognize the existence of a higher power, however you define it, and to ask it/her/him for help. There's an uncanny mix of the secular and religious. It's heady and powerful.

Although I'm new to AA, I think there are larger political lessons for the world here.

I think one of the biggest myths in our culture is that people are friendly to you in bars. *Cheers* reruns are such bullshit—this idea that there's a bar somewhere where "everybody knows your name." Where everybody loves you. That myth is so insidious because it dangles something it knows you really want. And then it hits you in the gut. It hits you hard with its own emptiness. We go into bars looking for community and human contact, and instead we are shocked to rediscover that alcohol is a depressant. It makes people even more egocentric, violent, and suspicious than they have already been conditioned to be. No wonder the agenda of war, xenophobia, and scapegoating is so often served in our media diet, broadcast on cable news stations in bars.

That said, I love bars. I love beer and pot. But I also have a chance now to look back and see the stories I was making up and living out with those substances. I loved an "idea" of what a bar was, but I wasn't rigorously honest about what actually happened in bars.

STRAIGHT AND TRUE

Revolution literally means "the shape of a circle." It feels good to have come full circle to the branch of punk I grew up in. Straight edge was huge in D.C. and the Northeast in the '80s. It was a decentralized movement (but maybe not a "Movement," per se) inside hardcore punk. It expressed dissent against the American culture of drinking and habitual intoxication as well as the violence and cheap sex they lead to. The nonmovement's reluctant "founder," Ian MacKaye, made an interesting connection to religion. With sweeping vitriol, he extended the comparison between addiction to drugs/alcohol to religious fervor. (Despite his adamant refusal to think of straight edge as a movement, it clearly was a quite grassroots force. It was more real than he knew. It was meeting a need.)

I didn't get this either at the time, but now I see that what MacKaye was doing was quite Zen, in a way. He was protesting clinging to delusion. In the words of Gandhi, "renounce and enjoy."

We can become the people we were meant to be if we renounce our bad habits. Perhaps it's time to somehow reunify and revive straight edge as a way to blend punk rock and sobriety. Sobriety gives us so much more time for music, for realizing our creative potential, for political activism, for spiritual development, for truth and peace. AA has shown that there's a way to practice the compassion and fellowship at the heart of Christianity with none of the power and hierarchy that lead to corruption. AA was founded by people influenced by Carl Jung, who said that it's human nature to be religious. The Oxford Group, a liberal Christian group in the UK, also influenced AA's founders.

I urge anyone who is at all curious to try sobriety. But don't go it alone. Maybe you have a raging problem or maybe you have a mild one—it doesn't really matter. The blast waves of magical love you get from meetings are the same, and you can't get them from a book—you have to feel them in person. Thanks to these meetings, I haven't had any serious cravings to go back to the way I was. I used to think I couldn't give up smoking pot every day. Now, it's just not a part of my life anymore. Instead, calling my son, playing guitar, writing songs, and building the Truth Party take priority.

If you go to AA meetings, you get to see a glimpse of human beings as they really are. You see that human beings really are naturally loving, generous, and sensitive, especially when they are sober, inside this culture of mutual support. Beyond the *Cheers* myth, the magic of AA is that human fellowship is real. You feel the warmth of Jesus and the angels in the concern of other people. Jesus becomes alive. AA resurrects the dead.

The capitalist nightmare preaches that human beings are naturally egocentric, greedy, and selfish. I have always *theorized* that this is a lie, but now I can prove it. Or what I have seen in AA proves it. AA works, without hierarchy or a big centralized home office. It functions based on some very heartening facts about human nature. It calls forth the community and fellowship we seem to have been built for.

AA works against a disease and succeeds where other treatments fail. It shows that the mainstream view of "human nature" is just a delusion. It proposes a spiritual solution for a spiritual problem. It hooks up addicts with other addicts who can empathize and help. AA has grown like a grassroots vine to two million members and counting in just eighty years.

For me, AA has been revolutionary. The real experience of AA shows that what we were taught about human nature is a myth, fake and outdated, like a TV rerun. Once you discard delusion, the possibilities are infinite, both spiritually and politically.

ZEN, ANARCHISM, AND THE TRUTH PARTY

How un-Zen my mind still is, wrapped up in problems of its own creation. Is it weird that an "anarchist" is also founding a political party? I worry about this.

But I have no idea what other people may think, and it's not my problem. In all my life, my best moments are when I forget to worry about what other people think.

Anarchism is scary to some, but it needn't be. It's the best antidote to a bloated national security state. It's a vision of peace. The best way to be antiwar is to envision life without a terror state. What anarchism has historically needed is some kind of spiritual life. Zen can help.

The concept of anarchism is close to the core Zen ideas: There is no true authority outside your own truth-loving nature. Watch what you believe. Examine what you've been told.

If you work on polishing the lens to see your Buddha nature, you are the freest person you can possibly be. You are free even to start a new political party, or a new culture, or a new federation, based on simple, good ideas: a sober peace, a loving truth.

When you sit *zazen*, you free your mind. The worries get slain. The freedom and the peace flow like a river. The river was always there, always moving. You grow in compassion and deepen your connection to the universe. You realize that your concept of self is itself something you are clinging to. You let go of it a little, and dissolve into the bigger picture. By having no self, you have a bigger self, a better self. The contradiction proves the rule.

I think that Zen is the best way to understand the essence of the 9/11 Truth Movement. Remember, Zen seeks to polish our perception of the root of all religion. The Truth Movement seeks something similar: the root of all politics—the human desire to *be* freedom, to live freedom, to practice freedom.

We know now that the riverbed is not the river. Human beings have shown that constructing elaborate national security states only makes things worse. We waste our money building bombs and war machines based on a mental illusion. We have no enemies, so we create the illusion of them.

The actual reality of the national security state proves the necessity for a radical reworking of the state. The state itself shows that the most ethical thing to demand is its own dissolution. Not the dissolution of America or the Bill of Rights—in fact, that document is a step in the right direction, as we will explore some more in the next chapter.

Human beings have this tendency to make the riverbed into the river, in terms of spirituality as well. The human tendency to mix religion and power is toxic. Zen keeps it simple. I stay connected to the real Jesus of peace and truth by sitting in silence, letting him come to me.

23 A NEW KIND OF COUNTRY: USA AS TRUTH MACHINE

The United States was built to be a truth machine. We are the product of the subversive and scientific thinking that was called the Enlightenment.

For too long, I have seen it become unfashionable to point out anything positive about American history. But since Zen asks us to slow down and check what we assume to be "real," let's do that for a second here with American history itself.

It's true that this country committed crimes as it struggled to be born: the genocide of native peoples, slavery, Hiroshima, 9/11. But there's another half of the story. When I think of the United States's greatest legacy in the past one hundred years, I think of Martin Luther King, César Chávez, or Dorothy Day. The greatest advocates for social justice couldn't have existed without a free flow of information. The First Amendment creates a social context for the success of great activists. Social justice and freedom of information go hand in hand.

These peace revolutionaries are the real American heroes. King and Chávez used a kinetic form of direct-action nonviolence, based on faith, to seek justice. It's their legacy that is the future. What if we now pushed this further and used freedom and the First Amendment as a model for badly needed financial reforms?

What if love for the United States was the stimulus for this country to heroically confront its own violence?

We are not fated to rise and fall as just another bloody empire. The fate of the United States is to become number one at peaceful, enlightened conflict resolution. If the United States returned to constitutional principles, it would become the leader in "truth-force" and nonviolence.

As I stated in the opening invocation of this book, this vision is of a revolutionary change from what we are doing. But it's not a change from what we are. It will be hard work. But with mindfulness, work becomes a joy.

This is how we answer the 9/11 Commission's challenge for the United States to figure out "what it stands for." This is how we regain our moral dignity. This is how we rip ourselves off the path of torture, secrets, and war. This is how we can create something for the United States to stand for, at home and as an example to the world.

This idea is not overly ambitious. It's in our DNA. The freedom of religion clause in the First Amendment is a kind of antiwar document in itself. The interminable wars of postmedieval Europe were based largely on the miscegenation of religion in a bad romance with state power. The first words of the First Amendment abjure the United States's ability to practice any one religion. The founders were setting us on a trajectory toward peace and freedom.

A NEW KIND OF COUNTRY

At its founding, the United States was not only a new country, but also a new *kind* of country. We weren't defined by a single national, ethnic identity. America then was chartered to become committed to a certain kind of antiracist federation.

The Bill of Rights is a radical document in that it seeks to *limit state power*. It seeks to protect the people *from* the government. America is a place where radicals, peace lovers, progressives, anarchists, and libertarians should be seen to be at the center of the American spirit, not marginalized.

The problem, then as now, is that the money power in this country remains to be confronted. The Founding Fathers delayed tackling slavery and set the stage for the Civil War. They also delayed tackling what we could call banking/financial justice, a problem that is ongoing. Jefferson didn't want a central bank to control the currency and credit, and he predicted dire consequences if one was allowed to. But Hamilton and the Federalists won out and created a national bank, which began to use debt as a growth mechanism. (The idea was that it's better to have some national debt and pay interest on it because the alternative is to have inadequate capital with which to grow. Of course, too much debt cripples an economy—look around you.)

The financial-justice issue also haunted Abraham Lincoln. He had the audacity to have the federal government directly mint and print currency, another way he saved the Union in the Civil War. Today, we have a private, bank-controlled system, the Federal Reserve, through which the big banks control currency.

We have two political parties on the same side when it comes to all the key issues: war, torture, secrecy. But it may be even more relevant that they are also singing from the same hymnal on Wall Street's influence, the Federal Reserve, the 9/11 official story, etc. People don't know that the IRS is actually illegal, if you read the U.S. Constitution. It turns out the Founding Fathers never said that taxing personal income was legal. Taxing corporate profits was the original idea. Taxes were supposed to be "apportioned"—i.e., shared evenly and fairly. But the IRS allows megacorporations to get off scot-free, while the working people carry a burdensome load.[67]

One of the most radical ways to resist right now is to read the U.S. Constitution. There, you'll see a reasonable blueprint for a peaceful country. There, in its naked, innocent vision, you'll find a discussion of "if" the United States needs to create a standing army. I love it! "If." This is light-years away from an insane monster that spends $700 billion of fiat currency it borrows from China to blow up brown people.

Is having a permanent "standing army" really a good idea? Even the "paleo-conservative" American historian Forest McDonald points out that the Founding Fathers believed:

> Once a nation started down the road to a love of luxury, it was doomed . . . A related danger was the resort to standing armies—

partly because a standing army was inherently inimical to liberty, partly because it required a large and continuous public expenditure, which increased debts and taxes and thereby contributed to luxury—but mainly because it entailed a most unmanly shifting of responsibility for one's own defense to the hands of others.

In the material on attorney William Veale, we first discovered that the framers of the Constitution wished us to have a way to remain free from being manipulated into wars. To hoodwink the people into a war was the framers' definition of "treason." Today, it seems that ignoring the Founding Fathers' recommendations not to have a standing army has lead to a treasonous series of illegal wars.

We have in our country a grassroots movement that has not only asked the right questions about the War on Terror but has also influenced U.S. and world opinion with its skepticism. This movement is honoring and working for the spirit of the U.S. Constitution. It needs to further clarify that the spirit of peace and truth lies at the heart of the Bill of Rights.

THE TRUTH PARTY

Over the course of nine years, I have seen the emergence of a new politics inside the model of the 9/11 Truth Movement. The Truth Party is not something I "founded" so much as something that reflects an already emerging political reality. The Truth Movement has showed me that people on both the Right and the Left unite against huge U.S. government falsehoods. We have been inspired to take up the tools of free speech to combat "state crimes against democracy," a new term sociologists have coined to describe an almost unimaginable set of political atrocities.

This Truth Movement has created the beginnings of a broad mass movement for peace through truth. We have lived for freedom through action.

I'm not proposing an authoritarian, hierarchical, militarylike party structure. I don't think that would last. Books on social organizing show that flat-hierarchy, grassroots movements are more lively and life-giving. In *The Starfish and the Spider*, the authors point out that people united around common values are much harder to beat than movements or cultures reliant on lockstep authority. The ancient classic *The Art of War* also says that a small organization will defeat a larger one if the smaller one has "the fullness" or the unity of spirit. The Internet has shown us that good ideas spread virally and that hierarchies are no longer assets.

In fact, if you look at the way the FBI's COINTELPRO targeted the top of black-power and white-leftist organizations, you'll realize hierarchy is a liability. If a revolution can be stopped just by killing the leader, then this time around we all need to be the leader in certain ways. At Occupy Wall Street, there is no "leader" for the media and government to drive crazy. But there is organization. Key decisions are made at a "general assembly" that meets every night. Participation is open to everyone.

Before he died, in 2010, historian Howard Zinn said he'd like to be remembered "for getting more people to realize that the power which rests so far in the hands of people with wealth and guns ultimately rests in people themselves and that they can use it." Occupy is using it.

There are huge, untapped creative powers in all of us as well as in our collective democratic endeavors. We can tap back into our country's founding principles. We can unite a mass movement for change around the ideas of peace and truth. It's already under way.

There's no telling where the energy unleashed in fall 2011 will take us. But it needs to be made a permanent part of American political life. The Truth Party could be a part of that. As it takes form, it could be a blend of Occupy and AA.

In AA, we say that only an addict can understand another addict. The Truth Party needs to have that kind of humility and raw, honest connection between souls. We are all addicted to Truth, and our sickness is that society has starved us of what we need. We should hold regular meetings: "Hello, my name is Sander, and I'm a truth addict." They would be like open-mic events, at which people listen to and support each other. We would begin to share skills—to share the lessons we have learned through experience: how to raise money, how to run candidates, how to build new businesses that serve people's needs. You come to gatherings of the Truth Party, you share your own challenges with truth seeking, you teach and learn, and you get support from fellow truth addicts.

I have begun to achieve my sobriety. It has been great for me to do so. I would like to invite the country to try a new form of political sobriety.

When the time is right, we should run political candidates, both at the microlocal level and at the national level. We should democratically build up this party together. It's so new; there's so much room to grow.

One idea I have is to develop a public interest venture fund as a way to reform the economic system. Everyone from anarchists to Goldman Sachs brokers can understand this.

We learn from Zen that the mind is an illusion-maker. Our assumptions are often false. One tragic assumption that revolutionaries have often made is that religion is oppressive and that's there's nothing good there. Another big illusion is that the interests of capital—i.e., big money—are always in opposition to the interests of the people.

What if neither of those is true? What if there were a way to work with money but also put it toward the public interest? Not through the communist approach—i.e., by seizing the assets and cash of the rich and putting it in the hands of "the people"—but by being a little more suave and seductive and luring the fox out of his hole? There's a way to make capital serve both the public interest and its own interest.

The framers of the Constitution couldn't figure out a solution to the need for financial justice. As a result, we have hobbled from one financial-disaster institution to another, from Hamilton's national bank to the Federal Reserve. But the nascent Truth Party is out to hybridize divergent schools of thought. We propose two major economic ideas:

1. A system of "public interest venture capital," which will help people save the world, create meaningful green jobs, and also create a good return for the owners of capital.

2. The Occupy Business School, which will teach people the skills they need to start innovative, compassionate, disruptive new ventures, without incurring the debt of traditional business school tuition.

PUBLIC INTEREST VENTURE CAPITAL: A CREATIVE ALTERNATIVE TO THE FED RESERVE

We saw in the excellent 2010 film *Inside Job* that the forces that destroyed the global economy in 2008 went unpunished. I think the best scene is when the dean of Columbia Business School, R. Glenn Hubbard, is asked on camera about his conflicts of interest. Suddenly, his genteel facade drops like a rock, and what is revealed is a belligerent, threatening bureaucrat caught in a lie.

Columbia is also deeply connected to New York finance and the New York Federal Reserve. Faculty at the business school coolly defend the hopelessly corrupt and manipulative bankers at Goldman Sachs. Columbia president Lee Bollinger is the chairman of the board of the New York Federal Reserve.

In truth, the Federal Reserve system is an even bigger, longer-running cover-up than anything related to 9/11. Reading *Web of Debt*, by Ellen Brown, and hearing G. Edward Griffin speak have been eye-opening for me. The Federal Reserve is not in fact a federal animal at all. The American people and the U.S. government own none of it; 100 percent of its stock is owned by big American banks. It was created through an act of subterfuge in 1913, the same year in which Congress created the IRS and the FBI.

Today, the U.S. dollar has shrunk to one-twentieth of the value it had in 1913, according to the Consumer Price Index.[68] That's ironic, because the Federal Reserve was set up in 1913 to control inflation, not create it.

Like so many, I have suffered in this "Great Recession." It's been painful, but I'm trying to use the pain for something useful. Let's scheme up some new alternatives to the U.S. cronyist economy, with its corrupt, unconstitutional systems: the IRS, the Fed, and the military-industrial vampire complex.

What if we had a big, grassroots, community-focused "green venture capital fund" in every town in America? What if new money were available to all the creative souls out there yearning to quit their lousy job or get out of the army of the unemployed and start a company that does something in the public interest?

We could do this. We could create a PIVOT, a "public interest ventures organic trust." Commercial banks would invest in the fund and reap both financial rewards and social goodwill (they already have plenty of the former and desperately need the latter). A few brave voices inside the U.S. government have begun to question the secrecy and the efficacy of the Federal Reserve (especially U.S. representative Ron Paul and former representative Alan Grayson). Whether or not we "abolish the Fed" in our lifetimes, we definitely need to try something different. The PIVOT plan would give the Fed a run for its money. It would simply say, *Hey, we have a plan to add more value to people's lives. We won't abolish you—you are already abolishing yourself. We will beat you on the free market.*

Our fund would back cool new companies, ones that offered a nice financial return on investment but also a serious social return to the public. We're talking here about a hybrid of progressive social values, environmentalism, and American hustle. What if the U.S. federal government started thinking of itself as an investor instead of as a reluctant donor? Instead of a handout, the U.S. government should expect a return (either social or financial) on whatever money it put into a venture marketplace.

As a presidential candidate, Barack Obama voted for the $700 billion bailout. He showed his true colors, and it only made things worse. It rewarded the system's criminals who had pumped up illusions and preserved the status quo. Obama's economic team of Summers, Geithner, and Rubin are the same characters who got us into this mess.

When he was president-elect, Obama said, "We'll put people back to work rebuilding our crumbling roads and bridges, modernizing schools that are failing our children, and building wind farms and solar panels, fuel-efficient cars, and the alternative energy technologies that can free us from our dependence on foreign oil and keep our economy competitive in the years ahead." None of that has happened.

But I'm not asking for a New Deal–style program. Wouldn't it be better to give the people access to the credit and capital they need to do it themselves, to create their *own* New Deal? Despite the $700 billion bailout, banks are still not lending, and there's a sharp hunger for credit. According to Ellen Brown, 71 percent of entrepreneurs today say they lack access to adequate credit. The system is killing itself, but it's too heartless to care.

WHAT IS VENTURE CAPITAL?

Commercial venture capital is a form of finance unique to the United States. A venture capital firm takes a piece of ownership in a new and growing firm and looks forward to when that company's growth provides an opportunity to "exit" in about five years. When the investors exit, they sell their stake, usually for five to twenty times what they paid for it. It's a great deal, but only around one in three investments grows to that point. So a venture capital firm is ready to write off losses on most of its investments. Experimentation and risk are built into the system.

The exit, though, is a triumphant experience for the founders, the original shareholders, and the VC firm. Often, the exit takes the form of the company's getting acquired by a bigger firm, or, even better, the company goes public by selling shares on a public stock exchange. This represents a triumph of economic democracy: The people have supported the products or services of a particular firm by choosing to spend their money with that firm. The original entrepreneurs sacrificed for years to get the firm going. The big payoff is the explosive growth in the value of their shares at the moment of the public offering.

The PIVOT plan would advance a whole new way of thinking about finance. It would take the best aspects of free-market economics and principled government planning and would fund new ventures in the public interest, like the infrastructure and green-energy projects Obama promised. But PIVOT could eventually be expanded to include new-media companies, to enrich our democracy through new technology and a freer exchange of ideas and information. We could use PIVOT to reindustrialize the United States and retool our plants and factories. We could use it to rejuvenate American agriculture, to move away from pesticide-laden crops and get away from genetically modified factory farming. All of which would boost employment and put the whole U.S. economy on steroids, so to speak.

Here's a real-world example: I met this guy, Bob Nape, who runs a solar panel company in Ithaca, New York. He's been established for a good couple of years, but he really wants to grow. Let's say he goes to PIVOT with a good business plan. PIVOT could choose to invest $2 million in Nape's company and own 45 percent of it. With that $2 million, in five years Nape's company will grow. He will hire more people and buy more goods and services for his company. The local economy in Ithaca will feel the love.

After all, alternative energy is bound to be a hot stock in the Obama era. Nape's firm is a sound investment in light of increasing demand. In five years, there could be an exit, at which time 45 percent of Nape's company would be worth much more than the investment PIVOT put in. There could be a public offering. PIVOT (i.e., the U.S. government in partnership with private-sector lenders) would get back something like $5–10 million for the $2 million it put in. Then PIVOT would have more money to invest in the next round of companies in Ithaca.

PIVOT could eventually be a self-sustaining government entity, or a quasi-governmental entity that is part public, part private—kind of like the Fed, but vastly different in terms of whose interests it serves. In time, it wouldn't even need an annual budget from Congress. It's time for the government to use the power of the markets. The PIVOT plan would be an incubator for thousands of new companies producing things that people need. It might save the planet. It would help people feel good about doing meaningful work, saving their country, realizing a larger purpose.

This is *not* a top-down infusion of cash into the financial sector. I'm interested in figuring out how we can unite workers and entrepreneurs to transform this global economy and get everyone back to work. And why not go beyond that? Let's think of everyone not just working, but building a better world.

So, rather than another $700 billion for the banks, or tens of billions for the Big Three carmakers, let the market run its course. Those firms made their choices. Now they have to live with them. The same banks lobbied former president Bill Clinton to repeal the 1933 Glass-Steagall Act. Then they engaged in that unhealthy mix of commercial and investment banking, which led to the subprime mortgage crisis, which led to the credit markets' shriveling up, which led to this recession. In Detroit, the Big Three helped kill the electric car by resisting fuel efficiency and ignoring a changing world. Now they want a blank check? Their SUVs heated up our planet; Congress was right to rebuff them. But how do we create their replacements? Through the PIVOT plan.

Cantankerous voices in the old right wing might say this sounds like socialism. Au contraire—the socialists kicked me out of their party for saying stuff like this. Since then, I have become an award-winning capitalist with two successful and unique ventures under my belt.

What I'm proposing here is the future of capitalism. It's Capitalism with a Soul. In purely capitalistic terms, this is a plan to use market forces and public equity markets to create an exit for the original investors, even if one of the original investors happens to be an experimental public-private entity.

It's not about the state holding on to assets and companies; it's about the state helping to create the companies we must create for the public good and then letting them grow on their own. For the PIVOT plan, it's all about the exit; it's all about starting cool new companies and then looking to recoup the original investment in about five to ten years.

Another possible problem with this PIVOT plan is that it might sound "too corporate" to some. Well, I know from personal experience that the Left in this country is plagued with psychological hang-ups about money. (I'm working on my own, believe me.) We resent money; we feel weird about it.

There's a basis for some of this. We have seen an extreme form of Machiavellian capitalism in recent years, symbolized perfectly by Bush and Cheney, Enron and Halliburton. Capitalism unregulated creates an elite, and that elite creates monopolies that squelch competition.

But the PIVOT plan is not the old capitalism. It's the future of capitalism. It's a plan to democratize this brutal system, share wealth, spread opportunity, and use the explosive power of public equity markets.

It's not the New Deal, but it is new, and it's quite a big deal. Finance all too often is a thing shrouded in mystery, the exclusive domain of the elite. But really, all people of truth should learn the language of finance. Remove the mystery, and you'll see that it's not really all that complicated.

To fund a company, to invest in something, is to show hope, to show a faith that the basic human creativity, the light inside us all, will get us beyond a time of fear, violence, and despair. PIVOT is a way to say that we believe we all have a light within, and that we are going to use our faith, and our brains, and our hard work to save the world.

OCCUPY BUSINESS SCHOOL!
THE PEOPLE'S UNIVERSITY OF
DISRUPTIVE CAPITALISM

The Occupy Wall Street movement has struck a nerve by putting up entrenched resistance to the nexus of financial and political power in the United States.

We want to get away from a world of hoarding and secrecy, and so we practice a world of free sharing and compassion . . . and the idea has caught on!

But what will we all be doing a year from now? What will you be doing in five?

We need a way to make the spirit of Occupy a permanent force in our lives.

I have found that as corrupt as capitalism has become, one of the best ways to resist the system is to create your own alternative machine—entrepreneurial ventures that are "corporations," yes, but ones that care about much more than just profit. According to economist Joseph Schumpeter, the "perennial gale" force of the entrepreneur is supposed to be the dynamic engine in capitalism. This is what he wrote in 1942, borrowing a term from Karl Marx: "creative destruction."

> *"The process of industrial mutation . . . incessantly revolution-izes the economic structure from within, incessantly destroying the old one, incessantly creating a new one . . . [The process] must be seen in its role in the perennial gale of creative destruction; it cannot be understood on the hypothesis that there is a perennial lull."*
> —Joseph Schumpeter, The Process of Creative Destruction

Running a progressive business gives you an opportunity to make revolutionary, ethical, creative, productive activity a daily practice. You can liberate yourself from working a job you hate.

If you really want to zap the murky and mysterious problem of how financial power controls political power in this country, then study how money and the economy work, in a direct way. Practice a new economy daily. By joining the Occupy Business School network, you learn to run your own business, but you also become part of a bigger dialogue about a new economy, as we build it together.

There are certain skills that most political activists know nothing about. They are the basics of running a business, and they are great skills to have in life, no matter what you do. The Occupy Business School curriculum will include:

- Business Plan Creation
- Capital Raising
- Triple Bottom Line Business: People, Social Impact, and Profit
- Low Cost, High-Impact Marketing
- How to Hire Great Talent
- How to Buy Assets, Cheap
- Bare-Knuckle Accounting: P&L Management
- Return on Investment and Investor Relations
- The Revolution of the Internet

We are creatures of light. But all too often, we work jobs we hate, and we become what we hate when we do what we don't really want to. It's time to turn away from constant compromises. We have wellsprings of talent and creativity that we neglect. Some of us are called to start the companies of tomorrow, companies that practice a higher code of justice, fairness, healthiness, and environmentalism.

We need a new systemic analysis of the U.S. economy. It is in deep crisis because of systemically skewed priorities. The tax system, the military-industrial complex, the Wall Street power brokers, and the hedge funds are not even practicing "capitalism" these days so as much as "cronyism." They have become unable to create enough new jobs, because they can't create enough new entrepreneurs. Six out of seven new entrepreneurs fail. There's not enough credit out there, but what's more, there's not enough love. Part of Occupy Business School's mission is to create a new social network. We are beyond winners and losers. Someone who has started and run a business that has failed has won a great life lesson in business, the hard way. OBS will create a "network of experience" to pair new entrepreneurs with a "sponsor," who will be a guiding mentor to that new entrepreneur (or group of entrepreneurs).

Occupy Business School will launch with the launch of this book. I will tour the United States and the world in 2012, talking about setting up Occupy Business School events.

With other speakers I will invite, we will teach some hard-won lessons in creating socially progressive community businesses and ventures.

We are talking about both for-profit and not-for-profit ventures here. OBS will have guest speakers from the nonprofit field and from successful social ventures. The different classes of corporations can be formed as collectives, cooperatives, or corporations designed for fast growth. Different forms can serve different needs. We'll go over this in class.

What's important is that we try something new. This economy sucks—it sucks the life blood out of us—and it's time we all tried an experiment in peace, truth, and adventure.

It's time for more radical social ventures. It's time to create the machines that create jobs, create learning experiences, and create wealth. The more wealth that is created by radical lovers of truth, the more wealth we will have to invest in each other.

Mainstream business school is a sham. Do the math: The tuition is $200K. If you finance that, that's $200K worth of debt, plus interest. With that debt load to service, you can't *dare* do anything that is truly disruptive, innovative, world-changing, or entrepreneurial. The few good things about capitalism are increasingly shrouded and obscured by the very system that is supposed to be training the business creators of tomorrow.

It's time to *Occupy* Business School.

It will be free for the unemployed and will scale up from there. It will be a great show and a great education.

We can replace the old financial institutions in this country with ones that work, are empowering, and are life-giving. We can share wealth by sharing how wealth is created.

24 THE TRUTH PARTY

Whew! What a whirlwind tour this book has been: 9/11 Truth, anthrax, and the CIA, but then also Gandhi, Jesus, Zen, and public interest venture capital. What could possibly be next?

It seems clear to me that we need a new political party to foment this peace revolution. We need an organization to make these words flesh. I have already started one, but honestly, it's only just started.

I believe in your inner light. I believe in open-source collaboration. I believe that the Truth Party and Truth Gathering ideas are just beginning to get off the ground. You are invited to join in. I will be touring the country for a year or more to talk about all the ideas in this book. I would like to do a Truth Gathering in your town soon.

In March and April of 2011, I toured the country, announcing that this book was coming out and planting the seeds for local branches of the Truth Party in ten major cities.

The first thing I wrote about the Truth Party was the "Three Simple Virtues" below.

Take a look:

1. PEACE LEADERSHIP

It's time for the United States to become the leader in peace. We should be the top expert in nonviolent conflict resolution. We should stand for the science of advanced human communication. This is our true legacy as Americans: Martin Luther King, César Chávez, and Dorothy Day, who showed that nonviolence is more effective than violence.

America was the first country to put the ideals of the Enlightenment into practice. We were the first complex representative democracy.

The original core mission of the United States was to be the first "antiwar nation." Jefferson said, "If there is one principle more deeply rooted in the mind of every American, it is that we should have nothing to do with conquest."

The freedoms of the First Amendment therefore are a blueprint for peace and freedom. It's time for progressives to act like prophets and return America to the original promise, the original covenant we made with history, at the Enlightenment.

2. PEACE ECONOMICS

The war economy has bankrupted our country. The dollar is in decline, our debts are enormous, and our creditors are getting nervous. Stay on the path we are on, and the dollar will collapse.

We need to audit the Federal Reserve. We need to abolish it by surpassing it. We can create something better: new public interest banks to make capitalism more democratic. A federally funded public interest capital bank could directly fund progressive and green entrepreneurs. This would be a real economic stimulus, and it would show an innovative way some market mechanisms can be used in the service of the public.

3. FREEDOM FROM LIES

Despite Obama's promises, the federal government relies on deception and subterfuge. The Iraq War, 9/11, anthrax, torture and murder at Guantánamo Bay, and rendition are all crimes against humanity that need full investigation and prosecution of the guilty.

The alternative is the death of the country. Ancient history teaches us that countries fall due to moral failure. Our empire is an empire in crisis, expanding abroad but bankrupt at home.

The United States aches for answers, and they will come from me, and you, through this new political formation, the Truth Party.

Look not just at American history for its slavery, the theft from the Natives, and the current imperialism. Never forget America's contributions: democracy, the Internet, jazz, hip-hop, and rock and roll.

What's next? What are the next big ideas from our country, for the world?

These are the things that will save us and save the planet:

Peace Leadership
Peace Economics
Freedom from Lies

TRUTH PARTY TEN-POINT PROGRAM

On that March–April 2011 tour, I also listened to people, and out of the discussions we had at each speaking gig, I started to hear and repeat certain truths. Those statements form the basis for the Truth Party Ten-Point Program.

I. The Truth Party Has a Positive Vision

We stand for something substantial. We define ourselves in terms of what we are for, the way the positive symbols in the logo carry our message. The Truth Party has three core values: USA Peace Leadership, Peace Economics, and Freedom from Lies. It's time to expand upon this. Note: Many groups define themselves in terms of what they are against. Our logo and our core message are positive.

II. The People Can Be United

On certain issues, people are moving beyond the same old political categories: the bailouts, the cover-ups that create war, etc. This is a huge strategic advantage—let's unify around these issues. This has never really been tried before: a political movement based on the big ideas that unite people, people from the Left, the Right, and beyond.

Politics as usual is the addiction, and truth politics is a new form of political sobriety. Together, we are developing a program that is uniting a mass movement: patriots, populists, and real progressives.

III. Economics Is a Vibrant Form of Direct Action

On my March–April 2010 tour, Jack in "Free State" New Hampshire talked about "agorism" (i.e., "marketism"). At the end of the tour, in Vista, California, I found the Twelve Tribes community doing something very similar: living by example, showing the world a better way, not through scolding, but by doing. They create ventures, vessels to carry the message. Twelve Tribes has an amazing café/restaurant in Vista that is packed from 9:00 PM to 2:00 AM everyday. Isn't it funny that the people who are best at "business" are the ones who don't do business primarily for money, but who have put their mission first?

I personally have found that I'm happiest when I follow the axiom "never work a job you hate." We need to make it easier for people to find this kind of economic happiness. We need to make the credit available. We need to move beyond the Federal Reserve and the government of, by, and for Wall Street. We need public markets to work for the public. We need to make capital available to more people.

IV. There Has to Be a Way Out

The temptation with deep research work is to get overwhelmed by the data. Every problem has a solution. And remember, the Truth Movement can't go anywhere if it's just a conspiracy-theory club. What we want is to spread this realization: The days of war are numbered. *War is obsolete.* You see this by studying the fabricated provocations that have started all the wars. September 11 is a good place to start. But it's not the place we end.

V. Everyone's Creative Capacity Is Infinite

Jim in Madison, Wisconsin, gave me a book on Nicholas of Cusa, a forgotten fourteenth-century mystic who states that the universe is the unfolding of the divine. Also in that book is the assertion that the creative powers of each human being are infinite, despite the pessimism and the limits we are taught. The First Amendment seems to know this truth. The Bill of Rights is built to protect our "inner light" from the darkness of tyranny. There's a link between the free exchange of ideas and the life of a democracy. The more we nurture our "inner light," or what the Buddhists call "everyone's Buddha nature," the better we become as a people, as a republic, and as a democracy.

VI. We Are All in a Dialogue with the World's Great Religions

The First Amendment seems to encourage freedom of religion, as a cousin of the right to free speech and the right to dissent. So, religion and spirituality are languages that every working intellectual-activist in the Truth Party needs to be able to speak, although no particular belief system is required. The essential values we have—peace, truth, fostering divinity, and emancipation—are also at the core of the Judeo-Christian tradition and its descendant religion, Islam, not to mention these faiths' distant godfather, Buddhism. We are all for the separation of church and state while acknowledging that religion, politics, and philosophy all stem from the same tree.

Consciousness changes the world. "The power of unity changes history."—Daisaku Ikeda

VII. The Call for a New Political Culture

At one point during my 2011 tour, a 9/11 Truth Activist posted on the tour's Facebook page, regarding the larger movement: "No more drama! No more arguing!" Unfortunately, conflict and disagreements will always be with us. We can try to be of "one mind and one spirit," but at the same time, we must be able to deal with conflicts. You can't outlaw them, unfortunately. One thing that has worked for me in my own life is compassionate communication techniques, in which I get away from making accusations and instead learn to clarify my own needs. If everyone's needs can be "held equally," then together people can create a new strategy to meet all of those needs. This has been a good way to get away from the usual dramas and into some serious conflict-resolution success. This has to be a part of the lively culture we develop inside the Truth Party.

VIII. Cause and Effect

It's the age-old law. You get what you give. You become what you focus on. Keep voting for deceptive politicians, you get more heartbreak and economic suffering. Vote for the corrupt, get corruption. Some say to work within existent parties, but we say that ground is toxic, and we won't plant there. We can see the toxicity of too many bad compromises in that soil. Time to break new ground! A new party with a new vision, a new culture, a new spirit has arrived!

IX. We Have a Winning Viral Strategy

A smart guy in San Diego said, make it an "organism," not so much an "organization." We need a starfish, not a spider. This is *not* about one man, one ego, or one political career, and this is not the Sander Hicks Party. Instead, we should seek to create a network of equals, not an authoritarian hierarchy. We should seek to be empowering, rather than covetous of power. We should seek to listen before seeking to speak.

X. Micro- and Macropolitics

The Truth Party strategy, for its first ten years or so, will be to run candidates at the micro level: neighborhood council, school board, city council, etc., as well as to nominate a national candidate, or slate of candidates, in order to gain national stature.

25 CONFRONTING DICK CHENEY: TRUTH PREVAILS

For this last chapter, let's go back to the beginning. There is one more Goliath story to tell. One more monster to confront. Now it's time for all of us to become David.

I want to use what we've discussed thus far to tell the story of my first major confrontation regarding 9/11 Truth.

I want to tell you the story of the time I asked vice president Dick Cheney about 9/11 being an inside job. I met Cheney personally. I felt his cold sickness. I got the sense right away that he had even more health problems than the many we already knew about. I felt his soul frightened by his guilt. Maybe the most radical thing we can do is try to save this man's soul.

It was a catalyzing event, and it was so draining. I felt it was a failure at the time, but over the long haul, I see now that it led to other, better confrontations. It was stupid in some ways, what it took to pull this off, but in the big picture, it led to this book. I learned from my mistakes. Leibniz is proven right here: There's just enough evil in the world to give us the right amount of work to do.

After meditating on this, I had an insight. When you think about love and the love of God, when you empty out your ego in Zen practice, when you imagine the justice of Jesus's realm of God on Earth, something different happens. Even though Dick Cheney is "indictable" for 9/11, it makes more sense for us now not to seek his punishment. Rather than revenge, let's desire truth. This is a more practical goal, and it's more ethical.

In South Africa, and in North Carolina, we have seen truth and reconciliation hearings use this practice. Each sought to find out the truth about apartheid and racist killings of leftist activists, respectively. A truth and reconciliation conference is an extrajudicial process that asserts that the truth of what happened is more important than punishing the guilty.

Like Special Agent Hayes, Dick Cheney is obviously suffering, writhing in his guilt for his illegal wars, mass killings, and 9/11 cover-up. He claims that he believes in never apologizing, but that's the kind of thing a person says when he's repressing a huge apology to the world.

It is Dick Cheney whom William Veale and the Center for 9/11 Justice want to indict first in a court of law, or a citizens grand jury for 9/11. Cheney is the "arch enemy" of 9/11 Truth, it's true. But Gandhi would say not to indulge in the fantasy of "evil enemy" and instead to reach out to Cheney's humanity. Cheney likes to have people think of him as a Darth Vader type of character, but to do so is only to play into his own mythmaking. Really, what we have here is a troubled, hurt, and hurting human being.

In Cheney's last years on Earth, we can find out the truth about 9/11 by simply asking him more questions, free from reprisals. That way, we indict a system, not a lone mad gunman. Maybe Cheney can turn state's evidence and become an informant on the whole plot. There is certainly enough evidence against him personally to compel him.

CAST-IRON STRENGTH

In an article for *Time* magazine about his then-forthcoming memoir, *In My Time*, Cheney said his guiding principle is to show "cast-iron strength at all times—never apologize, never explain."

Cheney has done many things, but he has not always maintained this facade of "cast-iron strength." In a 2006 Texas hunting accident, Vice President Cheney shot a seventy-eight-year-old attorney, Harry Whittington, with two hundred pieces of birdshot in the face and heart. Cheney, who at formal dinners has made a great show of refusing wine, admitted to park rangers that he'd been drinking beer earlier that day. Instead of an apology at the time, it was Whittington who chose (or was compelled) to publicly apologize *to Cheney*, even after Whittington suffered a heart attack from the birdshot in his heart. At defining points in Cheney's life, then, "never apologize" begins to look like a severe weakness, not cast-iron strength.

In 2011, Cheney was a vocal critic of President Obama, breaking tradition and the bonds of civility. But he then praised President Obama for his extrajudicial murder of Osama bin Laden.[69] That's strange, because in an interview with Tony Snow in 2009, Cheney himself let this slip: "So, we've never made the case, or argued the case that somehow Osama bin Laden was directly involved in 9/11. That evidence has never been forthcoming."[(69)]

Cheney later clarified that he had meant Saddam Hussein, whom the host and he had been discussing. But the administration's claims that Hussein and bin Laden were both behind 9/11 were never proven.

According to Cheney's memoirs, even President Bush himself was "pulling away" from Cheney in the second term of their administration. Bush was alarmed that their actions had resulted in a severe drop in the polls. (Cheney's own approval rating of 63 percent in April 2001 fell to 13 percent by the end of his term.) When Turkish television asked Cheney about this drop, his response was "So?"

Recall that Dick Cheney was tasked by then-governor Bush with heading the vice-presidential selection committee for the Bush campaign in 1999. Cheney had the audacity to pick himself as Bush's running mate. In Bush's first term, he had taken a lead role as a policymaker and spokesman for the preemptive attacks of the Bush doctrine. "My belief is we will, in fact, be greeted as liberators," he said of the Iraqi invasion, before it turned into a bloody, protracted disaster. His cast-iron strength is a tinhorn machismo. Even the *New York Times*'s review of his memoir notes that Cheney is rather pithy about 9/11, the defining event of his administration. But in that review I learned that the CIA used to call Cheney Edgar, a reference to Edgar Bergen, the ventriloquist puppeteer famous in the mid–twentieth century.

CHENEY, RUMSFELD, AND THE FABRICATED SOVIET THREAT

Zen masters tell us to "face reality and annihilate fantasy." Throughout his career, Cheney has done the opposite: He hides reality and creates false enemies. In the Ford administration, he was chief of staff alongside long-time friend Donald Rumsfeld. They felt Nixon was too soft on the Soviets with the SALT II treaty and détente. They believed William Colby and his CIA lacked the correct, right-leaning take on "reality."

Cheney and Rumsfeld wanted big spikes in defense spending. But the CIA said the Soviet Union was crumbling. So Cheney, Rumsfeld, and other budding neoconservatives created PFIAB, the President's Foreign Intelligence Advisory Board, an intelligence group that said what the hard Right wanted it to say, over the protestations of William Colby.

Donald Rumsfeld, President Ford, and Dick Cheney, plotting to overthrow the CIA.

PFIAB (aka Team B) got approval only when CIA Director Colby was fired. The new CIA director, George H. W. Bush, signed off on the policy with enthusiasm. Colby later died mysteriously after appearing in the suppressed documentary *Conspiracy of Silence* regarding the Bush White House/CIA/Catholic Church pedophilia scandal. His body was never found.

CHENEY ON 9/11

Dick Cheney made a political legacy out of 9/11. It created a widespread feeling of fear and insecurity, continually renewed by a series of different, uninvestigated terror incidents: the anthrax attacks, the Shoe Bomber, the London Tube bombings, the Underwear Bomber, etc.

For some odd reason, today, Dick Cheney's Wikipedia page has nothing about 9/11. His official biography, at the fan site DraftCheney2012 .com, has only one line about 9/11. (Cheney does not maintain an official website.)

September 11 was the dominant event of his vice presidency. Yet someone wants us to not look too closely at Cheney and 9/11: where he was and what he did.

Recall that on the morning of 9/11, Norman Mineta, the secretary of transportation, went down to the White House bunker, the Presidential Emergency Operations Center (PEOC), where he had been called to do crisis management alongside Dick Cheney early in the morning. Mineta, a Japanese American, had been interned in the World War II–era round-up of Japanese Americans during his childhood in California. He was the only Democratic member of Bush's cabinet.

Thanks to C-SPAN, we have video of a clearly concerned Mineta describing how Cheney seized presidential powers on 9/11. Mineta relates that Cheney's orders were of grave concern to those around him. At around 9:25 AM, Mineta testified, the following happened:

> During the time that the airplane was coming into the Pentagon, there was a young man who would come in and say to the vice president . . . the plane is fifty miles out" . . . "the plane is thirty miles out" . . . and when it got down to "the plane is ten miles out," the young man also said to the vice president, "Do the orders still stand?" And the vice president turned and whipped his neck around and said, "Of course the orders still stand; have you heard anything to the contrary?!"

The 9/11 Commission suppressed this testimony. Video of it was deleted from the commission's video archive but survives on YouTube.

Cheney claimed that he was not in the PEOC until 9:58 AM, but Mineta placed him there at 9:20 AM.

Cheney testified to the 9/11 Commission only behind closed doors, with no media, no public accountability. The commission members were not even allowed to take notes. Cheney was not under oath, perhaps to skirt a perjury charge—the commission had earlier heard from Mineta that Cheney had been in the PEOC a significant thirty-eight minutes prior to when he claimed he had arrived there.

The "order" that "still stands" was likely an order not to shoot down the plane (or object) that was coming across the radar, headed for the Pentagon. Cheney had been given the legal ability to shoot down commercial aircraft, and Mineta testified that his experiences that day made that apparent: Cheney was using his new power at his own discretion. Cheney had given orders that were so odious to his White House aides, they double- and triple-checked that the orders still stood.

Dick Cheney played a lead role in the Project for the New American Century, the think tank of neocons and centrist Democrats who in 2000 said that "rebuilding America's defenses" would be a long and slow process unless a "cataclysmic and catalyzing event," like a "new Pearl Harbor," occurred to galvanize and polarize American popular opinion. On 9/11 itself, America's air defenses were paralyzed, by four or more "war games" or military drills that filled the NORAD and FAA radar systems with extra "blips" and false targets.

Four months before 9/11, on May 8, 2001, President Bush signed an order that placed Dick Cheney in charge of "all federal programs dealing with weapons of mass destruction consequence management within the Departments of Defense, Health and Human Services, Justice, and Energy . . ."[70] This order included all "*training and planning . . . seamlessly integrated.*" It's possible that the May 8 order put former secretary of defense/vice president Cheney in charge of the military drills. The Mineta testimony tells us that Cheney was directing a stand-down. The orders still stand.

That May 8 presidential directive is important for another reason. Recall that Jerry Hauer and Rudy Giuliani were holding the biochemical drill Tripod II on the morning of 9/11 in NYC. Their Office of Emergency

Management issued a press release that said Tripod was being run with the federal Office of Domestic Preparedness. Dick Cheney was in charge of that office, thanks to Bush's order of May 8.

Later that morning, when Flight 93 crashed in Pennsylvania, Mineta asked himself, aghast, "Oh, my God, did we shoot it down?" Later, Mineta "got the memo" and hewed to the company line. The 9/11 official story later claimed, absurdly, that the Flight 93 terrorists chose to crash the plane all by themselves, due to the "heroic" actions of Todd "Let's Roll" Beamer outside the locked cockpit door.

However, while working for a Japanese news agency, I interviewed Indian Lake, Pennsylvania, mayor Barry Lichty. He let slip that multiple Flight 93 garbage bags of human body parts and plane wreckage were pulled out of the lake in front of his home. This was about two miles away from the Shanksville-area crash site.

We asked Lichty, if the plane was *not* shot down, if it did *not* explode in the air, how could so much debris from Flight 93 have landed *two miles away*? With a kind of wink and a nod, he said that the official story tells us that it was the wind, that calm day in September. No plane parts were found aboveground in the "crater" in Shanksville.

Struggling with his humanity, Cheney later mused aloud to Tim Russert on this topic, without admitting outright that he had allowed the Pentagon crash or authorized the shoot-down of Flight 93: "Now, people say, you know, that's a horrendous decision to make. Well, it is. You've got an airplane full of American citizens, civilians, captured by . . . terrorists, headed . . . and are you going to, in fact, shoot it down, obviously, and kill all those Americans on board?"

Cheney said he was willing to pull the trigger on that decision.

CONFRONTING CHENEY

In November 2005, my wife and I were running the Vox Pop café in a struggling neighborhood that was beginning to respond to our book-store-coffeehouse business. I had just gotten elected president of the Cortelyou Road Merchants Association. The GOP, it turns out, automatically sends you information if you're a merchants association head.

They assume that all businesspeople are Republicans, even in the blue state of New York.

I had also just published a small book of 9/11 investigations, *The Big Wedding: 9/11, the Whistle-Blowers, and the Cover-Up.* The National Republican Congressional Committee wrote me a thank-you letter for joining their "Business Merchants Circle." They sent me a souvenir gavel. They asked if I would like a chance to meet and have my photo taken with vice president Dick Cheney. I wrote them back, and said, *Why,* yes, *I would.* They said, *Great, that will be $5,000.*

Now, I don't want you to think that what happens next was a decision I made lightly. Nor do I want anyone to think I regularly have $5,000 lying around. But I had just gotten married. We did have some extra money from buying a co-op in Brooklyn. It was impulsive, yes, but I talked it over with my wife and decided to buy two tickets and get some access to Cheney. I felt like I had only begun a real 9/11 investigation. I needed to do some postpublication research.

Later, people in the Green Party and people in my family felt anger over my decision to give the GOP $5,000. I, too, have often asked myself whether it was worth it. In hindsight, I know this: No one else need feel guilty. I take full responsibility for my action. I admit, it sure didn't seem worth it immediately afterward. But it's worth it now, because it helped create this book.

The event itself was like a circus. I walked into the glitzy, gold-plated Grand Hyatt on Forty-second Street and Park Avenue. I played the part of a young GOP operative by wearing my best suit and a white tie, just like Dubya.

Fox News host Sean Hannity spoke first that morning. He got few laughs for his stale Clinton-sex and drunken–Ted Kennedy jokes. "These jokes are funnier after you've had a few drinks," he said to an unconvinced, partially filled ballroom. I kept seeing 9/11 come up. Hannity and other speakers linked GOP anti-immigration policies to 9/11. Iraq, they claimed, was a just war, and that, too, was all about 9/11.

Then they lined us up for the Cheney meet and greet. I asked Cheney during our photo op, "What do I say to all these people who tell me 9/11 was an inside job?" I was smiling when I said it, leaning over him and grinning at the camera. In the moment when the shutter clicked, he heard the joy in my voice. I think it angered him. You can see some glumness in the photo:

To Sander
With Best Wishes,

Calmly, he turned his whole body and gave me this wave of cold energy.

"Just look at the evidence," he said evenly. "It's not true."

Cheney's calm was eerie. He sounded like he was trying to project confidence, but really there was a deep sadness inside him. His spoke softly. He was trying to exude "cast-iron strength." He wasn't strong as iron, but he was cold the way iron is, the way it takes heat out of your hand. It all seemed like an act. His face looked translucent, like that of someone in the hospital. I could see tiny veins in his puffy cheeks and nose.

I felt greasy and disoriented for twenty-four hours after that moment. Most people react with dramatic emotion when you bring up the "9/11 inside job" talk. Cheney was not surprised at all. He knew it all.

Cheney wasn't surprised some guy had just popped up in the $5,000 donors' photo-op line at a GOP fundraiser and started talking about 9/11 being an inside job. He didn't detail what "evidence" he had to the contrary, or where one could find it to prop up his besieged official story. He didn't care what I thought I knew. He didn't want to hear what "all these people" were saying. He had a quick answer prepared and was ready for the next photo.

THE REAL STORY IS WHAT THE PEOPLE ARE SAYING ABOUT 9/11

Even Ronald Reagan's old assistant secretary of the treasury, Paul Craig Roberts, is a 9/11 Truther. In 2011, he wrote, "The real story is what the people are saying about 9/11."

Cheney doesn't want to know. But that's okay—we know enough about Cheney, and Bush, and the American government on 9/11, to know now where to go.

We need a 9/11 Truth and reconciliation hearing. We need a 9/11 citizens grand jury. We need to build the Truth Party.

We need a new politics that blends spiritual wisdom, compassion, and mercy with a progressive social vision. We need public interest venture capital to unleash and empower our creativity.

The 9/11 Truth Movement is the path that has led me to know about many things, not just 9/11. The truth is compelling, it is beautiful, and it is its own reward.

Thank you, Dick Cheney. Now we know a few things for certain, such as that "cast-iron strength . . . never apologize" is light-years away from being a good motto. It's the opposite of what anyone would say if they knew anything of Divine Mercy, Gandhi, Jesus, Zen, or good politics.

Now we know that Cheney and all his Cheney-isms, like "cast-iron strength" and "war without end," the myth of U.S. military might, and the 9/11 official story are all bankrupt illusions. You should be proud, Dick Cheney, because you have helped to create a beautiful future for the world and the United States. But it's a path that is very different from what you intended for us. Life is like that. God is like that. Truth is like that: full of curveballs.

Now we need to throw away our weapons, our bombs, our lies, and our illusions. The new arsenal is love, mercy, democracy, empowerment, real spirituality, truth, truth politics, and real human fellowship. And that's just the beginning.

26 FINAL INVOCATION

I'd like to close this book with the Lord's Prayer. No, I'm not kidding.

A lot of people use this prayer. For example, it usually closes a lot of AA meetings. But in its traditional, King James version, some find the language rather archaic.

I have found this new translation more useful. The Sufi poet Neil Douglas-Klotz created it by studying Jesus's mother tongue, Aramaic. He found a deeper truth there: double meanings and hidden wisdom embedded in the ancient language.

From *Prayers of the Cosmos*:

The Lord's Prayer

O, Radiant One,
You shine within us
You shine outside us
Even darkness shines when we remember.

Your name, Your sound, Can move us if we tune our hearts
As instruments for its tone

Create Your reign of unity now
Through our fiery hearts and willing hands

Help us to love
beyond our ideals
and sprout acts of compassion
for all living creatures.

Grant us what we need each day in bread and insight:
Loosen cords of mistakes binding us,
As we release the strands we hold of other's guilt.
Don't let surface things delude us,
But free us from what holds us back.

Sealed in trust and faith, Amen.

NOTES

Chapter 1

1. Psalm 68.

2. See the overview of these poll data at: http://en.wikipedia.org/wiki/September_11_attacks_opinion_polls.

3. World for 911 Truth, "New Poll: 48% of New Yorkers Support a New 9/11 Investigation into Building 7's Collapse," June 8, 2011, http://world911truth.org/new-poll-48-of-new-yorkers-support-a-new-911-investigation-into-building-7s-collapse/.

4. JoAnne Allen, "No consensus on who was behind Sept 11: global poll," *Reuters,* September 10, 2008, www.reuters.com/article/idUSN1035876620080910.

5. (Even if David was later also a conquering military king and a big cheater on his wife. My hero is the early David, presellout.)

Chapter 2

6. On my special page for this book, www.sanderhicks.com/slingshot.html, I have published the twenty five-page report by the "referee" of this dispute.

7. As Veale told Kevin Barrett of No Lies Radio, http://noliesradio.org/archives/35231.

8. Debra Cassens Weiss, "'Fantastical' 9/11 Lawsuit Could Lead to Sanctions for Lawyer, 2nd Circuit Says," ABA Journal, April 28, 2011, www.abajournal.com/news/article/fantastical_9-11_lawsuit_could_lead_to_sanctions_for_lawyer_2nd_circuit_say/.

Chapter 4

9. Jordan Green, "The Strange Death of Dr. David M. Graham," *Yes Weekly,* October 23, 2007, www.yesweekly.com/triad/article-4160-the-strange-death-of-dr-david-m-graham.html.

10. FBI memo dated March 4, 1968, available widely online, e.g., at http://whatreallyhappened.com/RANCHO/POLITICS/COINTELPRO/COINTELPRO-FBI.docs.html.

11. See archival new footage as preserved by the excellent documentary *9/11: Press for Truth.*

12. See highlights from these videos at www.sanderhicks.com/graham.html.

Chapter 5

13. See the indie noir film Able Danger, by Paul Krik, to watch some of the actual mainstream-news footage that exposed Able Danger that week. The film is based in part on my previous 9/11 history, *The Big Wedding: 9/11, the Whistle-Blowers, and the Cover-Up.*

Chapter 6

14. Daniel Hopsicker, "The Secret World of Jack Abramoff," *Mad Cow Morning News,* June 21, 2005, www.madcowprod.com/06202005.html.

15. Daniel Hopsicker, "FBI Flubs Terrorist's Timeline," *Mad Cow Morning News,* September 18, 2002, www.madcowprod.com/issue29.html.

16. Hopsicker describes the "9/11 Truth Movement . . . a group which has been aggressively spamming on the Internet for several years . . . ," at http://www.madcowprod.com/mc6612004.html.

17. From SourceWatch.org: "The Committee on the Present Danger (CPD) is a hawkish 'advocacy organization' first founded in 1950 and re-formed in 1976 to push for larger defense budgets and arms buildups, to counter the Soviet Union. In June 2004, *The Hill* reported that a third incarnation of CPD was being planned, to address the War on terrorism."

18. *The Big Wedding: 9/11, the Whistle-Blowers, and the Cover-Up* (Brooklyn, NY: Vox Pop, 2005).

19. See Chapters 2 and 11 of *The Big Wedding,* available for free at www.sanderhicks.com.

20. See the September 24, 2001, issue of *FOCUS,* published in Germany.

21. *Los Angeles Times,* September 15, 2001; *Washington Post,* September 16, 2001; Gannett News Service, September 17, 2001.

Chapter 7

22. For an excellent report that asks serious questions about the official story, see *The London Bombings: An Independent Inquiry,* by Nafeez M. Ahmed. A reader on Amazon UK said, "Ahmed's research and analysis is exhaustive, prodigious and profound; demonstrating the very highest academic protocols."

23. I am indebted to the research of Canadian professor Michel Chossudovsky for some of this material on Visor Consultants, www.globalresearch.ca/index.php?context=va&aid=821.

Chapter 9

24. See more in the edited selection of key-eyewitness testimony at http://letsrollforums.com/world-trade-center-task-t15012.html.

25. *New York Times,* "World Trade Center Task Force Interview: EMT Richard Zarrillo," http://graphics8.nytimes.com/packages/pdf/nyregion/20050812_WTC_GRAPHIC/9110161.PDF, October 25, 2001.

26. NFPA fire safety manual, 921–19.2.4.

27. *Daily Kos,* "WSJ Op-Ed: 'Bruce Ivins Wasn't the Anthrax Culprit,'" August 5, 2008, www.dailykos.com/story/2008/08/05/562764/-WSJ-Op-Ed:-Bruce-Ivins-Wasnt-the-Anthrax-Culprit.

Chapter 11

28. In Shreveport, after speaking with FBI agent Steve Hayes, I, too, felt that there was deep corruption inside the FBI. I called the Department of Justice's Office of the Inspector General (OIG). They recommended I file a complaint with the FBI's own Office of Professional Responsibility. I pointed out that I already knew that complaint would go nowhere, based on the Lin DeVecchio case. They conceded that I was probably right, and agreed to accept a letter directly to the OIG. But I never received a response.

Chapter 12

29. www.timesonline.co.uk/tol/news/world/europe/article7069826.ece

Chapter 13

30. Joseph Goebbels, *The Goebbels Diaries,* 1942–1943 (Garden City, NY: Doubleday, 1948), 86, 147–48.

31. *Der Spiegel and Die Zeit,* in October 2002. My activist colleague Nick Levis speaks German, did translations, and published them online.

32. For more information, see www.fromthewilderness.com/timeline/popups/011212.html.

33. Marc Perelman, "Spy Rumors Fly on Gusts of Truth: Americans Probing Reports of Israeli Espionage, *Jewish Forward,* March 15, 2002, www.american-buddha.com/911.spyrumorflyongustoftruth.htm.

34. John Mintz and Dan Eggen, "Reports of Israeli Spy Ring Dismissed." Washington Post, March 6, 2002. Notice that John Mintz has the lead by-line here, this same reporter suppressed FBI informant Randy Glass's information about the Michael Chertoff link to an Al Qaeda money man. Mintz was also hostile to this book's author, on the phone.

35. *Jane's Intelligence Digest,* March 13, 2002.

36. Yossi Melman, "Israeli firm blasted for letting would-be plane bomber slip through,"*Haaretz,* October1,2010,www.haaretz.com/print-edition/news/israeli-firm-blasted-for-letting-would-be-plane-bomber-slip-through-1.261107.

37. Ezekiel 36:26, *New Living Translation Bible.*

Chapter 15

38. Executive Order 13489.

39. As told to author Douglas Valentine (the Phoenix Program) at www.consortiumnews.org.

40. *The Wayne Madsen Report* is subscription based, but a near-complete sample of his research on Obama's CIA history is available at www.reallyreality.com/f7/barack-obama-conclusively-outed-cia-creation-522/.

41. ibid

Chapter 16

42. The full text of Ryan's letter to the NIST is available at www.911truth.org/article.php?story=20041112144051451.

43. Niels H. Harrit, Jeffrey Farrer, Steven E. Jones, and others, "Active Thermitic Material Discovered in Dust from the 9/11 World Trade Center Catastrophe," *Open Chemical Physics Journal,* April 2009, www.bentham science.com/open/tocpj/articles/V002/7TOCPJ.htm.

44. Church Committee Reports, "Volume 1: Unauthorized Storage of Toxic Agents," 1975.

45. Judith Miller, Stephen Engelberg, and William Broad, *Germs: Biological Weapons and America's Secret War* (New York: Touchstone/Simon & Schuster, 2001), 287–99.

46. Ibid., 308–09.

47. Rick Weiss and Susan Schmidt, "Capitol Hill Anthrax Matches Army's Stocks," *The Washington Post,* December 16, 2001.

48. From www.bnbi.org/.

Chapter 17

49. Colin Moynihan, "At On-Air Haven for Dissent, a Dissenting Voice Is Silenced," *The New York Times,* May 26, 2011, http://cityroom.blogs .nytimes.com/2011/05/26/an-insistent-voice-is-gone-but-only-from-the-airwaves/?scp=1&sq=moynihan%20weinberg%20wbai&st=cse.

50. Published in Weinberg's own zine, *World War 4 Report.*

51. See this topic expanded upon at length by Marxist and Hegelian academics: D. MacGregor and P. Zarembka, "Marxism, conspiracy, and 9-11," *Socialism and Democracy* 24, no. 2 (2010): 139–63.

52. Webster Griffin Tarpley and Anton Chaitkin, *George Bush: The Unauthorized Biography* (Joshua Tree, CA: Tree of Life Books/ProgressivePress .com, 2004). From Chapter XX, "The Phony War on Drugs": "The Iran-contra drug-running and gun-running operations run out of Bush's own office played their role in increasing the heroin, crack, cocaine, and marijuana brought into this country."

53. former AP reporter Robert Parry's excellent journalism on this topic at www.consortiumnews.com/2000/092300a.html.

54. *JFK Murder Solved,* www.jfkmurdersolved.com/bush.htm.

55. Von A. Weist, "Hinckley-Bush Family Friend Nears Release," *Rense. com,* March 28, 2011, www.rense.com/general45/hink.htm.

56. Alex Constantine, "David Icke Is a Neo-Nazi (Part Three): My Shadow, or the 'Turd in the Punch Bowl,'" April 26, 2009, http://aconstantineblack

list.blogspot.com/2009/04/david-icke-is-neo-nazi-part-three-my.html.
57. *Project Censored,* www.projectcensored.org/top-stories/articles/16-no-hard-evidence-connecting-bin-laden-to-9-11/.

Chapter 20
58. Samantha Power, *New York Times Book Review,* January 3, 2004: "We rebuff the complaints of foreigners about the 650 people who remain holed up in Guantanamo kennels, denied access to lawyers and family members, with not even their names released."
59. King, Martin Luther. Stride toward Freedom: The Montgomery Story. New York: Harper, 1958. Print.
60. Matthew 5:5, 44, 38–39.

Chapter 21
61. Matthew 10:26.
62. *The Zen Site,* www.thezensite.com/non_Zen/Was_Jesus_Buddhist.html.
63. Matthew 6:24–34.
64. Matthew 6:25.
65. Luke 17:21

Chapter 23
67. Freedom to Fascism film by Aaron Russo, also Bill Schultz, We the People foundation,
68. Cheney's "mistaken" remarks on Bin Laden's innocence were March 29, 2006, on The Tony Snow Show, on Fox News Radio. The next month, Tony Snow became White House Press Secretary.

Chapter 25
69. Jonathan Karl, "Dick Cheney Says 'Obama Deserves Credit' for Osama bin Laden's Death," *ABC News,* May 2, 2011, http://abcnews.go.com/Politics/dick-cheney-osama-bin-ladens-death-obama-deserves/story?id=13509547.
70. Michael Kane, "Crossing the Rubicon: Simplifying the Case Against Dick Cheney," *From The Wilderness,* January 18, 2005, www.fromthewilderness.com/free/ww3/011805_simplify_case.shtml.

WORKS CITED

9/11 Commission. *The 9/11 Commission Report: Final Report of the National Commission on Terrorist Attacks upon the United States*. New York: Norton, 2004.

Allison, Aimee, and David Solnit. *Army of None: Strategies to Counter Military Recruitment, End War, and Build a Better World*. New York: Seven Stories, 2007.

Avrich, Paul. *Anarchist Portraits*. Princeton, NJ: Princeton University Press, 1988.

Bernstein, Carl. "The CIA and the Media: How America's Most Powerful News Media Worked Hand in Glove with the Central Intelligence Agency and Why the Church Committee Covered It Up." *CarlBernstein .com*. www.carlbernstein.com/magazine_cia_and_media.php (accessed January 24, 2012).

Blum, William. *Killing Hope*. Monroe, ME: Common Courage, 2004.

Brafman, Ori, and Rod A. Beckstrom. *The Starfish and the Spider: The Unstoppable Power of Leaderless Organizations*. New York: Portfolio, 2007.

Brown, Ellen Hodgson. *The Web of Debt: The Shocking Truth About Our Money System—the Sleight of Hand That Has Trapped Us in Debt and How We Can Break Free*. Baton Rouge, LA: Third Millennium Press, 2007.

Bryant, Nick. *Franklin Scandal: A Story of Powerbrokers, Child Abuse & Betrayal*. Springfield, OR: Trine Day, 2010.

Bugliosi, Vincent. *The Prosecution of George W. Bush for Murder*. Cambridge, MA: Vanguard, 2008.

Clermont, Betty. *The Neo-Catholics: Implementing Christian Nationalism in America*. Atlanta, GA: Clarity, 2009.

The Coming Insurrection. Los Angeles: Semiotext(e), 2009.

Crossan, John Dominic. *Jesus: A Revolutionary Biography*. San Francisco: HarperSanFrancisco, 1994.

Dear, John. *A Persistent Peace: One Man's Struggle for a Nonviolent World*. Chicago: Loyola, 2008.

de la Vega, Elizabeth. *United States v. George W. Bush et Al*. New York: Seven Stories, 2006.

Douglas-Klotz, Neil. *Prayers of the Cosmos: Meditations on the Aramaic Words of Jesus*. San Francisco: Harper, 1994.

Douglas-Klotz, Neil. *The Hidden Gospel: Decoding the Spiritual Message of the Aramaic Jesus*. Wheaton, IL: Quest Books the Theosophical Publishing House, 1999.

Douglass, James W. *JFK and the Unspeakable: Why He Died and Why It Matters*. Maryknoll, NY: Orbis, 2008.

Dunayevskaya, Raya. *Philosophy and Revolution*. New York: Delacorte, 1973.

Friel, Howard, and Richard A. Falk. *The Record of the Paper: How the* New York Times *Misreports US Foreign Policy*. London: Verso, 2004.

Gandhi, Mohandas, and John Dear. *Mohandas Gandhi: Essential Writings*. Maryknoll, NY: Orbis, 2002.

The Gnostic Society Library. "The Gospel of Thomas Collection—Translations and Resources." *The Gnosis Archive*. www.gnosis.org/naghamm/gosthom.html (accessed January 24, 2012).

Graham, Bob, and Jeff Nussbaum. *Intelligence Matters: The CIA, the FBI, Saudi Arabia, and the Failure of America's War on Terror*. New York: Random House, 2004.

Graham, David M. "The 9/11 Graham Report: The True Story of Three 9/11 Hijackers Who Were Reported to the F.B.I. Ten Months Before 9/11." Unpublished. Available as a public-interest free download at sanderhicks.com/graham.html.

Griffin, G. Edward. *The Creature from Jekyll Island: A Second Look at the Federal Reserve*. Westlake Village, CA: American Media, 2002.

Hatfield, J. H. *Fortunate Son: George W. Bush and the Making of an Ameri-*

can. New York: Soft Skull, 2000.

Hicks, Sander. *The Big Wedding: 9/11, the Whistle-blowers, and the Cover-up*. Brooklyn, NY: Vox Pop, 2005.

Hopsicker, Daniel. *Welcome to TerrorLand: Mohamed Atta & the 9-11 Cover-up in Florida*. Eugene, OR: MadCow, 2004.

Kaplan, Justin. *Walt Whitman: Poetry and Prose*. London: Fitzroy Dearborn, 1997.

Levine, Noah. *The Heart of the Revolution: The Buddha's Radical Teachings on Forgiveness, Compassion, and Kindness*. New York: HarperOne, 2011.

Lipstadt, Deborah E. *Denying the Holocaust: The Growing Assault on Truth and Memory*. New York: Free Press, 1999.

Mader, Julius, and Mohamed Abdelnabi. *Who's Who in CIA: A Biographical Reference Work on 3,000 Officers of the Civil and Military Branches of Secret Services of the USA in 120 Countries*. Berlin: Julius Mader, 1968.

Marx, Karl. *The Eighteenth Brumaire of Louis Bonaparte: With Explanatory Notes*. New York: International, 1994.

McDonald, Forrest. "Founding Father's Library: A Bibliographical Essay." *Online Library of Liberty*. http://oll.libertyfund.org/index.php?option=com_content (accessed January 24, 2012).

The New American Bible. New York: Catholic Book Publishing, 1970.

Pagels, Elaine H. *Beyond Belief: The Secret Gospel of Thomas*. New York: Random House, 2003.

Paul, Ron. *The Revolution: A Manifesto*. New York: Grand Central Publishing, 2008.

Shaffer, Anthony. *Operation Dark Heart: Spycraft and Special Ops on the Frontlines of Afghanistan—and the Path to Victory*. New York: Thomas Dunne, 2010.

Shenon, Philip. *The Commission: The Uncensored History of the 9/11 Investigation*. New York: Twelve, 2008.

Smith, Morton. *Jesus the Magician*. San Francisco: Harper & Row, 1978.

Spencer, Lloyd, and Andrzej Krauze. *Introducing Hegel*. Thriplow: Icon, 2006.

Suzuki, Shunryu, and Trudy Dixon. *Zen Mind, Beginner's Mind*. New York: Walker/Weatherhill, 1970.

Tarpley, Webster Griffin. *9/11 Synthetic Terror: Made in USA*. Joshua Tree,

CA: Progressive, 2006.

Trento, Joseph John. *Prelude to Terror: The Rogue CIA and the Legacy of America's Private Intelligence Network*. New York: Carroll & Graf, 2005.

Trento, Susan B., and Joseph John Trento. *Unsafe at Any Altitude: Failed Terrorism Investigations, Scapegoating 9/11, and the Shocking Truth about Aviation Security Today*. Hanover, NH: Steerforth, 2006.

Tzu, Sun. *The Art of War*. Middlesex, U.K.: Echo Library, 2006.

Urantia Foundation. *The Urantia Book*. Chicago: Urantia Foundation, 2001.

Warner, Brad. *Hardcore Zen: Punk Rock, Monster Movies & the Truth About Reality*. Boston: Wisdom Publications, 2003.

Wright, Brian. *The Sacred Nonaggression Principle*. East Lansing, MI: Freeman Press, 2010.

Yuanwu. *Zen Letters: Teachings of Yuanwu*. Translated by J. C. Cleary and Thomas F. Cleary. Boston: Shambhala, 1994.

Zinn, Howard, Mike Konopacki, and Paul Buhle. *A People's History of American Empire: A Graphic Adaptation*. New York: Metropolitan, 2008.

BIG THANKS:

The author wishes to thank the following without whom this book would not be possible.

First of all, Thanks be to God: the Spirit of Change, of Revolution, of Truth. You are the true Dharma, the eternal law. "You shine within us, you shine outside us."

Thanks to Luke Gerwe, my developmental editor, for his sensitivity and eloquence. Thanks to the leadership of Laura Mazer, the executive editor at Soft Skull, and Annie Tucker, the copy editor. Thanks to Charlie Winton, publisher at Soft Skull, for his passion for the truth, no matter what taboos must be broken to find it. Charlie provided useful feedback on an earlier draft, and really connected the bat to the ball.

Thanks to everyone helped me to live while I was writing this book. Especially, thanks to Michael Galinsky and Suki Hawley, who gave me their house in the Catskills for the lions share of the writing. They were kind beyond reason. Thanks to Esther Bell, Yana Landowne, Amy Jones, Nathan Griggs, Brian Gage, who also gave me a place to live at various times, in Brooklyn and LA.

Thanks to everyone in Shreveport, LA, who helped guide Jordan Green and I in our investigation of the death of Dr. David Graham. Especially thanks to Richard Wilkes, John Milkovich, and private investigator Rick Turner. Thank you FBI Special Agent Steve Hayes for stumbling into the pages of this book. Our interview was clearly the best.

I am in debt to Barry Kissin, Esq. for his research around the anthrax cover-up, to Nick Bryant for his research into Obama, and to William Veale, Esq. and Mustafa Ndusa, Esq. for their valiant attempts to get 9/11 justice through the courts.

Thanks to Joshua Holland my editor at Alternet, where a few pieces of this book first appeared, in a different form. Thanks to everyone who worked at Vox Pop's New York Megaphone newspaper, where other stories herein first appeared, in shorter form. Thanks to Carl Person, Esq. and his wife Lu Ann Person, for providing the Eliot Spitzer/Silverstein Amicus Brief. Thank you Chris Baima, for a great front cover design, on this book and at the Megaphone.

Thanks Caroline Savage, who provided feedback on the chapter on zen. Thank you, Jim Fitzgerald, my agent. Thanks Kazumi Sakurai for a great author photo. Thank you, Jeff Teitleman, for the lap top and the introductions. Pax Christi be with you.

Thanks to my parents, Norman Lee Hicks and Ann Marie Hicks, for their love, and the models of their independent social consciences.

Thanks to all 9/11 Truth activists, We Are Change confrontation artists, and Occupiers everywhere. Keep at it. We are the revolution.

Finally, it's 10:10 PM on February 24, 2012 and my feet are wet and cold. I spent the day in the rain building a loft bed in a yard in Bushwick. But tonight, for the latest round of proof corrections for this book, I decided to come back across the bridge to the old Kinko's on East Houston Street in Manhattan.

ABOUT THE AUTHOR

© Kazumi Sakurai

Sander Hicks is the founder of Soft Skull Press and Vox Pop Inc. Raised in the Washington, D.C., area, he is the son of Norman Hicks, a progressive economist and anti-poverty specialist, who is retired from the World Bank organization. Hicks has worked as a playwright, editor, carpenter, and journalist. He was a producer and interviewer for the television program INN World Report and has been covered in *CounterPunch*. You can learn more about Sander Hicks and the Truth Party at www.sanderhicks.com.

Here, I want to say thank you to the entire staff of this store, now called a Fed Ex Office. I wrote a lot of this book here, in the self-serve LapNet station. But more than a simple "thank you", I want to say something to you, in this book, directly. Back in 1992 I started a publishing company inside a Kinko's. And you can too. It's not hard. The rules are yours to break.

I used to work here, I was this store's first overnight shift leader. And now I have a little book you should read . . .

Sander Hicks
February 24, 2012
Brooklyn, NY